# The Son Conceived In Drunkenness

# The Son Conceived in Drunkenness

## Magical Plants in the World of the Greek Hero

Carl A.P. Ruck

REGENT PRESS
& ENTHEOMEDIA
Berkeley, California

Copyright © 2018 by Carl A.P. Ruck and Mark Hoffman

HARDBACK
ISBN-13: 978-1-58790-423-3
ISBN-10: 1-58790-423-3

PAPERBACK
ISBN-13: 978-1-58790-424-0
ISBN-10: 1-58790-424-1

E-BOOK
ISBN-13: 978-1-58790-426-4
ISBN-10: 1-58790-426-8

Library of Congress Control Number: 2017957092

All rights reserved under International and Pan-American Copyright Conventions.

No part of this book may be used or reproduced in any manner whatsoever without the written permission of the publisher, except in the case of brief quotations embodied in critical articles and reviews.

The authors and publisher gratefully acknowledge the permissions granted to reproduce the copyrighted material in this book. Every effort has been made to trace copyright holders and to obtain their permission for the use of copyrighted material. The publisher apologizes for any errors or omissions and would be grateful if notified of any corrections that should be incorporated in future reprints or editions of this book.

2 3 4 5 6 7 8 9 10

Manufactured in the U.S.A.
REGENT PRESS
Berkeley, CA 94705
www.regentpress.net
regentpress@mindspring.com

# Table of Contents

Introduction ............................................................................. xi

**Chapter One**
**A Classic Case of Nuptial Debauchery**
    Ulterior Motives ................................................................... 1
    Disjointed Realms ................................................................ 2
    Misguided Persuasion ......................................................... 4
    At Home and Abroad .......................................................... 5
    No Child of Mine ................................................................ 6
    Toxic Mates ........................................................................... 7
    Two Fathers ........................................................................ 10
    A Pious Deceit ................................................................... 10

**Chapter Two**
**Making the New Olympia**
    The Marriage of the Horse-mistress ............................... 17
    The Marriage Bed in the Magical Garden .................... 19
    The Great Altar of Olympian Zeus ................................. 21
    The House of Oenomäus ................................................. 22
    The Grove of the Altis ...................................................... 23
    The Cretan Herakles ......................................................... 25

**Chapter Three**
**The Child of Fortune**
    The Creature Found Growing on the Mountainside ........ 29
    Worthless Prophecies ....................................................... 30
    Matriliny and Patriliny .................................................... 32
    Pharmakon ......................................................................... 33
    Mushroom-town ................................................................ 34
    Thunder Stone ................................................................... 35
    The Drunken Parents ....................................................... 37
    Ecstatic Herbalism ............................................................ 39
    Jocasta's Brooch ................................................................ 40

## Chapter Four
## Fall Guy for the God

- The Alphabetic Plays .................................................... 43
- Picking the God's Flowers .......................................... 44
- The Cave of the Long Rocks ...................................... 45
- The Trial of Orestes ..................................................... 46
- The Cave of Pan ........................................................... 47
- The Empowered Female ............................................. 49
- The Birth of Erichthonios .......................................... 50
- The Wicker Hamper .................................................... 51
- The Shrine of Aglauros ............................................... 53
- Plynteria Festival ......................................................... 55
- The Mystery Hamper .................................................. 55
- The Maidens' Dewy Basket ........................................ 59

## Chapter Five
## Cleansing the God's Image

- Cleansing the God's Image ........................................ 61
- The Crown Matrimonial ............................................. 62
- Lycian and Hyperborean Apollo ............................... 64
- Tribal Rivalries ............................................................ 65
- The Drunken Revel ..................................................... 66
- Plucking Plants in the Cave ....................................... 68
- Chrysokomes Apollo ................................................... 69
- The Cave of Triphonios .............................................. 70
- Ion's Other Name ........................................................ 71
- Viola Boy ...................................................................... 72
- Saffron Boy ................................................................... 74
- Prismatic Color ........................................................... 74
- Ionic Column ............................................................... 76
- Kreousa as the Gorgon Queen Medusa .................... 78
- The Court of the Delphinium .................................... 79
- Weaving a New Identity ............................................. 80
- The Birthday Party ...................................................... 83
- The Horoscope ............................................................. 85

## Chapter Six
## The Riddle of the Sphinx
    Jocasta as the Sphinx ................................................................ 87
    Two Names ................................................................................. 87
    The Zoomorphism of the Sphinx ............................................ 90
    Consuming Goddess ................................................................. 91
    Sexual Conquest ........................................................................ 93
    The Drunken Sphinx ................................................................ 95
    The Daughter of Laïus .............................................................. 96
    The Rapture of the Golden Steed ............................................ 97
    The Sacrosanct Body ................................................................ 99

## Chapter Seven
## The Problem of Thebes
    The Purity of Bloodlines ........................................................ 101
    To the Left of Laïus ................................................................. 103
    Promethean Fire ...................................................................... 104
    Shamanic Rapture ................................................................... 108
    Chthonios ................................................................................. 109
    The Grove on Mount Kithairon ............................................ 110
    Regency of the Wolf ................................................................ 113
    Amphion and Zethos ............................................................. 116
    The Marriage of Cadmus and Harmonia ............................ 118
    The Divine Mother ................................................................. 119
    The Milk of the White Goddess ........................................... 121
    The Necklace of Harmonia ................................................... 125

## Chapter Eight
## The Hero's Weapon of Choice
    Tools of the Trade ................................................................... 127
    The Pruning Hook of Perseus ............................................... 127
    Mithraism ................................................................................ 129
    The Container for the Pruned Monster .............................. 131
    Baby Bunting ........................................................................... 133
    Golden Mushroom ................................................................. 139
    Golden Pluck ........................................................................... 141

Salamander ............................................................. 143
Cold Fire ................................................................. 144
For Love of a Salamander .................................... 147

## Chapter Nine
## The Pruned Olive

The Conquest of Primitivism ................................ 151
The Wild Olive and the Cultivated ....................... 152
The Deer Hunt ........................................................ 153
Arboreal Hosts ....................................................... 155
The Olive as Pacified Toxin .................................. 156
The Secret Offering ............................................... 157

## Chapter Ten
## The Club of Herakles

The Olive of Nemea .............................................. 161
A Crown of Parsley ............................................... 162
Deadly Hemlock .................................................... 163
Lycanthropy ........................................................... 164
Herakles as Wolf .................................................... 166
Rabies ..................................................................... 167
Wolfsbane ............................................................... 169
Divestiture of Mortality ......................................... 170
Mistress of the Chambers ...................................... 171
The Line Dance of Humanity ................................ 172

## Chapter Eleven
## Arrow Toxins

The Venom of the Hydra ....................................... 175
Lake Halcyon ......................................................... 177
Priapus .................................................................... 184
The Dermatological Affliction .............................. 185
The Rust Potion ..................................................... 189
Ass's Ears ............................................................... 191
The Sting of the Medusa ....................................... 192

## Chapter Twelve
## The Club from the Volcanic Caldera

The Club-man with a Single Foot ................................ 199
The Healing Spa ................................................ 201
An Eyewitness Account ......................................... 202
The Birth of Apollo's Son ..................................... 203
A Good Place for Dying ........................................ 204
Dog Mount ..................................................... 205
The Rod of Asklepios .......................................... 206
Never Do Harm ................................................. 207
Viper's Venom ................................................. 209
The Alchemical Serpent of Renewal ............................. 210
The Asklepia Festival ......................................... 211
The Sword of Aegeus ........................................... 213

# Acknowledgment

I am indebted to my editor Moira Luthin, who more than checking the manuscript for errors and consistency of format, repeatedly amazed me by her knowledge of the subject and often led me into new areas for investigation.

# INTRODUCTION
# Botanical Empowerment

An essential aspect of the traditional stories or myths about the Greek heroes has been intentionally overlooked in the study of Classical literature and religion, specifically, the pivotal role accorded to magical plants and religious sacraments derived from psychoactive botanical and venomous animal sources, serpents, reptiles, and the like. Although the heroes were commonly assumed to have been real historical figures, their biography, if they ever did actually exist, is mythologized history, transitional in the evolution of the cults and culture over which they often preside as etiological founders. They are not creatures like ordinary people, magnified to greatness of stature and prowess, as befits the heroic persona, but pawns in the power play of opposing forces aligned with traditions of male or female dominance and the supporting realm of gods and goddesses.

Deities have only the anthropomorphized personae and iconography evoked by the humans who worship them. Men create the gods and they are mutable, changeable over time as the societies of humans over which they reign evolve and project new demands for the numinous beings to authenticate, empowering the leaders with divine sanction.

These deities and the heroes both have botanical and animal attributes that relate to the societies and their modes of communication with the numinous realm. Toxic plants and animals reverently honored and correctly accessed have the potential to alter consciousness, allowing direct mystical communion between gods and humans in rapturous trance or shamanic ecstasy. To call such visionary experience a drug-induced hallucination is doubly pejorative in describing both the outcome as a hallucinatory delusion or falsification of reality and its cause as a drugged or malfunctioning mind. This is particularly true when the leaders of the religion or its allied government claim empowerment from such drugged hallucinations.

Toward the end of the great expansion of consciousness now known as the Psychedelic Revolution of the 60s and 70s, I proposed a new word for such mind-altering substances to free them from the implications of irreverent recreational abuse and the irresponsible marketplace of New Age pseudo-scientific theologies. This word is *entheogen*, a substance that allows the deity to reside within the human.[1] The most direct mode of access is the simple ingestion or other method of application of the sacrament so that the entheogen forms the mediating pathway between the human and the divine.

This induces a state of consubstantiality in which the deity, the entheogen, and the human share common attributes as magical plants or shamanic animal familiars. Consubstantiality differs from the rite of transubstantiation, in that the latter aims at producing the former as merely a symbolic imitation. To claim the opposite was persecuted in the twelfth century of the Church as a heresy labeled impanation, the embodiment of the true presence of the deity in the Eucharist. In such a theological context, it is not risible to notice that even so great a hero as Oedipus has characteristics descriptive of a mushroom, or that the divine iconographic persona encoded in the complex metaphoric configuration of the great Gorgon queen known as the Medusa was similarly a mushroom.

A common motif in the tales of the heroes is the drunkenness of his parents at the moment of his conception. In the case of Persephone's abduction by Hades and their subsequent son, the

---

1 Carl A.P. Ruck, Jeremy Bigwood, Danny Staples, Jonathan Ott, and R. Gordon Wasson, "Entheogens": 145-146, in *Journal of Psychedelic Drugs*, vol. 1, no. 1-2 (1979).

plant that precipitated the event is clearly named as the 'narcotic' *narkissos* that the maiden plucked while out gathering herbs with the sisterhood of her attendants. This altered state of consciousness forms part of an entire scenario descriptive of shamanic rapture induced in a context of ritualized herb gathering or the extraction of venoms from living creatures. The child born from the amorous encounter of his parents becomes the etiological founder of his peoples. He bears the double role of potentially representing his mother's offspring, as her matrilineal son, or that of his patriarchal father. Upon the assignation of his parents depends the nature of the ensuing society as beholden to the religion of the dominant female or that of the male.

The heroic career of the child will establish the mode of empowerment. Typically, he will confront a sequence of monsters, whose conquest (or the opposite) will confirm which of his parents was the dominant operative principle. The weapons of choice for this combat are implausible for actual warfare and betray the shamanic experience of his parents at the moment of his begetting. Typically, the weapons are botanical constructs, such as a special club pruned from a sacred tree, or an agricultural tool, like a pruning hook, a harvester's bag, or even a shovel. The monsters are zoomorphic or anthropomorphized entheogens, and the weapons employed to counter them are appropriate only in the context of mastery of their toxins or its opposite in succumbing to their intoxication.

Thus, Perseus employs a pruning hook as his weapon of choice, implying that his foe is a plant. Herakles (Heracles, Latin Hercules) uses a club pruned from an olive tree as his weapon and arrows dipped in the venom of the Hydra. For Theseus, the olive club has undergone alchemical metallurgy to emerge recast in bronze. Ultimately, this magical club that is the hero's weapon of choice will emerge as the rod of Asklepios, wielded by the modern profession of medicine in the battle waged with drugs and toxins on the frontier of the battle between life and death.

THE SON CONCEIVED IN DRUNKENNESS

CHAPTER ONE

# A Classic Case of Nuptial Debauchery

**Ulterior Motives**

Even though Laïus (Laïos) had been warned by a Delphic prophecy that if he had a son, the son would murder him, he forgot himself in a bout of drunkenness and begot Oedipus (Oidípous) with his wife Jocasta (Iokásta).² This drunken fit has received considerable psychoanalytical exegesis as an element in the Freudian Oedipus Complex or in its complement, the Jocasta Complex. Laïus must have tried to defy the Fates by avoiding his wife's conception, either by finding other sexual partners or engaging in nonproductive modes of intercourse. Jocasta, on the other hand, seems to have known of the prophecy, but nevertheless seems to have seduced her husband and was apparently complicit in the attempt after the fact to save him from the inevitable outcome of the unfortunate parturition. As for the son, he inevitably became a pawn in the power play for dominance between the parents.

It deserves noting, however, that it is historically anachronistic to suppose that husbands and wives in Classical antiquity—or, even more so, in the mythological age of heroism—engaged in ordinary convivial marital drinking. Laïus and Jocasta are not ordinary parents, but mythical constructs, with millennia of ritual ancestors. Two other heroes, moreover, were similarly conceived in

---

2 For a comprehensive compilation of the traditions about Oedipus, see Lowell Edmunds, *Oedipus* (London/New York, NY: Routledge, 2006).

drunkenness. A comparison with the heroes Ion—founder of the Ionian tribal group—and with Theseus—the culture hero of Athens—offers a new perspective on the Oedipus myth and on the role of heroism in Greek religion and culture, with particular reference to the psychoactive substances for accessing ritual drunkenness and the theological symbolism and implications of the ceremony.

## Disjointed Realms

The earliest mention of the drunkenness of Laïus occurs in Euripides' *Phoenician Women* (*Phoenissae*), dated to around 409 BCE. Sophocles' *Oedipus Tyrannus* is similarly of uncertain date. On the basis of the prominence given to the plague in Thebes, many scholars have opted for a date around 429 BCE to make it correspond to the plague that visited Athens shortly after the beginning of the Peloponnesian War, although the mythical Theban plague has symptoms that are clearly symbolic and that in no way correspond to the symptoms that Thucydides recorded with medical exactitude for the Athenian plague.

Sophocles composed two other tragedies on the Oedipus myth: the *Antigone*, of uncertain date, but probably the first to be written, around 441 BCE; and the *Oedipus at Colonus*, written shortly before his death in 406 BCE and first produced by his grandson at the City Dionysia in 401 BCE. The late composition of the *Coloneus* in the playwright's career is perhaps substantiated by the tradition that his son accused his father of neglecting the family's finances and the great tragedian defended himself in court against the charge of senility by reciting passages from the play in progress.[3] The common source for the Oedipus myth is the *Theban Cycle*, a collection of lost epics probably written down between 750 and 500 BCE. The narrative of Oedipus and the Sphinx, and presumably the hero's marriage to his mother, was recorded in the *Oedipodea*, attributed to Cinaethon (Kinaithon), a legendary eighth-century persona of an oral poet from Sparta. The three

---

3 Cicero, *De senectute*, 7.22.

extant fragments add nothing to our knowledge of the hero's conception and claim that he had no sons from his mother, contrary to the tradition of the warring brothers Eteocles and Polyneices.

The Sophoclean plague in Thebes consists solely in the cessation of birthing: the crops wither in the bud; the herds and women are without offspring.[4] The Athenian plague, in contrast, despite the detailed description of Thucydides,[5] has not been definitively ascribed to any known disease, but it differs from the symbolic plague of Oedipus's Thebes in that it spread from an outside source, specifically Ethiopia, Egypt, and lands of the Persian Empire, and that some of the afflicted survived, and it affected animals only by contagion with the human victims and it had no effect upon the crops. Nor does it have any specific symptom causing infertility or stillbirth. The dating of the Oedipus tragedy to the year after the onset of the plague is a misguided and desperate attempt to impose a political or philosophical agendum upon a purely mythical event. It also isolates the Theban plague from its earlier occurrence in the predations of the Sphinx, from which Oedipus previously had rescued the city. This is particularly unfortunate because the plague of the Sphinx involves sexual predation and the theme of drunken rapture.

In 467 BCE, Aeschylus had won first prize at the City Dionysia with an entire trilogy on the theme of the Oedipus myth (*Oedipodeia*). Its first play was entitled *Laïus*, the second *Oedipus*, the third, which alone survives, is the *Seven Against Thebes*, in which the war between the sons and heirs of Oedipus is the subject, an episode totally lacking from the account by Cinaethon. The final satyr play was entitled the *Sphinx*. Since Aeschylus was accorded the honor of posthumous performances, it is possible that a revival presentation was offered closer to the performances of his theatrical successors. This seems likely since Euripides and Sophocles appear to have critiqued or further developed themes

---

4 Sophocles, *Oedipus Tyrannus*, 25-26.
5 Thucydides, 2.47.1-55.1.

of their predecessor, which would otherwise have fallen from the memories of an audience not accustomed as yet to reading the classical works of a canon of acknowledged masterpieces, as evolved in the later Hellenistic Age.

## Misguided Persuasion

The *Seven Against Thebes* mentions only that Laïus begot Oedipus, despite the Delphic warning, because he was overcome by 'misguided counsels', in the plural (choral Doric *aboulían*, 750). The text states that it was his 'friends' who offered the counsel (*philon*), but this has been corrected, probably rightly, to *philan*, making it an adjective, implicating Jocasta as the agent offering 'loving wrong counsel', which is to say in tragic poetic diction, that she seduced him into having sex. This is, of course, an amended version of the manuscript tradition.

In the prologue to Euripides' *Phoenician Women*, Jocasta glosses over her possible culpability, stating simply that Laïus 'fell into a bacchanalian rapture' (*es te bakcheian peson*, 21). Obviously, she was present since she conceived the child. A bacchanalian rapture, however, is not a drink with dinner. It describes a ritual of drug-induced shamanic rapture.

The loving misguided counsel similarly implies an experience, not simply of forgetting his resolve to avoid sex with Jocasta, but an alteration of consciousness such as would occur in the ritualized bacchanalia. Ascribing ulterior motives to Jocasta, such as chafing at imposed chastity or plotting to have offspring, is nowhere extant in the ancient sources and would probably be inappropriate to the mythical scenario, and considered unseemly in fifth-century norms for wifely behavior. Presumably, moreover, the married couple had been having sex before the Delphic prophecy since the lack of offspring was precisely the reason for consulting the oracle. The rejected child that resulted is the product of a ritual event in which Apollo as the patron of the Delphic oracle is thematically implicated. Oedipus is a Dionysian child, the reciprocal antithesis to Apollo. Thematically this dichotomy establishes the symbolic parameters of his heroic persona as two opposed states of mind, within which he functions as some kind of mediation.

## At Home and Abroad

Aegeus (Aigeus) of Athens was similarly without offspring when he consulted the Delphic oracle. His response was the riddle that he should not untie the protruding foot of the wineskin until he returned to Athens.[6] Unable to solve the riddle, he visited Pittheus of Troezen (modern Troizena), who apparently understood the prophecy quite well, but nevertheless introduced him to his daughter Aethra (Aithra) and 'persuaded' him into a drunken bout of sexual concourse.[7] The result was the birth of Theseus, born abroad in a foreign land, alone with his mother, since Aegeus had left for Athens, not knowing he had begot a son.

The meaning of the riddle is actually quite etymologically transparent. Aegeus is named as a 'goat-man', and the wineskin with its phallic foot is both a metaphor for his genitals and a reference to the use of the skin of a slaughtered goat as the container for the wine. The Delphic oracle had warned Aegeus neither to get drunk nor succumb to the persuasions of sex until he returned home. The 'foot' is a common euphemism for the penis, to the extent that the Bible refers to urine euphemistically as 'foot water'.[8] The same phallic connotations occur in the interpretation of the name of Oedipus as the 'swollen foot'.

Euripides, in his *Medea* tragedy (produced in 431 BCE), follows a tradition where Aegeus on route to Troezen first consulted Medea in Corinth about the meaning of the riddle.[9] Medea is

---

6 Plutarch, *Life of Theseus*; Apollodorus (often cited as Pseudo-Apollodorus since he is a post-first-century BCE author incorrectly identified as the second-century BCE Apollodorus of Athens), *Bibliotheke (Bibliotheca)*, 3.15.6.
7 Scholion to Euripides' *Hippolytus*. Plutarch, (*Theseus*, 3.4), glosses over the drunkenness as 'persuasion or misleading him' (*epeisen auton e diepatese*).
8 *Isaiah*, 36.12: *meymey regaleyhem*; *2 Kings*, 18.27.
9 Neophron, frag. 1 (scholion to Euripides, *Medea*, 666). E.A. Thompson, "Neophron and Euripides' *Medea*": 10-14, in *The Classical Quarterly*, vol. 38, no. 1/2 (Jan. – Apr., 1944). Other accounts make Aegeus arrive in Corinth after his visit to Troezen, on his return route to Athens.

actually his sister-in-law, since her sister Chalciope (Chalkiópe) is recorded as the second wife of Aegeus.[10] Thus she greets him as a familiar friend in the play. Presumably, it is with her sister that Aegeus has failed to beget a child. Medea, as a notorious sorceress, doubtless had no trouble unraveling the riddle, but she does not explain its meaning for him. Instead, she arranges for Aegeus to offer her asylum in Athens after she finishes her revenge upon her mate Jason in Corinth. She promises Aegeus to use her spells to end his childless state. When Aegeus returns to Athens, Medea has sex with him and produces the son Medus. Thus, the childless Aegeus now has two sons, neither his: Theseus, who doesn't yet know his father and was born abroad in his mother's land; and Medus, Medea's son, born from the wine-sack untied at home, doubtless also in a drunken revel aided by the drugs of the foreign sorceress.

## No Child of Mine

The curse of the father's infertility masks a symbolic problem. It is not that there is no offspring, but it is rather the situation that whatever child is begotten is the mother's child, ascribed to the matrilineal tradition. Thus, Medea's Medus (Medos) is named after her and destined eventually to become the etiological ancestor of the foreign Iranian Persians or Medes, the traditional barbarian antithesis of the Hellenes, at least as experienced in the two Persian invasions of Greece at the beginning of the fifth century. In such a mythical scenario, Oedipus plays a pivotal role, empowered both as son of the king Laïus, and as consort (and son) of the queen Jocasta. As early as our hominid ancestors, power over the group was in the hands of the alpha male or the alpha female supported by her chosen son.[11]

The recognition of Oedipus as the lineal descendent of the Theban Laïus, instead of the Corinthian Polybus, although unfortunate

---

10   His first wife was Meta, a name like Metis, who was the pregnant female that Zeus swallowed to beget the goddess Athena.
11   Linda Marie Fedigan, *Primate Paradigms: Sex Roles and Social Bonds* (Chicago, IL: University of Chicago Press, 1992, reprint of Montreal: Eden Press, 1982).

for the hero, who finds himself married to his own mother, nevertheless has the optimistic outcome of reasserting patrilineality. Although supposedly an outsider empowered by his marriage to the queen, he is actually a native Theban, empowered as male heir of the deceased king and his wife. Thus, Oedipus is doubly legitimate as heir, a pawn mediating between the traditions of matrilineal and patrilineal descent. The recognition of his true identity is the event that lifts the plague that is visiting the city of Thebes.

In the case of Theseus, the recognition of him as the son of Aegeus will occasion the exile of Medea and her son Medus. The newly recognized son of the king supplants the mother's child, both being born at approximately the same time. Moreover, Theseus will eventually join his father to defeat the 'sons of Pallas', the Pallantidae (*Pallantidai*, anglicized as Pallantids). They are the sons of Aegeus's brother Pallas, who is evidently named in matrilineal fashion after the goddess Pallas, a primordial version of Athena. Pallas as the brother of Aegeus is probably actually a product of mythological exegesis, obfuscating the true situation that the children, like Pallas himself, are all called after the female deity or queen. Similarly, the wife from whom Aegeus could beget no child of his own was named Meta. She is a version of Metis, the persona of the goddess that would become subjugated in the birthing of Athena as the motherless daughter of Zeus. Athena assumed the epithet of Pallas Athena after she accidentally slew Pallas, distracted by the aegis *(aigis)* or goatskin, which she henceforth wore as a commemoration of her former identity. The oldest images of Athena, moreover, were called palladiums (*palladia*), natural objects not yet molded into an iconic form anthropomorphized as Athena, commonly identified as a meteorite or *baitylos*, a stone fallen from heaven and enshrined as deity.

## Toxic Mates

The aegis as a goatskin with serpent fringe is emblematic of the goat-men and serpent-men that represented the attendants or mates of the primordial goddess of Athens. Since Aegeus is named as a 'goat-man' (*aig-eus*), he belongs to this same tradition. His father Pandion was a serpent-man, like the king Erechtheus and Athena's foster-child Erichthonios (Erichthonius). The aegis goat-skin as the wine-sack implicates the theme of toxic drunkenness in their ritual attendance upon their goddess. Since a goat-man in Greek mythology was visualized as an ithyphallic satyr, ecstatic drunkenness, interpreted as sexual rapture, is indicated. The satyrs were the way that Bacchus materialized to his female devotees or 'brides' (nymphs) in their maddened bacchanalian revels. These women allegedly handled serpents in their rituals. Both the goats and the serpents are emblematic of psychoactive toxins. The serpents were milked to extract venom,[12] and the goat was similarly symbolic of magical venoms since goats commonly graze on toxic plants, which renders their flesh an analogous source of the plant toxins, whose psychoactive potential the goatherd frequently observed in the maddened or ecstatic behavior of the grazing herd. Thus, these goat-men and serpent-men of the goddess indicate her toxic mates, the zoomorphism of the toxins whereby the sisterhood of the goddesses' priestesses accessed shamanic rapture, and probably also the form in which the shamanic animal familiars materialized or were visualized during the ecstatic experience.

The conflict of Aegeus with Pallas is the common theme of oppositional traditions aligned as warring brothers. The ascendency of Aegeus with a son of his own indicates the transition of the primordial Pallas goddess to a transmuted or pacified version remade in the image of her as Athena, the daughter of her Olympian father. The same scenario of oppositional traditions imagined as warring brothers will be played out more extensively in the conflict between the two sons (and half-brothers) of Oedipus, Polyneices (Polynices, Polyneikes) and Eteocles (Eteokles), who

---

12   Demosthenes, De corona, 18.260: pinching the cheeks of snakes (toús ópheis toús pareías thlíbon) ['stroke, massage', apparently to milk their venom]. David Hillman, Hermaphrodites, Gynomorphs and Jesus: She-Male Gods and the Roots of Christianity (Berkeley, CA: Ronin Publishing, 2013).

will inherit the disputed kingship of Thebes.

A third brother of Aegeus was named Lykos (Lycus) as a wolf. The same wolf-man occurs in the lineage of the Theban aristocracy, as the Lykos who was regent for the young Labdacus (Labdakos), the father of Laïus, both when Labdacus was too young to rule and then again after Labdacus was torn to pieces by women in a bacchanalian frenzy, just like his cousin Pentheus. It was supposedly a son or more likely a grandson[13] of this Lykos who assumed the regency of Thebes again in the time of Herakles.

The wolf is traditionally associated with the motifs of marginality, expulsion and reintegration, inhabiting the dangerous realm between civilization and the wilderness. The wolf-men who act as interim regents at Thebes are pivotal in the dichotomous opposition between Apollonian and Dionysian realms of consciousness as mythologized in the bacchanalian frenzy of the hero's drunken conception. Apollo himself was a 'wolf-god',[14] and bore the epithet Lycian, which despite its connotations of lycanthropy also yielded the Lyceum as synonymous with a gymnasium as a place for male education. The conjunction, of course, derives from the fact that as early as the sixth century BCE, a gymnasium was built in the grounds of Apollo Lykeios ('Wolf-god') in Athens and used for military training. It was here that Plato and eventually Aristotle and a long list of successors conversed or taught their disciples. The subsequent fame of the Academy obscures the reality that the Lyceum gymnasium was a place for indoctrination of warriors into the cult of the wolf, which implies the marginal space that armies must enter in opposing the threat to the civilized realm encountered as the enemy forces invading from the foreign wilderness. The gymnasium thus serves as the place for cultural indoctrination in its broadest theological significance, which is to say, the mystical perception of alternative modes of cognition.

---

13  It was customary not to name a child after a living ancestor, but to skip a generation.

14  Daniel Gershenson, *Apollo the Wolf God* (Institute for the Study of Man: *The Journal of Indo-European Studies* Monograph Series, no. 8, 1992).

## Two Fathers

The hero myth is composed of recurrent themes or motifs as variations upon a fundamental pattern that Joseph Campbell termed the 'monomyth',[15] with multiple references into anthropological, cultural, religious, and psychological dimensions. The most basic of these recurrent motifs is that the hero is liminal,[16] as in rituals of initiation, betwixt and between, belonging to two worlds, and is defined by an array of antithetical characteristics, comprising two versions of the heroic persona with two divergent scenarios, one for each of the two worlds.[17] The opposition of descent from maternal or paternal ancestors yields a heroic persona ascribed to two different fathers and represents the historical situation of societies based upon female or male dominance.

Thus, while Aegeus remains in his drunken slumber, Aethra rose from her bed, roused by Athena, and swam across the narrow straits that separate Troezen on the mainland from the tiny island of Poros-Sphairia to sleep also with the god Poseidon.[18] In the two versions of Theseus' identity, he is either the son of the drunken mortal Aegeus or of the god Poseidon. The same dual paternity is represented in the myth of Oedipus, the assumed son of Polybus who actually was the son of Laïus.

## A Pious Deceit

The island of Poros is of volcanic origin and lies like a rock ball narrowly separated from the larger island of Kalavria. It marked the endpoint of the race that Pelops ran with Oenomaüs (Oinomaös) of Olympia for the marriage with Hippodamia

---

15 Joseph Campbell, *The Hero with a Thousand Faces* (Princeton, NJ: Princeton University Press, 1949). Campbell borrowed the term 'monomyth' from James Joyce's *Finnegans Wake* (1939).
16 Arnold van Gennep, The Rites of Passage (Chicago, IL: University of Chicago Press, 1960, first published as Les rites de passage, 1909). The concept of liminality was further developed in Victor Turner, The Ritual Process: Structure and Anti-Structure (New York, NY: Aldine de Gruyter, 1969).
17 Carl A.P. Ruck and Mark Hoffman, Mushrooms, Myth, and Human Consciousness (Berkeley, CA: Ronin Publishing, 2013), 104-118.
18 Pausanias, *Description of Greece*, 2.3.1.

(Hippodameia) and the control of the Peloponnesus. The transition of control from Oenomaüs to Pelops reflects a historical evolution in the dominant culture of the Peloponnesian peoples from female to male dominance, historically recorded as the ascendancy of the Mycenaean culture over the earlier Minoan-Pelasgian peoples. The island was named for Sphaerus (Sphairos), the charioteer of Pelops in the race.[19] Aethra poured a libation to him there on his tomb, when Poseidon erotically possessed her, and she founded a temple on the spot dedicated to Athena Apaturia,[20] renaming the island as 'Holy' (*Hierá*).

The epithet of Athena as Apaturia is supposedly derived as the 'Deceitful', indicative of a persuasive trick that Athena had played, essentially as pimp, in bringing Aethra together with Poseidon. This motif is the same loving persuasiveness that Jocasta exerted upon Laïus for the drunken debauchery that resulted in the birth of Oedipus. Troezenian maidens dedicated their menstrual belts to the deceitful goddess there upon the tomb of Sphaerus on the day of their marriage. Thus, their anticipated marital pregnancy was cast in the paradigm set by the birthing of Theseus as transitional to the assignation of the child to the agency of the legally recognized husband. The etymology from *apáte* or 'deceit, leading off the path', however, is fanciful. The chariot race of Pelops represents the abduction of the 'horsewoman' Hippodamia (so named as the 'horse-mistress') away from her father and the transition to patriarchal control over a woman's offspring. The true etymology of Apaturia was recognized in antiquity as derived from 'together' (*háma*) with the 'fathers' (*patéras*).[21]

Thus, the three-day Festival of the Apaturia in Classical times

---

19  The island's name as Poros is of Byzantine derivation as the 'crossing', by comparison with the crossing between Byzantium and the land across the Golden Horn, Galatia. The mainland shore opposite Poros is the village today of Galatea, assimilated with the 'milk-maid' who was the object of the Cyclops Polyphemus's amorous devotion, although the villagers assume that it alludes to the mainland as the transit point at some time in the past for the delivery of milk to the island. (Personal informant.)

20  Pausanias, *Description of Greece*, 2.33.1.

21  Xenophon, *Hellenica*, 1.7.8.

centered upon the initiatory acceptance of male children as legitimate offspring of their acknowledged fathers into the male brotherhoods or *phratries*. The food of choice for the festival was the communal dining upon grilled sausages, which cannot be divorced from their obvious similarity to the male sexual organ.[22] This is the obscenity that defines the role of the sausage-seller in Aristophanes *Knights* as a rival to Kleon the dildo-maker to serve the anally receptive Demos or populace of Athens.[23] The same obscenity probably lurks in the *Acharnians* episode since the ambassador from the court of the Thracian Sitacles claims that the king's son is doting in homoerotic love with Athens and has a hankering to eat the Apaturia sausages. It was this initiation that qualified the boys as citizens rather than as unclaimed and disenfranchised matrilineal bastards, like the Pallantids with only an identifiable mother acknowledged. Laïus never accepted Oedipus as his son, but abandoned him in a state of marginality and hence was justified in exposing the infant on the mountainside, free from the guilt of infanticide. Jocasta was the child's only acknowledged parent, a certifiable birth witnessed from his mother.

According to Plutarch, who rationalized the myth of Theseus a millennium and a half later as a historical event, the deceit of the Athena Apaturia consisted of a rumor that Pittheus spread about Aethra and her supposed sexual union with Poseidon, so that the Pallantidae would not murder Theseus as the son of Aegeus and the rightful patrimonial claimant to the kingship of Athens. According to the deceitful rumor, Theseus, like the Pallantidae, had only a mother.

The charioteer Sphairos is etymologically named as a 'ball' or sphere (*sphairos*), hence descriptive of the tiny island where he

---

22  Aristophanes, *Acharnians*, 145-146. Each father, moreover, offered a sacrificed goat or sheep, and if any man objected to the acceptance of the father's son into the brotherhood as legitimate, the victim was removed from the altar. On the erotic connotations of the diet of sausages, see James Robson, "The Language(s) of Love in Aristophanes": 251-266, in Chiara Thumiger, Chris Carey, and Nick J. Lowe (eds.), *Erôs in Ancient Greece* (Oxford: Oxford University Press, 2013), 256.

23  Aristophanes, *Knights*, 150 *et seq.*

lay entombed. As a 'sphere', the charioteer's name is descriptive of the 'wheel' of his chariot. There was no reason, however, for him to have died there in the chariot race,[24] other than that he is a thematic double for the charioteer of the competitor Oenomaüs. His name was Myrtilus (Myrtilos). It was he who replaced the bronze linchpins on the wheels of the chariot of Oenomaüs with beeswax so that they would melt, releasing the whirling wheels and causing the fatal accident.

As charioteer, he would have been driving the chariot of Oenomaüs and there is no way that he could have avoided the same deadly outcome as his master. Instead, however, he was said to have claimed the *doit du seigneur* to sleep with the bride before her husband as his reward for the deceitful linchpins. Pelops, if he had ever promised this, reneged and tossed him from a cliff, presumably the mountain that looms above Troezen, into the sea beyond Poros-Sphairia, which is named as the Myrtoan Sea, after him. No cliff closer to Olympia could plausibly let him fall into the Myrtoan Sea. An Etruscan alabaster cinerary urn depicts Pelops slaughtering Myrtilus on an altar, while Hippodamia on the left holds the chariot wheel and the still living Sphairos, identifiable by his Phyrgian cap, stands on the right.[25]

The name of Myrtilus is derived from the 'myrtle' shrub, whose branches became emblematic of the marriage ceremony. Alternatively, he was assigned an Amazon named Myrto as a mother, hence making him a matrilineal child. The myrtle was sacred to Aphrodite, but with connotations of death, associated with her dead Phrygian lover Adonis and similar funereal contexts,[26] reflected in its common name as toxic dogbane, probably with

---

24  Some accounts (fourth-century BCE historian Theopompus) attempted to rationalize this problem by claiming that Sphairos died before the race and appeared in a dream requesting burial; this would implausibly place the Temple of Apollo Cillaeus on the tiny isle of Poros in the same spot as the Temple of Athena Apaturia. The later reappearances of Sphairos as still living after the eventful chariot race were further rationalized as ghostly materializations.

25  Museo Etruso Guarnacci, Volterra, MG 215.

26  Vergil, *Aeneid*, 3. 19-68. It grew on the grave of Aeneas' Phrygian/Trojan cousin Polydorus, and dripped with blood as the hero attempted to uproot it.

implications of the more sinister canines, the Phrygian/Thracian fox and the wolf, the psychoactive wolfsbane plant, and traditions of lycanthropy.[27] It signifies the death of the lover, replaced by the married husband, and was thus worn commonly as the bridal garland. It therefore testifies to the transition from female polyandry to the male's marital dominance. The 'ball' or sphere (or even more explicitly as a hoop) of the other charioteer Sphairos was similarly a traditional token of love and courtship. It ultimately symbolizes the apertures of the body through which lovers physically unite.[28]

Troezen itself was an entrance to the netherworld, reputedly the entrance from which Herakles returned with Theseus when he rescued him from the underworld. In the *Hippolytus* tragedy (428 BCE), which involves the thematic opposition between the matrilineal and paternal sons of Theseus, Euripides portrayed the chorus as women washing menstrual cloths in the stream that cascades in a series of pools down the mountainside from the netherworld entrance in the cliffs high up above, from which Myrtilos/Sphairos presumably plunged to his death. The symbolism of the 'hoop' as vulva of the goddess applied to such entrances to the world beyond. As Aphrodite, who delivers the prologue to the tragedy, declares, Hippolytus does not see that the gate to the underworld lies open to him. At the end of the tragedy, Artemis retaliates by predicting the death of Aphrodite's beloved Adonis.

The mythical kingship list for the Athenian dynasties is

---

27  Carl A.P. Ruck (ed.), Mark A. Hoffman, Evie Marie Holmberg, Stavros Kiotsekoglou, and Vassil Markov, *Dionysus in Thrace: Ancient Entheogenic Themes in the Mythology and Archaeology of Northern Greece, Bulgaria, and Turkey* (Berkeley, CA: Regent Press, 2014).

28  Compare the bawdy implications of lovers communicating through a 'chink in the wall'. In Shakespeare's *Midsummer Night's Dream*, act 5, scene 1, Pyramus and Thisbe communicate through 'chink', played by an actor, with the chink apparently, the space between the actor's legs. Gordon Williams, *Shakespeare's Sexual Language: A Glossary* (London: The Atlone Press, 1997), 189. See below on the Sphinx and the 'sphincter'; Euripides' *Hippolytus* and the presentation of the wreath to the effigy of Artemis. Eros is often portrayed with a (victory, bridal) wreath: Abduction of Europa, riding the bull, followed by Eros with two wreaths, Caeretan *hydria*, 520 BCE, Villa Giulia, Rome. On Eros as a ball thrower, see J.F. Davidson, "Anacreon, Homer, and the Young Woman from Lesbos": 132-137, in *Mnemosyne*, vol. 40, no. 1-2 (1987).

disjointed, with successive new beginnings, representing an attempt in later historical revisionism to force matrilineal descent into a patriarchal paradigm. Thus, the line of Theseus some two hundred years later terminated in a deceit that was also claimed as the etiology for the Apaturia Festival. In a single hand-to-hand combat between the kings of Athens and neighboring Boeotia, a certain figure named Melanthus (Melanthos) or 'Black Flower' replaced the Athenian as king by causing his defeat and death. The deceit consisted in throwing him off guard by shouting that a man in a black goatskin was aiding his opponent. The black flower and the black goatskin metaphorically represent the shift back to the drunkenness and Dionysian bacchanalia implied in the Troezenian conception of Theseus, against the warning of the Delphic prophesy.

# THE SON CONCEIVED IN DRUNKENNESS

# Chapter Two
# Making the New Olympia

**The Marriage of the Horse-mistress**

Implicit in the chariot race of Oenomaüs and Pelops is an opposition between Dionysus and Apollo. The name of Oenomaüs is formed from the word for 'wine' (*oínos*) and a verbal root that denotes 'eager yearning' (*má-esthai*), while Pelops' charioteer Sphairos is sometimes cited with the name Cillus (Killos), apparently, a companion from his native Anatolia named for the town sacred to Apollo. Chryseïs, the abducted maiden awarded to Agamemnon, and her father, the priest of Apollo, came from Cilla.[29] Similarly, a place near Thebes with the same name had a temple to Apollo. Pelops erected a temple on the site of the grave of the charioteer, and dedicated it to Apollo with the epithet of Cillaeus.

In mundane terms, the race was run on a track within the confines of the Olympian sanctuary at Pisa in the northwestern Peloponnesus, and it was so commemorated at Olympia by the gravesite of the charioteer within the sanctuary grounds, but mythically it conferred control of the entire Peloponnesus and its cultural traditions to the victor. Accordingly, the racecourse stretched across the entire landmass, from west to the east, ending at the isle of Sphairia and the Myrtoan Sea beyond. Thus, the gravesites of the two charioteers are also on the eastern coast of

---

29   Homer, *Iliad*, 1.37.

the landmass at the base of the looming mountain that marked the Troezenian entrance to the netherworld.

Vase paintings replace the charioteer for Pelops with Hippodamia in the vehicle with her lover as the abducted bride since the essential theme involves which male claims ownership over her and her offspring, her husband or her father, who was reputed to be also her lover.[30] Thus it was also told that Oenomaüs had received an oracle warning him that whoever received his daughter in marriage would replace him. This latter version is the common motif that signifies the transition to a new mode of cultural tradition. The same thing was said of Perseus at Mycenae and is implied in the marginal role of Oedipus.

In fact, the single charioteer, who was the competing athlete with his team of horses or mules, drove the chariot in a race. In combat, the second occupant of the chariot was the warrior driven by his charioteer. The race with Oenomaüs was actually intended to leave only one of the competitors living, ending in the death of the losing suitor, which had been the outcome with all of the opponents before the arrival of Pelops.

It is, however, not so much simply an opposition between the two gods, Dionysus and Apollo, who are half-brothers of each other, as it is a matter of the thematic transition from older more ecstatic forms of worship centering on female shamanism to the new evolving realm of Olympian male superiority and dominance, over which Zeus presides. Dionysus and Apollo are emblematic of this dichotomous opposition. Olympia was a sacred site as early as the tenth century BCE. The burnt remains of *Homo heidelbergensis* found at the site suggest that its sanctity may even extend to the hominid ancestors of *Homo sapiens* hundreds of thousands of years ago.[31] The conical hill at the eastern edge of the Classical sanctuary was where the mythical Oenomaüs would have had his supposed house. By the Classical times, the hill was assigned to

---

30  Apollodorus, *Epitome*, 2.4-6.5.
31  Katerina Harvati, Eleni Panagopoulou, and Curtis Runnels, "The Paleoanthropology of Greece": 131-143, in *Evolutionary Anthropology*, vol. 18 (2009).

Cronus (Kronos), as the predecessor and father of Zeus, symbolic of the pre-Olympian Age.

## The Marriage Bed in the Magical Garden

The sacred structures at the base of the hill maintained a thematic association with the female or primordial goddess of the site. These included a temple to the mother of the gods (presumably Rhea, the mate of Cronus) and the Temple of Hera, whose greater antiquity than that of the great fifth-century Temple of Olympian Zeus was architecturally maintained as essential to its symbolism. Among its antiquities was preserved the bed on which Zeus consummated the marriage to Hera that subjugated her as wife to him and endowed her thereafter as patroness of matrimony, the ritual by which the male claimed ownership over a woman's body and its offspring. Such marriage beds were a common item in temples of Hera elsewhere and suggest probable ritual enactments of a sexual nature.

In mythic tradition, this marriage was supposed to have occurred in the Garden of the Hesperides, implicating the golden apple of its sacred tree and its fungal analogue in the ecstatic orgasm.[32] A similar motif lurks in the figure of the charioteer Sphairos, as the 'wheel', inasmuch as a race of such magnitude implies more than physical transport; the chariot ride was a trip of mystical dimensions, especially since it occurred in the context of an entrance to other worlds and the Apollonian-Dionysian dichotomy, and the vehicle for the transport could be suspected of being a metaphor for a psychoactive agent that would access the shamanic flight. The wheel is a common metaphor for the mushroom's cap, with the gills on its underside presenting a good likeness of spokes. It is represented in the wheel of Ixion's torment, spinning like a solar disk, sometimes depicted with serpents binding the victim to its spokes as an indication of its toxicity. The wheel of Ixion is a

---

32  Carl A.P. Ruck, Blaise Daniel Staples, and Clark Heinrich, *The Apples of Apollo: Pagan and Christian Mysteries of the Eucharist* (Durham, NC: Carolina Academic Press, 2000).

fungal anthropomorphism. His crime was that he tried to undermine Hera's wifely devotion to her husband Zeus by sleeping with the goddess, but in his altered state of perception, he slept only with her hallucinatory likeness in the figure of the lady Cloud (Nephele). Since their offspring was Centaurus, born from a rainfall upon the mountainside from the cloud, and the subsequent ancestor of the whole race of equine anthropomorphisms known as centaurs, we might suspect that the mutable appearance of lady Cloud could assume the form of a Horse-mistress. Ixion himself is named for the mistletoe and he is hence involved in the whole complex of Druidic religion and the sanctity of the oak tree and its two analogous parasites, the mistletoe that infests its branches and the sacred mushrooms that sprout as fruits at its base, both inseminated by the fall of the bolt lightning during the rainfall of the thunderstorm. Zeus's marriage of Hera, like that of Pelops to the Horse-mistress Hippodamia, redefined the ecstatic rapture to the monogamous role of the wife, subservient to her polygamous mate.

The serpent Ladon that guarded the Tree of the Golden Apples was also a tributary of the River Alpheios (Alfeios), which flows through the Olympian sanctuary. Rivers in Greek mythology were not seen as the runoff of rainfall, but as welling up from netherworld pools and analogous to the seawaters of Poseidon or the springs or fountains of the water nymphs and their lovers. In Greek, the sea is named *thálassa*, with a word assimilated from the pre-Greek Minoan/Pelasgian language. Originally Poseidon was not associated with the sea, but with rivers, streams, sacred springs, and the like. His Latin equivalent as Neptune was derived in antiquity from the 'nuptial' of heaven and earth.[33] It is cognate with *nápe* in Greek for a wooded moist valley and *nepos* in Latin for a daughter's or a sister's son. As such, rivers were often anthropomorphized as bestial abductors of maidens, such as the Acheloös that courted the wife of Herakles. Ladon was eventually transported to the stars as the constellation *Draco* or *Serpens*, which is entwined like

---

33  Varro, *Lingua Latina*, 5.72.

a river around the northern pole. The pole star was seen as the immovable axis about which the cosmos rotated and as the gateway to the empyrean world beyond.[34] The river's metamorphism into the constellation is indicative of the psychoactive potential of the fruit guarded by the serpent, and the plucking of the magical plant symbolized the control over the shamanic rapture it induced, realigning its pathway from chthonic descent toward transcendental ascent. Thus, the serpent Ladon was a brother of the Gorgon sisterhood, and he is named as the rockrose, the *kísthos*, that lends its name and symbolism to the *Cista Mystica*, the basket that conceals the secret items for a Mystery initiation.[35]

## The Great Altar of Olympian Zeus

The accumulating burnt remains from the daily sacrificial offerings made at the great altar of Zeus closely adjacent to the hill resulted in an ever-increasing conical pile of ashes, to create a symbolic replacement for the old topographical site as a testimony to the new evolving age of the Olympian family. The ashes from the altars of the other deities of the family were regularly deposited on this main altar. The athletic contests inaugurated at the sanctuary in the eighth century were meant to reenact the mythical victory of Pelops over the previous divine orientation of the House of Oenomaüs. In chronological terms, Pelops would have been two generations before the Trojan War and hence his assumption of control over the Horse-mistress daughter of Oinomaüs should have taken place some five centuries before the first Olympiad in 776 BCE.

The heavily forested conical Kronion Hill was associated with the earliest shamanism as still commemorated in the rituals of the Classical period.[36] The prophetic Olympian priesthood claimed

---

34 Carl A.P. Ruck and Mark A. Hoffman, *The Effluents of Deity: Alchemy and Psychoactive Sacraments in Medieval and Renaissance Art* (Durham, NC: Carolina Academic Press, 2012), 177.
35 Ruck *et al.*, *The Apples of Apollo*, 51-54.
36 *Ibid.*, 46-49.

Iamos of Lake Stymphalos in northern Acadia just beyond Nemea as its hereditary founder. He was a bastard son of Apollo and his mother gave him his sacred name (*onyma athanaton*) as a 'drug-man' on the basis of the involvement of psychoactive herbalist motifs in his birthing: non-lethal serpent venom, bees, honey, and the violet flower, the last punning on the homonymous word for the violet and the arrow's toxin.[37] His mother Euadne (a 'flower' nymph, a dialectal version of *Eu-ánthos*) was a bastard daughter of Poseidon, abducted in the River Eurotas, where it springs up in the Arcadian mountains. When Iamos came of age, he waded into the Alpheios River, which flows down toward the Olympian plain, calling upon his two unacknowledged divine ancestors, his maternal grandfather Poseidon, and his father Apollo, to award him due honor. For the two preceding generations, there had been only children born with mothers. As acknowledgement of his divine paternal lineage, he was given control over the Kronion Hill, the 'steep rock of lofty Kronion'.[38]

## The House of Oenomaüs

Pausanias saw one of the wooden posts of Oenomaüs' house still standing in the second century CE. These were the pillars that were once topped with the supposed remains of the decapitated heads of the unsuccessful suitors for the hand of Hippodamia.[39] The authenticity of relics is of less importance than their identified existence, whether they be pious forgeries or relocated to more convenient places. The surviving post, reinforced by bronze bands and labeled, served as the turning point for the chariot races; and the ghost of the dead suitor, whose decapitated head had once served as its capital, was thought to materialize there to frighten the horses. It was also identified as a cenotaph of the charioteer Myrtilus, whose

---

37   Carl A.P. Ruck, "On the Sacred Names of Iamos and Ion: Ethnobotanical Referents in the Hero's Parentage": 235-252, in *Classical Journal*, vol. 71, no. 3 (1976).
38   Pindar, *Olympia*, 6.57 *et seq.*
39   Pausanias, Description of Greece, 5.20.7.

actual remains were presumably buried on the islet of Sphairia. The ruins of the supposed House of Oenomaüs, destroyed by a bolt of lightning, were preserved as well, and also what was left of the stables where he was said to have kept his horses.

It is these stables that Herakles (a great grandson of Pelops) cleansed when he, too, made over the sanctuary to his Olympian father, although by that time they were known as the Stables of Augeas (Augeias) and the defiling excrement came from his herd of cows. Cleansing the stables implies the equine and bovine creatures that produced the heaps of manure that had never before been cleaned away. This is probably the operable symbolism since both horses and horsemen like centaurs or horsewomen, like Gorgons and Hippodamia, are thematic bacchanalian motifs. The same is true of cows and cattle, which thematically are always in estrus, as the cow-maiden Io and even Hera, whose pre-Olympian manifestation endowed her with a cow face as *boöpis*. Hence cleansing the stables has the same goal of displacing the former bacchant shamanism.

## The Grove of the Altis

Herakles also planted the sacred grove of olive trees known as the Altis at the base of the Kronion Hill. He supposedly found the first olive among the mythical Hyperborean peoples, beyond the north wind, where he plucked its primordial sprout as the golden horn of a reindeer sacred to Artemis, known as the Ceryneian Hind. The olive grove supplied the wreaths that were awarded to the victorious athletes. The olive, which requires annual pruning to maintain its cultivated fruiting state, was emblematic of the triumph of cultivation over primitivism, and it was a symbolic surrogate for the same psychoactive plant or entheogen commemorated in the traditions of the Hesperid Garden. The cleansing of the stables and the planting of the olive grove represent the same motif as the chariot race. Herakles was even said to have had a son from Epikaste, a daughter of Augeas, and to have rescued a Hippodamia, who was the daughter of the king of Elis, one of the two towns in whose territory the Olympian sanctuary lay.

The thematic significance of the rescue of the 'horse-mistress maiden' Hippodamia to the reorientation of the Olympian sanctuary is clear from the pairing of two versions of the motif on the great fifth-century Temple of Olympian Zeus. The preparation for the chariot race of Pelops and Oenomäus is portrayed in the sculptural group of the eastern pediment above the entrance, with Zeus in central position flanked by the two contestants and with the Iamid shaman crouched in the corner nearest the Kronion Hill and distressed at foreseeing the death of his lord. This is expectable since the race is one of the etiological myths for the Olympic Games. The western pediment, however, depicts the same myth as the battle of the Lapiths and the drunken centaurs at the marriage feast of Hippodamia to Pirithoüs (Peirithoos), the heroic companion of Theseus. In central position, with the two heroes on either side, stands Apollo, looming above the others, unperturbed and extending an arm to preside over the battle whose outcome he, too, can foresee. The evolution of Olympian Apollonian transcendence over bacchanalian drunkenness is the theme in common between the two sculptural pediments.

The *metope* sequence for the temple depicts the twelve Labors of Herakles, the preeminent athlete and hence another etiology for the games. These were placed six at either end of the temple. The order in which Pausanias reported them indicates that the viewers as they walked around the temple before entering the *cella* or temple chamber would have begun with the Nemean Lion at the northern end of the western facade, the traditional first of the Labors, and ended back at the northern end of the eastwardly facing entrance of the temple with the Cleansing of the Stables, placed after the dog Cerberus, which traditionally was counted the first or the last of the Labors.[40] Thus, the cleansing of the stables was the culminating achievement of the hero's Labors since it, too, was the

---

40  Euripides, *Herakles*. Some sources, however, made Cerberus the first Labor to rationalize the ensuing Labors as expiations for the murder of the hero's wife and children.

reorientation of the sanctuary's religious tradition, analogous to his planting of the Altis olive grove at the base of the Kronion Hill.

## The Cretan Herakles

Herakles, however, had a far different role at Olympia before he rededicated it in the name of his Olympian father. He was once one of the Cretan dactyls who attended the goddess and this was commemorated at the Classical sanctuary by the identification of a cave there supposedly on the Kronion Hill as the Idaean Cave,[41] although the reference must be to an artificial construction since the hill is not geologically suitable for the formation of a natural cavern. Similarly, Joseph Smith, the founder of Mormonism, claimed to have found the golden tablets of the *Book of Mormon* in a cave on Cumorah in upper New York State, a wooded hillock where no caves exist.[42] At Olympia, there are many of these similar hills or drumlins close together along the plain of the Alfeios, and they were not formed by seismic uplift or volcanic activity, but the result of glacial drift and alluvial deposit. The Temple of the Mother of the Gods at the base of the hill symbolically represents this cave in the Classical sanctuary.

The most famous of the Idaean Caves was located on a hill on the slopes of Mount Dikte of Crete, an actual cave in ritual use, but there were several other of these so-named caves since the name is derived from the *ide* or 'wooded hill', or more simply from the wooden post, like the one preserved from the so-called pillared 'house' of Oenomaüs, with the decapitated head of a suitor

---

41   Noel Robertson, "The Ancient Mother of the Gods: A Missing Chapter in the History of Greek Religion": 239-304, in Eugene M. Lane (ed.), *Cybele, Attis and Related Cults: Essays in Memory of M.J. Vermaseren* (Leiden: Brill, 1996).

42   According to Brigham Young, "The hill opened, and they walked into a cave, in which there was a large and spacious room." Joseph Smith was engaged in 'digging for ancient treasure', which was a metaphor of root digging for medicinal herbs. Frank Sargent Hoffman, *The Sphere of Religion: A Consideration of Nature and its Influence on the Progress of Civilization* (New York: G.P. Putnam, 2008), 181. Robert T. Beckstead, "Restoration and the Sacred Mushroom: Did Joseph Smith use Psychedelic Substances to Facilitate Visionary Experiences?" Sunstone Symposium, Salt Lake, City, August, 2007, sponsored by the Sunstone Foundation and Magazine (not affiliated with the Church of Latter Day Saints).

as capital. The Kronion hill is too steep to provide a suitable plot for the construction of a house. The Cretan dactyls of the Idaean cave were tiny anthropomorphisms of the sacred woods or posts,[43] no bigger than a 'finger', a common euphemism for the phallus, a little zoomorphism of the fungal growths commonly found growing on such wooded hills. The destruction of the 'house' by lightning, leaving only its posts, suggests the common association of the growth of mushrooms from the fall of a bolt of lightning.

The dactyls were interchangeable with the *curetes* (*kouretes*, 'little men') and the *corybants* (crested 'helmet-walkers'), which indicates that they were not only botanical, also but ecstatic little dancing warriors, intoxicating like the 'wine-man' whose house it was, or more simply, entheogens involved in the rituals of shamanism. As *corybants*, the anthropomorphism endowed them with a shield to clash like cymbals, stamping their feet to the rhythm of the drum. The shield and the drum are descriptive of their hemispherical 'caps', which in folklore yielded figures like the *kaulomyketes*, 'shield/cover-mushroom' warriors. The shield or cymbal or drum borne above the heads of the tiny dancer-warriors is an easily visualized anthropomorphism of a mushroom. Bronze cymbals have been discovered in the excavation of the Olympian sanctuary, and drinking from the cymbal or the kettledrum was one of the code passwords for initiation into the mysteries.

> 'I have eaten out of the drum, I have drunk out of the cymbal, I have carried the *kernos* vessel, I have slipped into the bedroom'. Are these not tokens of disgrace? Are not the mysteries an absurdity?[44]

Needless to say, the mention of drinking and eating implies a mode of access to altered consciousness, which was apparently

---

43  Compare the Nordic sacred tree pillars (*Irminsul*, 'Irmin's pillar') and the materialized little people, the *alfar* (elves). These pillars were assimilated into Roman tradition as 'pillars of Heracles'. Tacitus, *Germania*, 1.34.

44  Clement of Alexandria (2nd century CE), *Exhortation to the Greeks*, 2.

interpreted as a sexual experience in the bedchamber.

The little Herakles at the old Olympia had four dactyl brothers from Crete, since these dactylic creatures occurred in groups of five, supposedly materialized from the fingers of Rhea as she grasped the earth in the agony of giving birth to Zeus. The analogue to an herbalist shaman bent over to pluck the mushroom men is unmistakable, especially since the magical procedures for gathering sacred plants often involve sexual mimesis.

Magical plants must be gathered by procedures that honor their indwelling spiritual powers.[45] Most ancient plants have common names with mythological or animal referents indicating that the gatherer was aware of such magical dimensions, which survive into the later languages of Europe, but were largely suppressed as mere pagan and hence diabolical and anti-Christian superstitions, except in the outlawed and persecuted traditions of witchcraft.[46] Where such procedures have survived at least until recently in the rural margins of civilized Europe, they indicate elaborate fantasies. The plant is hunted indirectly and by feigned misdirection, allowing it instead the opportunity to find the root-cutter, thereby signifying its willingness for the encounter. It is addressed with honorific and sacred names, as acknowledgement of its indwelling persona. It is given offerings of clothing and food as replacement for what is to be taken, sometimes replacing one psychoactive substance for another. Finally, it is approached with seductive gestures of sexual mimesis, with the root-cutter undressed and with genitals exposed.[47]

---

45  Wendy M. Geniusz, *Our Knowledge is Not Primitive: Decolonizing Botanical Anishinaabe Teachings (Iroquois and their Neighbors)* (Syracuse, NY: Syracuse University Press, 2009).

46  Ramón Gómez Fernández, *Las Plantas en la Brujería Medieval* (Madrid: Celeste Ediciones, 1999).

47  Mircea Eliade, *Zalmoxis, the Vanishing God: Comparative Studies in the Religions and Folklore of Dacia and Eastern Europe* (Chicago: University of Chicago Press, 1986, English translation of *De Zalmoxis à Genghis Khan* (Paris: Éditions Payot, 1970), 208 *et seq*. Carl A.P. Ruck, Blaise Daniel Staples, José Alfredo González Celdrán, and Mark Alwin Hoffman, *The Hidden World: Survival of Pagan Shamanic Themes in European Fairytales* (Durham, NC: Carolina Academic Press, 2006), 133 *et seq*.

There should be no doubt that there was no house of Oenomaüs on the Kronion Hill other than the woods themselves and the little psychoactive tree-men, capped and standing like pillars or posts. The anthropomorphism is so common that the *pileus* of the mushroom, so-called, is its 'cap', implying that someone, albeit 'one-footed', must be wearing it, and the stipe, so-called, is a 'trunk' (*stipes*), implying that the mushroom is actually a tree, although Latin *stipes* also means a 'leg' or a 'post'. The chariot race, moreover, was run between the termini marked by the Dionysian and Apollonian antithesis or the bacchanalian and transcendental states of consciousness, in a context of transition from female to male dominance.

# Chapter Three
# The Child of Fortune

**The Creature Found Growing on the Mountainside**

Oedipus, the swollen one-foot, with his feet pinned together, was such a creature that one might pluck off a mountainside. Sophocles' *Tyrannus* is a masterpiece of inevitable revelation in tracking down the footsteps toward the hero's identity.

Someone killed Laïus. Apollo, through Creon (Kreon), who has just returned from the Delphic oracle, tells Oedipus he must discover the murderer. Oedipus immediately enlists himself as an ally of the god in seeking out the truth. Tiresias (Teiresias) as a seer tells Oedipus that truth, that Oedipus killed the king, but Oedipus cannot see it, although he, too, has demonstrated that he was a seer in the previous crisis by solving the riddle of the Sphinx. This is now a new riddle, although it will turn out to be just a version of the former one.

Oedipus suspects a plot against him and quarrels with Creon. Jocasta intervenes to show that oracles are worthless. Laïus was supposed to be killed by his son, but she and Laïus prevented that by exposing the baby three days after its birth to die on the mountainside. Instead, it was a group of foreign highwaymen, as she claims, who murdered Laïus at a place where three roads meet. Apollo and the Delphic oracle are clearly worthless. No one will consult the oracle anymore. That is, of course, a blasphemous accusation since unless the oracle is true, Apollo's status as an Olympian god is jeopardized. This would cast Oedipus in the role of the god's antithesis, his ultimate enemy, unless the prophecy should prove true.

## Worthless Prophecies

The mention of the juncture of the three roads, however, rouses Oedipus's fear. He knows the place and inquires about the details. One eyewitness to the murder survived, pasturing sheep now as far away from the palace as possible, and Oedipus immediately has someone sent to fetch him. Oedipus explains his concern, how a drunken man at a symposium had claimed he was not the child of his supposed parents, the king and queen of Corinth. Could there be truth in drunkenness? The Corinthian royal couple, however, dismissed the rumor, but Oedipus set off in secret for Delphi to inquire about the tale.

The oracle told him that he would kill his father and marry his mother. To avoid this, Oedipus vowed never to return to Corinth. At that very same juncture of the three roads, *en route* to Thebes, he killed a man and, as he thinks, all his attendants. The father and unrecognized son had met coming from opposite directions on the same road. The intersection is called the *Schíste Hodós* or 'Cut (in the) Road'. The site is now identified as *Distomo*, 'double mouth'. Here the road from Delphi branches to Daulis and Ambrysus, the former going east on to Thebes and the latter south down the mountain on to the Gulf of Corinth. Presumably, the latter had been the route of Oedipus up to Delphi when he went to inquire of the oracle. In the dispute over the narrow passage, Laïus had even ratified the essential token of recognition by running his cart over the stranger's already maimed feet. Laïus was returning to Delphi to inquire whether his exposed son had actually died, and Oedipus was journeying to Thebes in order not to return to Corinth.

The eyewitness is essential, for only he knows that, according to him, it was a group of men and not a single man who murdered the king. Many cannot be one. A messenger arrives from Corinth with the news that Polybus (Polybos) has died of natural causes and Oedipus has inherited the kingship, by right of patriliny, supposedly the legitimate son of the king. The prophecy may be correct after all, only if Oedipus innocently caused the old king's death because he longed to see his self-exiled son. Clearly, as

Jocasta had declared, Apollo and the Delphic oracle are worthless.

Oedipus's Corinthian mother, however, is still alive. Oracles are tricky. If he returns to Corinth to claim the kingship, he might still marry the Corinthian queen, claiming the kingship doubly by right of matriliny. This is actually the unrecognized situation of Oedipus's double legitimacy at Thebes. The messenger sets his mind as ease. The Corinthian Merope is not his mother. The drunkard's tale is correct. *In vino veritas*, as the Latin motto claims. The messenger reveals that the Corinthian royal couple was not the parents of Oedipus. He had received the maimed infant from another shepherd, the very same man that Oedipus has already sent for, the surviving eyewitness to the murder.

Jocasta realizes the truth, but will not reveal it to Oedipus. He suspects that she is afraid he may be someone not noble enough to be her mate. She withdraws into the house, never to speak again.

It is at this point that Oedipus has no parents. 'I declare myself the son of Lady Luck', he says, 'the one who grants what is good'.[48] Luck or *Tyché* was honored as a goddess in cults. She was often indistinguishable from Demeter, and presided with a turreted crown over a city's wellbeing or was shown as the nurse of the child Plutos, who was the personification of the beneficent aspects of the netherworld as wealth and prosperity. She could, however, also hold a ball indicative of the unsteadiness of good fortune, because she was fickle and could easily roll in the other direction, where she became a companion of Nemesis, rightful indignation, at viewing excessive happiness or crimes that went unpunished.

Whatever the outcome, let the truth be told, Oedipus declares. 'I want to see my seed, however small'. *Tyché* is his mother—hopefully, the version that grants what is good; the seed or *spérma*[49] would be his father. Who is his father?

---

48   Sophocles, *Tyrannus*, 1080-1081.
49   *Ibid.*, 1076-1077.

## Matriliny and Patriliny

In the heroic monomyth,[50] the mother is always ambiguous.[51] The mother is obviously the more demonstrable of the parents since there were witnesses to see the child emerge from her body, but no one can be certain what kind of woman she was, subservient to her husband and the traditions of male dominance or a resurgence of the alliance of females bonded in a sisterhood serving the dominant goddess. There could be no mother more ambiguous than Luck, with her optimistic and pessimistic potentials.

The births of Athena and Dionysus are significant anomalies in that those deities were seen emerging from the body of their father. Aphrodite might be counted as another example, in the tradition that she emerged from the sea as the female metamorphosis of the severed genitals of her father Ouranos (Uranus); she was not, however, seen directly emerging from her father's body.

A similar motif of transition to verifiable patriliny defined the births of the immediate members of the Olympian family,[52] who were eaten as infants by their father Kronos (Saturn), 'digested' (with alchemical implications[53]) as transformation from their allegiance to their mother Rhea,[54] and regurgitated as Olympians through of the agency of the emetic potion or 'drug' (*phármakon*) administered along with the swallowed birth stone of Zeus.[55] Zeus himself was at first recognizably divine by right of matriliny. The

---

50   Joseph Campbell used the term monomyth to designate the archetype of the hero's journey (*The Hero with a Thousand Faces*, 1949), borrowing the word from James Joyce's *Finnegans Wake*.
51   Carl A.P. Ruck and Mark A. Hoffman, *Entheogens, Myth, and Human Consciousness* (Berkeley, CA: Ronin Publishing), 117-118.
52   Hera, Poseidon, Demeter, Hestia.
53   Alchemy as spiritual transformation paralleled by metallurgical procedures can be traced to the pre-historical period and underlies the myths of the *fire* thief and of Hephaistos and the volcanic forge and provided the ritual scenario for mystery religions like those of the Kaberioi. See Ruck *et al., The Hidden World*, 125-126; Carl A.P. Ruck, *The Great Gods of Samothrace and the Cult of the Little People* (Berkekey, CA: Regent Press, 2017).
54   John Davidson, "Zeus and the Stone Substitute": 363-369, in *Hermes*, vol. 123, no. 3 (1995).
55   Apollodorus, 1.4-5, 1.6-7.

ruse of the magical so-called stone-drug is the only proof of his patrilineal descent.

## *Phármakon*

The goddess Metis was responsible for the ruse of the emetic *phármakon*.[56] Zeus would subsequently ingest her herself when she metamorphosed into a fly[57] in the myth of Athena's conception. The metamorphosis into a fly suggests the mythical motifs associating the *Amanita muscaria* mushroom with the killing of flies, as well as the engendering of the same as the larvae commonly seen emerging from the harvested mushroom. In Judaic lore, the god of the Philistines worshipped at Ekron was called Ba'al Zebúb (Beelzebub),[58] interpreted as 'Lord of the Flies', an epithet also accorded to various Greek gods and heroes, including Zeus as *Myiagros* ('Fly-hunter') at Olympia. An inscription found at Ekron supplies the name of the goddess that the 'Fly-lord' there attended as *PTR*, which indicates that she was an anthropomorphized 'mushroom'.[59] Christianity identified this 'Fly-lord' as Lucifer and demonized him as the devil. It is extremely naïve to isolate these traditions from the shamanic context in which the psychoactive mushroom provided access to transcendent ecstasy, preferring instead to dwell upon the attraction of flies to the carcass of the slaughtered bull. The latter, moreover, is itself metaphoric for the fungal analogue.

The stone and the genitals both suggest a botanical metaphor

---

56 Hesiod, *Theogony*, 888-900; Apollodorus, *Bibiotheke*, 1.4-5.

57 Hesiod, *Theogony*, 886, with scholiast. Christian August Lobeck, *Aglaophamus, sive, De theologiae mysticae Graecorum causis libri tres* (Berlin: Gebrüder Borntraeger Verlag, 1829), vol. 1, p. 613. Lewis Richard Farnell, *The Cults of the Greek States* (Oxford: Clarendon Press, 1896-1909), vol. I, p. 283. See Carl A.P. Ruck (ed.), Mark A. Hoffman, Evie Marie Holmberg, Stavros Kiotsekoglou, and Vassil Markov, *Dionysus in Thrace: Ancient Entheogenic Themes in the Mythology and Archaeology of Northern Greece, Bulgaria, and Turkey* (Berkeley, CA: Regent Press, 2014).

58 *2 Kings*, 1.2-3, 6, 26.

59 Carl A.P. Ruck and Mark A. Hoffman, *The Effluents of Deity* (Durham, NC: Carolina Academic Press, 2012), 14-16.

since the genitals are always not so much severed as harvested with a pruning hook or reaping scythe, and the very stone itself that was the *phármakon* was preserved at Delphi as the sacred navel or ómphalos. This latter was probably the oldest relic at the sanctuary; the two marble replicas found at the site, egg-shaped with a flattened base, originally surmounted by golden eagles or gorgons, are pious forgeries of a later date. The primordial stone was probably phallic in shape or significance, representing the consort of Gaia and the gravesite of her intoxicating male attendant as the serpent Python or the god Dionysus. It may at one time have been fitted to channel the psychoactive ethylene fumes rising from the seismic fissure for the oracular consultation.[60] This clearly identifies the ómphalos itself as a symbolic replica of an entheogen.

Both the egg and the phallus stone are metaphors for the sacred mushroom. The stone was also called a 'disk',[61] suggesting the metaphor of the mushroom's cap. Zeus had the epithet of the 'Great Disk'. It was also supposedly a *baítylos* or meteoritic 'thunderstone' fallen from the heavens. Such thunderstones could also sprout from the ground as a type of 'thunder-mushroom'.

## Mushroom-town

In the myth of Perseus, parallel to his harvesting of the head of the Gorgon Medusa, a local tradition claimed that he picked a mushroom at the future site of Mycenae when the mushroom-shaped pommel (hilt) fell from his pruning hook. This latter manifestation indicates that the mushroom could be anthropomorphized as the Gorgon Medusa zoomorphism, a bearded female with added characteristics of pig, serpent, horse, fish, and cow. His encounter with her was ultimately sexual, in that his wife Andromeda, a doublet of the Medusa as a 'Man-queen', replaces her. Hence the mushroom or *mykes* was also a common

---

60   James Hastings, *Encyclopedia of Religion and Ethics*, part 18, (Whitefish, MT: Kessinger Publishing, 2003), sc. omphalos.
61   Scholiast on Lycophron, *Alexandra*, 397 et seq.

term for the erect penis.[62] His conquest of the dominant 'Queen' Medusa was the re-foundation myth that imposed male dominance upon the former Minoan or Pelasgian citadel of Mycenae, reinterpreting its name as the 'place of the *mykes*', instead of the plurality of its Gorgon sisterhood of Mykene maidens. If he had failed, he would have been metamorphosed into a pillar of stone, a thunderstone or *baítylos*.

An entheogen is a plant in which the deity resides. The deity and the worshipper are brought together at the site of the entheogen. The shaman hero and the deity become consubstantial with the mediating botanical sacrament. Most simply put, if you are looking for the deity, you can find it in the plant. If you eat the plant, you share an identity with it and its indwelling deity. The transcendent or ecstatic communion is accessed via the plant's psychoactive toxins, and the shaman and the deity often share aspects of the botanical specimen's iconography, such as have only a single foot or wearing a fungal cap.

## Thunderstone

Thus, these thunderbolt stones were endowed with prophetic properties, indicating their psychoactive potential as entheogens.[63] In the ruse of Rhea's substitution of the stone for the newly birthed Zeus, she wrapped the stone in woolen swaddling as a disguise. The wads of woolen swaddling are metaphoric for the white scabby remnants of the Amanita's shattered universal veil that give the mushroom cap its distinctive appearance. The *baítylos* (*baetulus*) was said to be a precious gemstone, zealously sought by the Zoroastrian magi priests for their mushroom cult, and it also provides the Latin name for the 'birch' tree (*betullus*, *betulus*), which commonly hosts the mushroom symbiotically parasitic upon its

---

62   Archilochus, frag. 34 (Diehl); cf. Hesychius, Herodian.
63   The fourth-century BCE Greek comedian Antiphanes makes specific mention (frag. 227, Edmonds) of a mushroom associated with the oak that was reputed to induce clairvoyance.

roots.⁶⁴ The narrow white trunk of the birch lent its symbolism to the tree as the shaman's mode of ascent through the realms. The mushroom was commonly thought to fruit where thunder struck the earth.⁶⁵ The etymology of 'birch' itself is ultimately traceable to its 'bright' appearance.

There was even a tradition that Rhea hung the infant Zeus upon a tree to hide him, while Kronos vainly searched the heavens and the earth, overlooking the intermediary realm lying in full sight.⁶⁶ Perseus was also claimed to have harvested the Gorgon head as the golden fruit of the magical tree growing in the western Garden of the Hesperides.⁶⁷

The ómphalos preserved at Delphi is sculpted as enclosed in a knotted woolen net with recurrent bunched wads. It was ritually anointed each day with olive oil, and spotted with additional actual scabs of wool for ritual occasions. The wads imitate the mushroom's wooly scabs. It also reflects the additional metaphor for the fly-agaric as the 'Golden Fleece', homophonous with `apple' (*mélon*, Latin *malum*, the latter also homophonous with the word for 'evil').⁶⁸ A parallel myth claimed that Rhea also tried to hide Poseidon from his child-eating father by disguising him in a flock of lambs.⁶⁹ The ritual anointment with olive oil, moreover, is the familiar mythic motif of supplanting the psychoactive nature of the primordial sacrament with the olive, which almost universally

---

64   John M. Allegro, *The Sacred Mushroom and the Cross: A Study of the Nature and Origins of Christianity within the Fertility Cults of the Ancient Near East* (London: Hodder and Stoughton, 1970, reprinted Los Angeles: Gnostic Media Research and Publishing, 2009), footnotes 2.24, 8.20, 8. 57, and 12.33.

65   Wasson, "Lightningbolt and Mushrooms": 83-94, in R. Gordon Wasson, Stella Kramrisch, Jonathan Ott, and Carl A.P. Ruck, *Persephone's Quest: Entheogens and the Origins of Religion* (New Haven, CT: Yale University Press, 1986).

66   [Pseudo]-Hyginus, *Fabulae* 139.

67   Perseus picking the mushroom in the Garden of the Hesperides, amphora, 3rd quarter of the 4th century BCE, Pergamonmuseum: Staatliche Museen zu Berlin, Antiken-Sammlung, inv. no. F. 3022. Figure 9, in Carl A.P. Ruck, Blaise Daniel Staples, and Clark Heinrich, *The Apples of Apollo: Pagan and Christian Mysteries of the Eucharist* (Durham, NC: Carolina Academic Press, 2000).

68   Ruck *et al.*, *Apples of Apollo*, 87-142.

69   Pausanias, *Description of Greece*, 8.8.2.

is depicted growing through the zoomorphic anthropomorphisms that serve as the object of the heroic quest. It is commonly seen depicted as growing at the site of the decapitated Medusa. Athena herself, with her sacred olive, is a pacified version of the Gorgon Medusa and the fungal entheogen.

The supposed meteoritic *baítylos* is a Semitic derivative from Bet-'el (Bethel), meaning 'house of God', the stone pillow upon which Joseph slept for his vision of the staircase leading to heaven. Upon awakening, he set it upright as a phallic pillar and anointed it with olive oil. This so-called pillow that was an aid for visionary slumber was a mushroom.[70] The Kronos stone was also called *abaddir*,[71] which is also apparently Semitic for 'mighty father' or 'stone of dir'.[72]

## The Drunken Parents

With Lady Luck as the mother for Oedipus, there could be no less decisive or more changeable a nature for the maternal persona. The two versions of the heroic identity in the monomyth are defined by two sets of parents, two different fathers, but a mother of questionable nature, either like the dominant women of her own family tradition or a submissive wife suitable for the New Age of male dominance. Both the Corinthian queen and Jocasta are women with the power of the crown matrimonial to confer the so-called 'kingship' of their lands to their mate or offspring. If Oedipus wasn't the son of Laïus, whose child was he, now that we know that he wasn't the son of the Corinthian Polybus, whose kingdom he has inherited in matrilineal fashion from the woman he had thought to be his mother?

The chorus develops the theme, claiming that they, too, now are prophets and endowed with knowledge.[73] This claim should not

---

70  Ruck and Hoffman, *The Effluents of Deity*, 9-20.
71  Priscian (6th century CE), *Institutiones grammaticae*, 7.32.
72  M.L. West, *The East Face of Helicon: West Asiatic Elements in Greek Poetry and Myth* (Oxford: Clarendon Press, 1997), 294.
73  Sophocles, *Tyrannus*, 1086.

be taken lightly, since it empowers their ensuing statement with divine authority or vision. Oedipus wasn't a foreigner after all, but indigenous, born from the earth, a native countryman (*patriótes*) of Mount Cithaeron, where the maimed infant was found. She, the mountain, was his mother and the one who nursed him.[74] The indigenous child of a mountain would be an autochthonous being sprouting from its sacred ground.

'Hail to Apollo, may everything turn out the best for Oedipus', they chant.[75] They address Apollo with the epithet of Phoebus, which is primarily associated with his sexual affair with the maiden Coronis and the birth of their son Asclepius (Asklepios, Latinized as Aesculapius) as the agent of Apollo for medical healing, hence the one who will alleviate the plague from which they are suffering. The amorous encounters with Apollo[76] present the god in his Dionysian mode, not as the supreme refinement of rational control, but its obverse, ecstatic possession.

These women of the chorus of Sopholces' *Oedipus* tragedy imagine the bacchanalian scenario for which the sacred mountain was noted. This is the same mountain, and probably the same location, where the cousins of his grandfather Labdacus, Pentheus and Actaeon, met their end. It is also where the twins Amphion and Zethos (Zethus) were exposed to die, and probably where they avenged their mother's maltreatment by tying her tormenter Dirce to a bull. The text of the *Tyrannus* as emended could refer

---

74  Ibid., 1086 *et seq*. Jebb's emended text changes Oedipus from genitive to accusative to make him the subject of the infinitive. In this reading Oedipus 'augments' or magnifies the fame of the mountain as his native land and his mother and nurse. Without the emendation, the mountain 'augments' the fame of a native son as his mother and nurse. The difference is negligible and not of concern here in simply establishing that Oedipus is not a foreigner, but indigenous and the native child of the mountain, who served as his mother and nurse.

75  Although they address the god in the vocative, the connective (*de*) indicates that the 'you' (*soi*) must be Oedipus.

76  Apollo's 'love' companions all mask the role of the beloved as the 'willing' sacrificial human victim offered to the god, often implicating the motifs of funereal, botanical, and prophetic symbolism: Daphne and Daphnis (prophetic 'laurel'), Cassandra, Coronis (funereal 'crow/raven'), Evadne ('flowery') and her prophet son Iamos ('violet, drug'), Cycnus (prophetic mourning 'swan'), Hyacinthus (mourning 'hyacinth'), Cyparissus (cemetery 'cypress').

to the other events: 'Surely you will magnify also the native Oedipus as both his mother and his nurse'. Even not emended, the text would read: 'Surely you will magnify also a native son as Oedipus's mother and nurse'. The *Phoenician Women* identifies the meadow of Hera as the specific site on Mount Cithaeron:[77] this means that it is probably also the exact place on the sacred mountain where Herakles was exposed and picked up and nursed by the goddess. This event was depicted on vases with the infant equated to a plucked herbal sprig and with the spilled milk from the goddess's breast converted into the heavenly elixir of the Milky Way.[78]

## Ecstatic Herbalism

The maenads in their mountain ritual enacted the magical procedures for gathering the sacred plants that figure in bacchant shamanism.[79] The emblem of their ritual was the *thyrsus* (*thyrsos*), which was synonymous with the *narthex*. Both are the ritual implement for containing the gathered plant, the latter transparent in its etymology as the 'narcotic-storage receptacle'.[80] This was well known to the audience of Sophocles' tragedy as a commonplace of the rituals of the god Dionysus/Bacchus, and hence Oedipus in such an environment was obviously an anthropomorphism of a suitable psychoactive botanical manifestation.

For father, perhaps it was the goat-man Pan who begot Oedipus by a bacchant, as the choral dancers in the *Tyrannus* attempt to visualize the scene so often depicted in the surviving Greek vases with ithyphallic satyrs sexually cavorting with the maddened plant-gathering women; or perhaps it was Apollo, in his materialization as a herdsman tending cows. Cows in Greek

---

77    Euripides, *Phoenician Women*, 24.
78    Hera suckling Herakles, red-figure Apulian *lekythos*, ca. 360-350 BCE, London, British Museum.
79    Carl A.P. Ruck, *Sacred Mushrooms of the Goddess: Secrets of Eleusis* (Berkeley, CA: Ronin Publishing, 2006), 85-110.
80    For the *thyrsos* as the container for gathered herbs, see Theophrastus, *Historia Plantarum*, 9.16.2; Ruck *et al.*, *The Apples of Apollo*, 8, 80-81, as synonymous with the narthex as the 'narcotic container', 133-134.

mythology are always in estrus and the one who tends them goads them into sexual ecstasy.[81] It should be noted that in the false account of Oedipus's family, both the Corinthian king Polybus and his queen Periboea are ascribed names identifying them as a 'cattle-lord' and his mate as 'luxuriate in cows'. Or perhaps it was Hermes or Bacchus who fathered him with one of the Muses from the intoxicating springs of the adjacent Mount Helicon.

In this imagined scenario, Oedipus was truly a child conceived in ritualized drunkenness. It was undoubtedly such a bacchanalian rite that led to Jocasta's insemination by Laïus. Oedipus was a child of a mountain maenad (Jocasta in her other persona, liberated from the strictures of patriarchy) with some pastoral god impersonating a satyr, such as Apollo, Hermes, or Bacchus. Jocasta is Iokaste in Greek, transparent in its etymology as a supposedly 'chaste'[82] version of the cow-maiden Io, maddened by the estrual prodding of the cow-fly's sting.[83] Iokaste is sometimes cited as Epikaste, which could be interpreted as 'very pure, clean, and chaste'. Being 'chaste' implies its dichotomous antithesis as 'profligate', the sexual abandon experienced by the bacchants in the mimesis of their seductive approach to the magical plants gathered on the mountainside. As mentioned, in the myth of Herakles and the remaking of Olympia, an Epikaste was the daughter of the cattle lord Augeias and a version of Hippodamia, the 'Horse-mistress', an analogue of the Gorgon queen Medusa.

## Jocasta's Brooch

The eyewitness arrives and is authenticated by the Corinthian messenger. The eyewitness reluctantly identifies Oedipus as the son of Jocasta and Laïus whom he had transferred to the Corinthian king and queen years ago, instead of exposing him to die on

---

81  Carl A.P. Ruck and Danny (Blaise) Staples, *The World of Classical Myth: Gods and Goddesses, Heroines and Heroes* (Durham, NC: Carolina Academic Press, 1994), 126 *et seq.*
82  Latin *castus*, Greek *kath-arós*, 'clean'.
83  *Tabanus bovinus*, the horsefly, called the 'cow-fly' in its scientific nomenclature, and the gadfly cow-prod oístros, which yields 'estrus' in English.

the mountainside. Oedipus rushes into the house, bursts into the bolted nuptial chamber, sword in hand, apparently intending to murder his mother, but he finds her hanged by suicide.[84] He grasps the brooch from her garment and pins his eyes together. Thematically this is the pin that pinned his two feet into one when he was exposed as an infant on the mountainside.

When he appears next on stage, the swollen one-foot creature is now a one-eyed being, endowed with seeing the truth, a seer, like the blind Tiresias.[85] The single eye, like the one-foot, characterizes the fungal dactylic creatures that are plucked from the mountainside, and the single eye also describes the swollen phallus.[86]

Oedipus had proclaimed himself an ally of the god in tracking down the footsteps of the old crime. The drunken conception of the hero Ion makes clearer what the god demands of his allies.

---

[84] The suicide of Jocasta is not a fixed element of the myth since Euripides presented her still living, with Oedipus hidden away indoors (64-66), as she performs the prologue of the *Phoenician Women* tragedy. She kills herself later in supplication to her (other) two sons to end their conflict.

[85] On the symbolism of the disembodied eye as metaphoric for visionary experience, see Jonathan Ott, "Carved 'Disembodied Eyes' of Teotihuacán": 141-148, in R. Gordon Wasson, Stella Kramrisch, Jonathan Ott, and Carl A.P. Ruck, *Persephone's Quest: Entheogens and the Origins of Religion* (New Haven, CT: Yale University Press, 1986).

[86] See the King's Eye, in Aristophanes, *Acharnians*, 91 *et seq*. The costume of the spy has made his comic phallus into the 'eye'.

# THE SON CONCEIVED IN DRUNKENNESS

# Chapter Four
# Fall Guy for the God

### The Alphabetic Plays

Euripides produced his tragedy about *Ion* sometime around 414 BCE. It survives as one of the 'alphabetic plays', tragedies with titles beginning with the letters *eta* to *kappa* from a single lost edition of the complete works of Euripides arranged in alphabetical order.[87] These plays represent a random selection, not influenced by the scholarly prejudices that produced the ten tragedies of the canonic group, as taught in the classrooms of the Hellenistic period, along with the seven canonic plays of Aeschylus and seven of Sophocles, the three dramatists who were selected as most representative of the three successive generations of playwrights active in what came to be considered the Classical Age of Athens. The inclusion of ten plays of Euripides in the canonic catalogue indicates his greater popularity, at least by the Hellenistic period. The random selection is uninfluenced by Aristotelian notions about tragedy and hence preserves types of plays more characteristic of the full range of compositions for the Theater of Dionysus. The *Ion* thus is somewhat unusual as a tragedy for its humor.

The myth, however, is very serious. Ion was the mythical founder of the Ionian Greeks, the tribal group to which the

---

87   *Electra, Helen, Heracles, Heracles' Children, Suppliants (Hiketes), Ion, Iphigenia in Aulis, Iphigenia among the Taurians,* and *Cyclops (Kyklops)*, the last being the only surviving complete satyr play, which was the traditional fourth production in each playwright's day-long offering of four works in the theatrical competitions.

Athenians belonged,[88] and hence his botanical identity and his relation to his father Apollo are of extreme importance to the bacchanalian motif of the hero's conception in drunkenness.

## Picking the God's Flowers

His mother Kreousa (Creusa) conceived the child while she was 'culling saffron-colored petals into her lap, to flower there reflecting golden light on her clothes', when Apollo, 'sparkling with gold in his foliage of hair', and with 'flashings of sacred lightning', forced her into the Cave of the Long Rocks beneath the Athenian Acropolis.[89] The sexual encounter with the god while plucking a flower with the same characteristic radiant leafiness as the deity's hair, accompanied with the flashing of sacred lightning, is unmistakably descriptive of a ritual of herbal ecstatic shamanism, in which the flowery petals blossoming in her lap induced her sexual possession.

The Acropolis has numerous caves around its base, all with archaeological evidence of their use since the greatest antiquity as sacred sanctuaries. Five caves of various sizes exist along the almost inaccessible terrace or ledge of the Long Rocks, on the northwestern flank, close to the westward facing entrance or Propylaea and opposite the hill of the Areopagos ('Hill of Ares'). Below the ledge is the fountain house of the Klepsydra (Clepsydra, 'Hidden Water'), with a grotto above dedicated to the nymph of the spring that rises deep within the rocky outcrop of the Acropolis. It served as the protected water source for the fortified citadel when under siege. The waters of the Klepsydra had a slightly brinish taste and the fountain was thought to have a connection to the sea and to be without bottom. Objects tossed into its waters were discovered in the sea beyond the Athenian port of Piraeus, or even as far away as Sicily, or at least, so it was claimed.

---

88   The four major eponymous tribal groups were the Ionians, Aeolians, Dorians, and Achaeans.
89   Euripides, *Ion*, 881 *et seq.*; 8 *et seq.*

## The Cave of the Long Rocks

The cave where Kreousa conceived Ion was the easternmost of the five along the ledge, east of the Klepsydra and its nymphaeum grotto below the ledge or terrace. This cave dedicated to Apollo was called *Hypo Makrais* ('Under the Long Rocks') or *Hyp' Akrais* ('Under the Heights'), sometimes cited as *Hypokraios*, 'All Mighty'. It had a sanctuary of Apollo within it.

The Cave of the Long Rocks and its symbolism would have been well known to the audience of Euripides' tragedy. Under the democracy, the archons (the group of ten annually selected 'rulers' who administered the government) swore an oath to Apollo in this cave, affirming that the god was indeed their paternal ancestor, and they deposited votive plaques in the sanctuary upon leaving office.[90] It was also called the *Pythion*, after the serpent python that Apollo slew in redirecting the religion of Delphi away from the Earth Goddess and reorienting its chthonic oracular voice as inspired instead from above by his Olympian father Zeus. The *Pythion* Cave at Athens was thus a parallel analogue of the Korykian Cave of the Python on Mount Parnassus, high above the sanctuary of Delphi. This latter lower sanctuary dated back only to the eighth century, when the cult was moved down the mountain to make it more accessible for the pilgrims consulting the oracle. As at Olympia, the older and newer locales figured in the traditions of the sanctuary's devolvement into historical times and the evolution of male dominance over a site previously devoted to the female and her sisterhood.

Adjacent to the Athenian *Pythion* Serpent Cave of the Long Rocks was a cave sanctuary of Zeus Olympios, with the epithet of the Lightning. From here certain priests known as the 'Pythiasts' (*Pythiastai*,[91] named for the Pythia, the oracular priestess at

---

90   Peter Edward Nulton, *The Sanctuary of Apollo Hypoakraios and Imperial Athens* (Providence, RI: Brown University, Center for Old World Archaeology and Art, 2003). *Hypoakraios* is *Hyp' Akrais*, made into an adjective.

91   Hesychios of Alexandria (fifth-century CE lexicographer), = *pythaïstai s.v., astrape di' harmatos*.

Delphi) would keep watch for three successive nights in each of three successive months for a lightning strike on the distant ridge called Harma on Mount Parnes to the northwest on the frontier with Boeotia, where there was an ancient cave sanctuary of Zeus. If a flash was observed, a sacrifice was dispatched to Delphi.[92] The Parnes cave lay on a direct line whose termini were the *Pythion* Cave of the Acropolis and the Korykian Cave on Mount Parnassus, the original site of the Delphic python and the earth oracle.

The symbolism of the Cave of the Long Rocks and the adjacent Pythian Serpent Lightning-bolt Cave of Zeus Olympios not only associated Athens directly with the Delphic sanctuary and the special metaphor of the flash of lightning, but it also commemorated the transmutation of Athena, from her previous role as a mother goddess or Queen, into her pacified version as a daughter of Zeus. She was so commemorated also at Delphi in the sanctuary of the *Pronoia* ('Beneficent', or *Pronaia*, 'Before or Below the Temple' of Apollo), on the slope just below the Classical Age precinct of Apollo above, with his Temple, treasuries, theater, and stadium. In contrast, the buildings in the *Pronoia* sanctuary were architectural versions of structures symbolic of the previous age of female dominance at Delphi: a circular *tholos* ('beehive') temple and a building representing a cave. The *Pronoia* sanctuary is constructed on a level platform achieved by excavating a portion of the steep hillside. Without the excavation, the temples would be underground. They symbolize the pacified version of the ancient rituals of the Korykian Cave higher up the mountain.

## The Trial of Orestes

Thus, in Athens at the beginning of the quadrennial celebration of the Panathenaean Festival, the wheeled ship that delivered the new *péplos* robe of the goddess passed into the city on the Sacred Way through the western sacred Double Gate (*Díplyon*) and was moored here below the Cave of the Long Rocks during

---

92   Jane Ellen Harrison, *Primitive Athens as Described by Thucydides* (Cambridge, UK: Cambridge University Press, 1906).

the ritual, supposedly as depicted in the Parthenon frieze.[93] It was on the adjacent hill of the Areopagos that Athena had cast the decisive vote in the trial of Orestes that determined that the father was the operative parent of a child, with the mother contributing only the vessel for the gestation of the fetus.

This view of procreation persisted until the seventeenth century CE, when the invention of the microscope seemed at first to confirm it. The spermatozoa were at first seen as the little humans, already living and complete, requiring only maturation within the mother's womb, which was analogous to an alchemical vessel.[94]

Conversely, ancient traditions of virginal birth may indicate that women had achieved control over their own bodies and were capable of stimulating the meiosis of the ovum through the administering of various toxins, perhaps derived from serpent venoms. This may be the true significance of the many depictions of goddesses and priestesses handling serpents.[95] Such a mode of procreation as parthenogenesis or cloning, although rare naturally, is possible and, in fact, is the norm for some animals.

## The Cave of Pan

A third cave to the west along the ledge of the Long Rocks had been dedicated to Pan after the victory over the Persians at Marathon in 490 BCE. The deity had materialized to the runner Pheidippides, asking why the Athenians had paid him no honor, despite his friendliness, and promising to aid them in the ensuing battle. He was thought to have inspired the so-called 'panic' fear in the enemy. The sanctuary of Pan was celebrated with an annual

---

93  The frieze is now convincingly interpreted as depicting the sacrifice of the maiden daughter of the primordial 'king'. Joan Breton Connelly, *The Parthenon Enigma: A New Understanding of the West's Most Iconic Building and the People Who Made It* (New York, NY: Vintage Books/ Random House, 2014). Compare *infra*, on the sacrifice of Kreousa's sisters.

94  Carl A.P. Ruck and Mark A. Hoffman, *The Effluents of Deity* (Durham, NC: Carolina Academic Press, 2012), 227-229.

95  Marguerite Rigoglioso, Virgin Mother Goddesses of Antiquity (New York, NY: Palgrave Macmillan, 2010); *The Cult of Divine Birth in Ancient Greece* (New York, NY: Palgrave Macmillan, 2011).

torch race and sacrifices. Because of its seclusion, it was a favorite trysting spot for lovers. A votive relief, now in the Acropolis Museum, shows the god making love to a mountain nymph. Panic and bacchanalian frenzy are both aspects of the maenads' ecstasy. The other two caves along the ledge of the Long Rocks may also have been dedicated to Pan. However, since the tale of the Marathon runner indicates that there were no sanctuaries of that deity before the invasion of Darius in 490 BCE, these caves must have served a different function at the time of Ion's conception, supposedly in the mid-second millennium BCE.

The fountain house of the Klepsydra itself below the Long Rocks, moreover, was associated with herbal shamanism and mystery religion. It is here that Socrates, in Aristophanes' *Birds* comedy (415 BCE), was scandalously depicted summoning up ghosts as a profane performance of the Eleusinian Mystery initiation, involving various anthropomorphisms of the sacred mushroom, as One-footed creatures or the Tongue-in-Bellies, beings whose whole body was comprised of the hemispherical cap in the likeness of the mystery dwarf Iambe or Baubo, who first served Demeter the entheogenic potion.[96] The reference is a pun, since the *klépsydra* ('water-thief') was also the timing device that limited the length of public speeches in the law courts, working like an hourglass with slowly leaking water instead of sand.

This conjunction of the five adjacent caves along the ledge of the Long Rocks is where Ion's mother encountered the god Apollo. As she reproaches the deity for his scandalous treatment of her in Euripides' tragedy, it is precisely in his role as a pastoral god like Pan and a tender of cattle that she identifies him as a pious fraud.[97] Thematically, this is the same imagined paternity for Sophocles' Oedipus as the child of Lady Luck, the drunken result of a bacchanalian orgy. Kreousa not only conceived the child in

---

96  Aristophanes, *Birds*, 1694-1705. Carl A.P. Ruck, "Mushrooms and Philosophers": 151-177, in R. Gordon Wasson, Stella Kramrisch, Jonathan Ott, and Carl A.P. Ruck, *Persephone's Quest: Entheogens and the Origins of Religion* (New Haven, CT: Yale University Press, 1986).
97  Euripides, *Ion*, 881 *et seq.*

the Cave of the Long Rocks, 'cavernous and full of secret recesses', however, but she returned to it to birth and abandon the newborn infant there in the same cave,[98] 'with Pan playing his pipes and a troupe of dancing maidens,'[99] apparently in the adjacent caves or before them on the rock terrace. This is surely a ritual scene. There she exposed the unwanted infant to die, placing him in a covered woven basket or hamper.[100]

## The Empowered Female

The mother's name Kreousa was not actually a name, but a title, the 'Ruling Female', a verbal participle, the feminine equivalent of Kreon, the male ruler. It was in this same Cave that her father Erechtheus, the so-called 'king', usually depicted like all these primordial kings of Athens as a serpent-man, had slaughtered each of his daughters when they came of age; she alone survived because he had died when she was still an infant, which probably means before her first menstruation. It was at puberty that humans qualified as ritual offerings.

The first legendary 'king' was reputed to be Kekrops, which means a 'face with a tail'. The primordial city was named after him as Kekropia. Although presumably it was a serpent's tail, he was also a merman with a fish's lower body. A serpent that embodied his spirit was housed in the fifth-century BCE Erechtheion (Erechtheum) shrine on the Acropolis and the Persians destroyed the serpent when they captured the Acropolis in 480 BCE, although the Erechtheion, like all the buildings on the Acropolis, was constructed after the invasion. The Erechtheion also contained the graves of both Kekrops and Erechtheus. The *Parion Chronicle*[101] sets the date of Kekrops as 1582 BCE, when the people of Attica

---

98   Ibid., 16, 949.
99   Ibid., 491 *et seq.*
100  Ibid., 19, 37, 40.
101  It is now in the Ashmolean Museum of Oxford University. It was deciphered and published among the Arundel Marbles (*Marmora Arundelliana*, London, 1628-1629), nos. 1-21, 59-119), Felix Jacoby, *Fragmenta graecorum historicorum* (1923-1959), 239A, epoch 39.

were the pre-Indo-European Pelasgians. Kekrops was 'king' before there was any patriarchal kingship of Athens, at a period when the matriarchal traditions of Minoan times prevailed.[102]

Since this is a myth, we may assume that the purpose of the sacrificed daughters was to prevent the very outcome that seems about to happen, a claimant to the role of ruler from an alien male lineage through his marriage to the queen. Erechtheus is a double for Poseidon as 'Poseidon Erechtheus', and he was counted the son of the autochthonous Erichthonios (Erichthonius).

## The Birth of Erichthonios

Kreousa's rejection of her new-born infant Ion repeats the same event commemorated in the birth of Erichthonios, Athena's foster child, inseminated in Gaia, as surrogate mother, from the ejaculated semen of Hephaistos (Hephaestus) that Athena wiped from her gown and threw to earth. His name was interpreted as combining the word for the wad of 'wool' (érion), with which Athena wiped away the semen, and the word for the chthonic 'earth' or ground (*chthón*), although it could just as easily be seen as simply an 'intensification' (with the prefix *eri*-, 'very') of 'chthonic'. He was a giant serpent like the Delphic python and was so depicted lurking beneath Athena's shield in Pheidias' chryselephantine (composed of gold and ivory) fifth-century Parthenon effigy of the goddess. Erechtheus, in contrast, is an agential derivative of the verb *eréchthein*, 'to rend;' and as an epithet of Poseidon, it probably implies the rending open of the earth as in an earthquake, not unlike, however, the rending occasioned by the sudden burst of the mushroom from the ground.

Erechtheus and Erichthonios, although separate in myth, are largely interchangeable, since the rending of the earth describes the manner of Erichthonios' birth, bursting up like a plant from the ground in mother Gaia's arms, as often depicted in vase paintings. Compare Erysichthon, the son of Kekrops and his daughter

---

102 See Jane Ellen Harrison, *Primitive Athens*, 43 *et seq*.

Aglauros. His name implies that he 'tore the earth' open at his birth. Erichthonios, in fact, appears to be a back-formation and etiological false etymology of Erechtheus to explain the strange manner of his birth. The wad of wool from the goddess's robe connects him with the motif of 'golden fleece' and the ritual of weaving. The mythical elaboration of the 'wad of wool' and the child sprouting from the fallen seed is transparently the same metaphoric botanical complex as the wads of wool that decorated the ómphalos navel-stone at Delphi.[103]

## The Wicker Hamper

Athena, like Kreousa, placed the infant Erichthonios in a covered woven wicker hamper,[104] intrusting it to the care of a sisterhood comprised of a trinity of maidens who were identified as daughters of the serpent-man Kekrops. They were collectively named in Euripides' play as the Aglauridae maidens.[105] Aglauros was apparently their leader, with her two sisters named as Herse and Pandrosos. These latter sisters are similarly named for the

---

103 Speculation about the significance of the wads of wool inevitably suggests the role of the wool used as a filter in preparing the Soma sacrament and its possible analogue for the motif of the Golden Fleece. Donald E. Teeter, *Amanita Muscaria: Herb of Immortality* (Manor, TX: Ambrosia Society, 2007), 18. The woolen fleece as a purifying agent also occurs as the 'little fleece of Zeus' (*Diós koidíon*), which was sacred to Zeus Meilichios, the euphemistic naming of the god that avoided his true chthonic aspect as anguiform Zeus-Hades. It is depicted full-size in art (Lovatelli urn, Torre Nova sarcophagus), but the diminutive 'little' probably indicates that it was a substitution for something more like a wad of fleece. It purified the stain of bloodguilt and functioned in the preparation of candidates for initiation into the Eleusinian Mystery (*Homeric Hymn 2, to Demeter*, 195-198). Daniel Ogden, *Drakon: Dragon Cult and Serpent Cult in the Greek and Roman Worlds* (Oxford: Oxford University Press, 2013), 280. The sacrificed ram that provided the fleece is a commemoration of what was originally a human offering as victim. Phrixos of the Golden Fleece was such a substitute. Carl A.P. Ruck, Blaise Daniel Staples, and Clark Heinrich, *The Apples of Apollo: Pagan and Christian Mysteries of the Eucharist* (Durham, NC: Carolina Academic Press, 2001), 105-112.
104 Depicted on an Attic red-figure *pelike*, by the Erichthonios painter, from Nola, Classical period, Mainfränkisches Museum, Würzburg H 4803. The illustration refutes all attempts to interpret the container as a baby carriage or perambulator. See Ruck et al., *The Apples of Apollo*, 54 et seq.
105 Euripides, *Ion*, 23.

'dew' (*hérse, drósos*), although their dewy nature could also imply their 'tender, young' pubescent state, menstruation, impregnation and offspring, with botanical implications. They danced in the Cave of the god Pan, with the epithet of the shepherd 'dwelling in the fields'.[106] Pan was a notoriously sexual deity, even copulating with goats.

Ion was placed in his wicker hamper with two golden serpents, preserving the custom derived from the exposure of Erichthonios,[107] along with a woven image of the Gorgon head. These are the tokens that will authenticate his true identity as the child of Kreousa,[108] these and a sprig of olive, whose botanical significance is the already mentioned motif of the olive as a transmutation and surrogate for the sacred psychoactive sacrament or entheogen, ultimately for a mushroom.

The Aglauridae (also called the Kekropidae) were told to tend the wicker hamper without peering inside. The sacred baskets traditionally hid obscene ceramics, and the 'basket' was metaphoric in comedy for the female's receptive genitalia.[109] The sexual implications are obvious in the myth of Pandora and her box, which she was forbidden to open. The *pyxis* or 'box' was ancient Greek slang

---

106 *Ibid.*, 496. *Agraulos* ('dwelling in the fields') is the reading of the manuscripts. Joseph Scaliger (sixteenth-century French scholar) corrected this to Aglauros. Although the interchange of *lambda* and *rho* is a common slip, the correction makes the maiden trinity (*kórai trígonoi*) into the daughters of one of the trinity, namely Aglauros, whereas the unmodified text as transmitted makes all three devotees of precisely the pastoral deity commemorated by the dancing in the Cave of Pan beside the Athenian Cave of the Long Rocks. *Agraulos* may also imply the *aulós* or 'flute', instead of the *aulé* or 'courtyard' of a dwelling place, the latter related to the former since the courtyard was open to the 'blowing of the wind', which is precisely what gives voice to the 'flute', and hence its name. If Aglauros has an etymology, however, it can only be the rhotacization of the *lambda*. More likely, however, the name is Pelasgian and without an Indo-European etymology.

107 Euripides, *Ion*, 20 et seq.

108 *Ibid.*, 1395 et seq.

109 Aristophanes, *Acharnians*, 253 et seq. Carl A.P. Ruck, "Aristophanes' Parody of Socrates as a Pothead and the Spartan Cult of the Wolf": chap. 4, in J. Harold Ellens (ed.), *Seeking the Sacred with Psychoactive Substances; Chemical Paths to Spirituality and God*, vol. 1, History and Practice (Santa Barbara, CA: ABC-CLIO, 2014).

for vagina.[110] When the Aglauridae disobeyed, the serpent-child bit them or the mere sight of the serpent so maddened them that they danced ecstatically until they fell, presumably by accident, off the Acropolis cliff. More exactly, only two of them disobeyed: Aglauros and her sister Herse. The good 'dew' sister Pandrosos consistently was identified as the one who was obedient to the prohibition. Unlike her sisters, whose tombs were in the Aglauros shrine, Pandrosos was buried in what became the later Erectheion, next to the sacred olive tree.

## The Shrine of Aglauros

The presumption of accidental death masks the ritual offering of human victims. Thus, in a parallel legend, a female with the same name of Aglauros voluntarily threw herself off the Acropolis since an oracle had declared that the Athenians would not be victorious in a long protracted war unless someone sacrificed herself for the good of the country. Similarly, human victims were still offered to Aglauros on the island of Cyprus at a late date.[111] All these Aglauros victims are probably offerings to Apollo with the herdsman epithet of Agraulos. The Athenians in gratitude built her a shrine on the Acropolis, or more precisely below it, in the Aglaurion Cave below the Erectheion and east of the ledge of the Long Rocks.

Kreousa, Ion's mother, who denied him nurture as an infant and tries to poison him at Delphi, is threatened with a similar deadly punishment, hurled down from the two shining cliffs (*Phaidriades*) that loom above the sanctuary,[112] a manner of sacrificial offering of human victims practiced there in the past and still on occasion at moments of crises on into the Classical period.[113]

Like Athena's role as the *Promachos* or 'leader in battle', young initiates into the Athenian military forces received their first suit

---

110 Leonard Shlain, *The Alphabet Versus the Goddess: The Conflict Between Word and Image* (London/New York: Viking Penguin, 1998), 129.
111 Porphyry, *De abstinentia*, 1.2.
112 Euripides, *Ion*, 1222 et seq., 1266-1267.
113 T. Dempsey, *Delphic Oracle: Its Early History, Influence and Fall* (Whitefish. MT: Kessinger Publishing, 2003, reprint of 1918), 127 *et seq.*

of armor and swore an oath of fealty before the Aglauros effigy in the cave shrine.[114] It is not hard to recognize Aglauros as a primordial pre-Olympian persona of the goddess Athena, similar to the one that lurks beneath the figure named as the 'Queen' of the Gorgon sisterhood, which is to say, the Medusa, or the same queenly epithet that names Ion's mother as Kreousa. Medusa (Medousa) is similarly a feminine participial for a verb designating empowerment. Aglauros was an epithet or byname of the goddess as Athena Aglauros,[115] like Athena's assimilation of Pallas, the goat goddess, as Pallas Athena, who like Athena is sometimes of indeterminate sex and depicted as a man.

Like Athena, Aglauros is more associated with young warriors than with the nursing of infants, and by one tradition, she was turned to stone when she tried to stand between Hermes and his amorous advances toward her disobedient 'dewy' sister Herse.[116] This metamorphosis into a herm or phallic pillar reveals her underlying hermaphroditic potential, analogous to Athena's bisexual iconography.

Aglauros is also a byname for Aphrodite, as a warrior goddess in her adulterous sexual union with Ares, the god of war. She can be portrayed with a spear, and her persona as a goddess of war is reflected in Homer and can be dated back to the Geometric or Archaic periods.[117]

The shrine of Aglauros lay halfway down the ancient Mycenaean stairway in a deep grotto. The Persians under Xerxes managed to storm the Acropolis in 480 BCE using this precipitous unguarded ascent.[118]

---

114 The oath of the ephebes in the shrine of Aglauros is quoted entire in Pollux, 8.105; Stobaeus 1.48, dated *ca.* 650-560 BCE.

115 Bion of Prokonnesos, FGH 332 F 1 = Berol. p. 19 1 Rei; Suda, *s.v.* Aglauros. Aglauros, identified by name, is preserved on several vases and pottery fragments.

116 Ovid, *Metamorphoses*, 2.710 *et seq.*

117 M. Valdés Guia, "The Cult of Aglauros (and Aphrodite) in Athens and in Salamis of Cyprus: Reflections on the Origin of the *Genos* of the *Salaminioi*": 57-76, in Gocha R. Tsetskhladze (ed.), *Ancient West and East* (Leiden: Brill), vol. 4, no. 1 (2005).

118 Herodotus, 8.53.

## Plynteria Festival

The past displaced persona of Athena as Aglauros was celebrated in Athens as the springtime (May-June) *Plynteria* Festival. The festival is so named since it enacted the 'Washing' of Athena's garments, recalling the wad of wool soiled with the semen of Hephaistos. This required removing them from the goddess, making her effectively no longer existent. The period of her ritual eclipse was labeled as unlucky 'days not to be spoken' or *dies nefasti*, when the temples were closed and no business could be transacted. Athena did not exist until her newly washed garments were replaced. In the meantime, her effigies were covered over and her temples roped off. A similar rite is enacted in the Roman Church during Lent and the Good Friday preparation for the Resurrection on Easter. In particular, the time from the third hour of Friday to the midnight of Saturday marked the divine interregnum, the *dies nefasti* when the deity languished in Hell.

What little is known about the *Plyntaria* indicates that it was a symbolic return to primordial times. The goddess's most ancient wooden effigy as Athena Polias, housed in the Erechtheion, was undressed of its robes and jewelry, wrapped and carried to the sea at Phaleron, some several miles distant, and bathed by two maidens, called the 'bathers' (*Loutrídes*). The procession was escorted by mounted ephebes (épheboi) or adolescent males and led by women carrying baskets of fig pastries, the fig being considered as the first food of mankind.[119] The fig, however, cannot be divorced from its sexual connotations.[120]

## The Mystery Hamper

The descent to the Cave of Aglauros was accessed through a gate down a subterranean passageway in the courtyard of the Arrephoreion, a house built close to the fortified northern cliff edge

---

119 *Hegetoria palathe* ('parading of the cakes'), Athenaeus, 3.74d; Porphyry, *De abstinentia*, 2.7.
120 Carl A.P. Ruck, *Sacred Mushrooms of the Goddess: Secrets of Eleusis* (Berkeley, CA: Ronin Publishing, 2006), 28 et seq.

of the Acropolis. The underground passageway no longer exists, but was sealed in an earthquake around 1200 BCE. The sanctuary of Aglauros may have subsequently been accessed via an ancient stairway below the Erechtheion. To the west, just outside the walled courtyard, a second gate afforded access to the flight of stairs, cut into the rock, which descended to the terrace of the Long Rocks and the Klepsydra further down the slope.

The House of the Arrephoreion provided lodging for the two prepubescent girls of noble lineage, as young as seven years of age, who wove the new *péplos* of Athena, under the tutelage of a religious sorority of older, probably post-menopausal women, for presentation to the goddess at the Panathenian Festival. The choice of prepubescent or not menstruating girls for the actual work indicates that the ritual involved a symbolic sexual initiation. It also was meant to isolate the weaving from its more sinister and sexual implications, as evidenced by the myth of the weaving contest between Athena and the spider-maiden Arachne.[121]

The girls also tended the sacred olive tree that Athena had caused to sprout in her contest with Poseidon for dominion over Attica. The maidens were called the *arrephóroi*, apparently named as 'bearers' (*phoreís*) of something secret or 'not to be named' (árreton), i.e., *arre(ton) phoreis*. A special rite they performed confirms this meaning. In addition to weaving the gown, on one night in midsummer, the priestess of Athena Polias, who tended the ancient wooden effigy of the goddess that by the Classical Age was housed in the Erechtheion,[122] entrusted them with a closed hamper to bear down the subterranean passage. They left the hamper unopened down below, and there they were given another hamper to bring back up. The contents of the hamper were never revealed. Neither the priestess nor the maidens knew it.[123]

---

121 Ruck and Hoffman, *The Effluents of Deity*, 241-242.
122 Previously, it would have stood in the Archaic Temple of Athena Polias, destroyed by the Persians.
123 Pausanias, *Description of Greece*, 1.27.3-4.

### The Maidens' Dewy Basket

The rite was called the Hersiphoria, after the disobedient dew-maiden Herse of the Aglauridae sisterhood. Thus, the Arrephoria was accorded a false etymology as the 'Bearing of the Dew', although no such meaning is attested for the root *arrhe-*. The girls were then dismissed of their task and replaced by others.

The rite was associated with the sanctuary of Aphrodite, with the epithet of 'in the Gardens', located along the descent to the Aglauros Cave. Aphrodite was sometimes depicted as present at the birth of Erichthonios, ready to endow him with the good qualities of abundance and governance.[124] The Aphrodite in the Gardens was an open-air cult site with shallow cavities cut in the rock face, like the one beyond Daphni on the Sacred Road to Eleusis, and it contained dedicatory inscriptions and many terracotta figurines of maidens, boy children, and sleeping babies, as well as votives in the form of male and female genitalia. One source claims that the hamper contained breads in the form of serpents and phallic symbols, as well as shoots of plants, probably, as with Ion's exposure, a twig of the sacred olive.

The rite explains the sexual implications of the two disobedient Aglauridae sisters named for the 'dew', and enacted the proper behavior of observing the probation against opening the hamper, which Herse (unlike Pandrosos) had violated. The sexual connotations of the 'dewy basket' should be obvious. Since Aphrodite had the epithet in this rite as 'in the Gardens', it enacted a sexual initiation of the maidens, whose proper behavior with their closed 'hamper' (like Pandora's box) assured fertility of offspring, probably linked to the health of the olive above and to the general fecundity of the crops in the Attic plain.[125]

The shrine of Aphrodite was apparently associated as well with the gravesite of Theseus' son Hippolytus, called 'Aphrodite in

---

124 Rachel Rosenzweig, *Worshipping Aphrodite: Art and Cult in Classical Athens* (Ann Arbor, MI: University of Michigan Press, 2004), 51 *et seq.*

125 Eva Cantarella, *Pandora's Daughters: The Role and Status of Women in Greek and Roman Antiquity* (Baltimore, MD: Johns Hopkins University Press, 1989).

Memory of Hippolytus'. Euripides identified it as the place Phaedra first caught sight of him upon a visit to Athens to be initiated into the Eleusinian Mysteries.[126] The extended poetic description of the dewy garden watered by the gardener named Pudendum, where the young hero is consorting with his beloved goddess Artemis and plucking flowers to weave into a wreath that he presents to her effigy on stage with explicitly sexual innuendos in the dramatic prologue of the tragedy, indicates the sexual symbolism that the playwright and his audience accorded to this area of the Acropolis slope that descended past the Aphrodite shrine down to the Aglaurion Cave.[127]

It is also probable that the mention of Phaedra's visit for the Mystery initiation is part of the entheogenic complex and not a convenient narrative invention on the part of Euripides. This is especially indicated by the fact that the poet pairs the death of Artemis's beloved Hippolytus with Artemis's retaliatory murder of Aphrodite's too ardently passionate Adonis. This latter was ritually commemorated in the planting of Adonis Gardens, flower pots planted with seeds that quickly sprouted but were left un-watered to perish in the heat of the summer sun, whereupon the women mourned his death.[128] The reluctant, virginal lover is contrasted with the one destroyed in the female's too passionate sexuality.

Hippolytus, himself, is a ploy in the transition to patriliny, since as the Amazon's son he was named after his mother Hippolyta and born out of wedlock, whereas Phaedra's suicide was

---

126 Euripides, *Hippolytus*, 28 *et seq*. The gravesite has been cited as overlooking the distance from Athens to Troezen, but the text does not say this. It is the Acropolis that overlooks Troezen across the Saronic Gulf, not the sanctuary of Aphrodite and the shrine in memory of Hippolytus, which being on the northern slope and below the summit of the Rock would obviously not afford a view of the distant town. This northern slope, moreover, is associated with mystery rituals. It is doubtful, moreover, that anything on the southern slope at the base of the Acropolis cliff is of sufficient altitude to be seen from Troezen.

127 Euripides, *Hippolytus*, 73 *et seq*.

128 Marcel Detienne, *The Gardens of Adonis: Spices in Greek Mythology* (Princeton, NJ: Princeton University Press, 1994, translated by Janet Lloyd from the French *Les Jardins d'Adonis: La mythologie des aromates en Grèce*, Paris: Gallimard, 1972).

intended to maintain the patriarchal inheritance of Theseus' two legitimate sons born to her in wedlock. One of these sons was Demophoön, who has the same name as the child that Demeter tried to burn in the hearth in the etiological myth for the Eleusinian Mystery.

# THE SON CONCEIVED IN DRUNKENNESS

# Chapter Five
# The Orgy in the Korykian Cave

**Cleansing the God's Image**

Meanwhile, across the great divide separating the Athenian Cave of the Long Rocks from the Korykian Cave on Mount Parnassus, aligned by the sighting of the lightning flash on the intervening Harma ridge of Mount Parnes, there was another scenario for the conception of the founding hero of the Ionian peoples.

Ion had been miraculously transported by Hermes as the infant exposed to die in the Cave of the Long Rocks from Athens to Delphi, where he has been tended as a foster child of the Pythian prophetess herself, like Erichthonios who became the foster child of Athena. There, Ion has grown to manhood and is now employed as a temple slave, sweeping away the droppings of the birds upon the temple steps. His actual rank is treasurer and the trusted guardian of the sanctuary's gold deposits.[129] His enactment in the tragedy is symbolically significant. He is cleansing the Olympian persona of his father Apollo and trustee of his golden image. It is also humorous, as he shoos away the quite sizable defecating birds (a swan among them), which might even have been visualized onstage by a troupe of bird dancers. He uses a broom of the sacred *daphne* or laurel plant, the entheogen associated with the priestess's shamanic rapture. This *daphne* represents the

---

[129] Euripides, *Ion*, 53-56.

transmutation of the psychoactive saffron crocus involved in the scandalous event of his own conception in the Cave of the Long Rocks. The *daphne* (*Laurus nobilis* or bay laurel) mythically represents the maiden Daphne who metamorphosed into the sacred tree to escape from the unwanted amorous pursuit by the god. Kreousa has similarly experienced the god's unwanted sexual pursuit. Although orphaned, without mother or father, Ion counts Apollo as the father that begot him.[130]

### The Crown Matrimonial

Kreousa and her husband Xouthos (Xuthus) have not managed to engender a child together, and they have come to seek advice from the oracle. Xouthos is not an Athenian, but has been awarded marriage to Kreousa in payment for his alliance in a battle over possession of Euboea (Évia), the long island lying along the northeast coast of Attica and Boeotia (Viotía).[131] In mythological time, the period is the transition from Pelasgian or Minoan traditions to Hellenic Indo-European culture. Xouthos is the son of Hellen, who lent his name to the Hellenes or Greeks and represents the first generation after the Great Flood, being the son of Deukalion (Deucalion) and Pyrrha. They were the sole survivors of the Flood and repopulated the devastated land by tossing the bones of mother Earth behind them as they walked forward into the New Age. They had interpreted the 'bones' as stones. Hence the Indo-Europeans could also claim, like the Pelasgians, that they were autochthonous. The *Parian Chronicle* set the time of the Great Flood at around 1528 BCE. Hellen, in the typical pattern of the 'two fathers' in the monomyth, may have been the son of Zeus, instead of his ostensible father Deukalion, and hence the invading

---

130 *Ibid.*, 136-140.
131 *Ibid.*, 59-64. The supposed battle is a piece of historical revisionism. The enemy is cited as Chalcedonians. Chalcedon, near the mouth of the Bosporus, occupied since 5500 BCE, was resettled as a Greek colony from Megara in 685 BCE. The island of Euboea passed into Athenian control in the early 5th century. It is an anachronism to imagine a battle over Euboea between Chalcedonians and Athens at the time of Xouthos.

Indo-Europeans could claim descent from their father god Zeus, who arrived with them.

Hellen begot his sons by union with a mermaid or fountain nymph in Thessaly, a mythic pattern that will survive into medieval times, where this mermaid has become the fish-serpent maiden Melusina, who empowered the ruling dynasties of Europe.[132] She is a version of the Classical Gorgon Medusa. In addition to fathering Xouthos, Hellen begot Aiolos (Aeolus) with the mermaid. Xouthos was reputed the father of Ion; and in the tradition that Euripides presents, he was the actual father with Kreousa of Doros and Achaeos.[133] Hellen's sister, named after the mythical primordial female Pandora, supposedly her grandmother, had three sons, Graikos, Magnetas, and Makedon. These seven sons (the two sons of Hellen and his two grandsons, together with the three sons of his sister Pandora) comprised the seven tribal groups of the Hellenes. His nephew Graikos (Graecus) supposedly colonized the Greek settlements in the southern Italian peninsula, and since these were the Greeks that the Romans first encountered, he lent his name to the Hellenes as Greeks. Magnetes and Aiolos were traditional founders of peoples in Thessaly, and Makedon was the eponymous founder of the Greeks of Macedonia.

The Dorians were the tribal group of the southern Peloponnesus (to which the Spartans belonged) and the Achaeans were the Greeks of the northernmost coastal shore of the Peloponnesus at the time of Euripides, but formerly once the inhabitants of the Mycenaean plain. The tradition, as presented by Euripides, that Doros was the actual son of Xouthos (instead of Apollo) probably represents an Athenian prejudice against their fifth-century Dorian rivals in the Peloponnesian War.

---

132 Ruck and González Celdrán, "Melusina of Plaincourault": 309-379, with DVD, in Carl A.P. Ruck, Blaise Daniel Staples, José Alfredo González Celdrán, and Mark Alwin Hoffman, *The Hidden World: Survival of Pagan Shamanic Themes in European Fairytales* (Durham, NC: Carolina Academic Press, 2006).
133 Euripides, *Ion*, 1589-1594.

## Lycian and Hyperborean Apollo

It is generally agreed that there are two deities assimilated into the Olympian persona of Apollo, an Anatolian Hittite god of flocks and a Hyperborean one, ultimately from the central Asiatic highlands,[134] perhaps, as now suggested, migrating into the Mediterranean area from Nordic lands southward via the Dnieper River.[135] Hence there are two major sanctuaries of Apollo, the Aegean island of Delos, where he was reborn into his Olympian identity as a son of Zeus, and the sanctuary of Delphi, where he reoriented the chthonic shamanism of the mother goddess. By mythical traditions, the Delian deity's pre-Olympian persona is associated with Minoan Knossos on the island of Crete; and the pre-Olympian version of Apollo at Delphi is associated with Anatolian Hittite Lycia. The Hittites were an earlier branch of the Indo-European migration, well established as an empire by the 18th century BCE. They had supplanted the previous non-Indo-European inhabitants around the beginning of the second millennium BCE. The Hittites may have known the mainland Greeks as Achaeans, which is to say, Mycenaeans.

The Dorians themselves had a special relationship to Apollo as a wolf god, both in their rituals of adolescent male indoctrination and initiation, and with their supposed lawgiver, Lykourgos (Lycurgus, 'who does the work of the wolf'), whom the Delphic oracle declared not a man, but a god. Lykourgos was probably not a single person, but a tradition of divine incarnations of their wolf-god Apollo as priests or shamans. Similar Spartan Dorian assimilations of Apollo are reflected in the Hyakinthos (Hyacinthus) myth (which associates Apollo Hyakinthos with a particular sacred plant (the hyacinth instead of the crocus);[136] and in the

---

134 Ruck, "The Secret Offering from the Hyperboreans": 225-256, in R. Gordon Wasson, Stella Kramrisch, Jonathan Ott, and Carl A.P. Ruck, *Persephone's Quest: Entheogens and the Origins of Religion* (New Haven, CT: Yale University Press, 1986).

135 Felice Vinci, *The Baltic Origins of Homer's Epic Tales: The Iliad, the Odyssey, and the Migration of Myth* (Rochester, VT: Inner Traditions, 2006).

136 Ovid, *Metamorphoses*, 13.395.

Spartan Apollo Karneios (a god of flocks), who was celebrated in the Spartan Karneia Festival, a pacified ritual of human sacrifice for which an animal victim was usually substituted. Wolves from Anatolian Lycia supposedly claimed the site of the Korykian Cave on Mount Parnassus at Delphi, whereas the secret offering of the Hyperboreans at the sanctuary of Delos associates the god there with the Nordic migration.

The Spartans' own view of their origins was that they were descended from the sons of Herakles, expelled from the ancient Achaean Mycenae, who crossed over into the Peloponnesus at Rhion (Naupactus) in rafts at the western end of the Gulf of Corinth.

## Tribal Rivalries

Euripides makes explicit that the descendants of Ion will colonize the Ionian Islands,[137] and Delos was the central sanctuary of their tribal group; but the Xouthos myth lays claim as well to a special affiliation with Delphi. In fact, the Athenians claimed to be autochthonous, and it is only in the generation after the Trojan War that the new Indo-European aristocracy supposedly entered Attica with Peisistratos (Pisistratus), the son of King Nestor of Peloponnesian Pylos. The Athenian claim upon Delphi, however, cannot be an element of the fifth-century city's propaganda, since the pre-historical affinity with the oracle is demonstrated by the complex of sacred caves dating back to Mycenaean times on the northern slope of the Acropolis.

It should, moreover, be pointed out that Athena was honored also at Sparta with a temple on the highest of its hills, which served as its Acropolis. She had the epithet of 'Athena of the Brazen House' (*Chalkioikos*), after the bronze dedicatory plaques that hung on its walls; she also had the epithet of the 'Guardian of the City' (*Poliouchos*, like *Polias* at Athens). The temple was supposed to date back to the time of Odysseus and Tyndareos (Tyndareus).

---

137 Euripides, *Ion*, 1581-1588.

It is highly unlikely that the Spartans accepted that Doros was simply the mortal son of Xouthos, especially since, as we shall argue, Xouthos is a byname of Apollo in the mythic motif of the two fathers.

## The Drunken Revel

Thus, Xouthos accepts the Delphic priestess's response that the first person he meets upon emerging from the Temple is actually his son. The scene is again humorous, with the young Ion at first repulsing the older man's effusive gestures as a pederastic proposition.[138] When they inquire into the details of the possibility, it turns out that about the right time ago to match Ion's age, before Xouthos married Kreousa, he had a sexual encounter with a woman at Delphi in a Dionysian revel. 'In you right mind?' asks Ion, 'or drunk?' 'In the pleasures of Bacchus', replies his supposed father. 'Then that's it; that's how I was begotten'.[139] Significantly, the insemination was accomplished out of wedlock. Making Ion only the illegitimate offspring of his supposed father.

The event is trivialized, as befits the mundane narrative. This was not, however, the tale of a Delphic host entertaining his foreigner guest with hetaeras. The occasion was a Bacchic torchlight procession and a *thiasos* or revel orgy of maenads. For three months every third winter (*Trieteris* Festival),[140] Apollo deserted the Delphic sanctuary, returning to the Hyperboreans, and the holy site passed into the patronage of his brothers, either Hermes[141] or Dionysus, and the sanctity reverted to its original site higher up the mountain to the Cave of the Python, which was sacred to the pastoral god Pan.[142] The cave has several chambers, forty according to local informants, hence its modern name as *Sarantavli* ('Forty

---

138 *Ibid.*, 517 *et seq.*
139 *Ibid.*, 553-554.
140 Carl Kerenyi, *Dionysos: Archetypal Image of Indestructible Life* (Princeton, NJ: Princeton University Press, 1976), 204 *et seq.*
141 *Homeric Hymn 4, to Hermes*, 550-568.
142 Pausanias, *Description of Greece*, 10.32.2-7.

Rooms'), and is enormous, the grandest that Pausanias had ever seen, and in use as a sanctuary since Neolithic times. A large rock formation within presents the likeness of a wolf.

Presiding over its rituals were the Thyiades, a triad of ecstatic maenads, as depicted dancing atop the colossal pillar erected before the Temple entrance as a commemoration of the winter orgy up at the Cave.[143] In fact, the portrayal of the Thyiades as a trio did not signify that the troupe was comprised of only three women, but that the females for the *thiasos* banded into the traditional three groups of bacchants based on their ages. The Delphic Sphinx, like the Acanthus Column of the Thyiades, has a similar commemorative symbolism,[144] representing the distant gravesite of Dionysus, whom the Titans were said to have dismembered in the Cave. The Greek cities sent biennial delegations of women to participate in the *thiasos* ritual. They entered a deep state of trance, as they danced on the mountain, and on one occasion, they were so out of their minds that they inadvertently wandered into the town of Amphissa that was at war at the time, and the women of the town formed a protective circle around them to protect them from molestation by the soldiers. The oblivious Thyiades passed out and slept through the night where they had fallen.[145] On another occasion they were caught by an unexpected snowstorm and men were sent to rescue the scantily clad women from the mountain.[146]

The point is that there were no men ordinarily in the *thiasos*. It was for women only. Everything that happened from the lighting of the torch for the procession to the rituals of the *thiasos* was a Mystery, involving prohibited knowledge.[147] The males depicted in these ceremonies always are only the god and his troupe of ithyphallic

---

[143] Acanthus Column, an Athenian offering to the sanctuary dated to *ca*. 380 BCE, Delphi Museum.
[144] Naxian Sphinx, *ca*. 570-560 BCE, a dedication presented by the wealthy citizens of Naxos, Delphi Museum.
[145] Plutarch, *Mulierum virtutes*, 249 EF.
[146] Plutarch, *De primo frigido*, 953 D.
[147] Scholion on Lycophron, *Alexandra*, 212.

satyrs, who represent the god's ecstatic possession of the women, but both the god and his henchmen can only be said to be materializations from a parallel mystical dimension accessed by the bacchanalian rituals. It would have been totally unacceptable in Greek society for the women to engage in sex with actual men. It should be noted also that wine drinking is never depicted in portrayals of the mountain revels. The women were encountering the god's herbal intoxicating antecedents from the primordial world before viticulture. Thus, although they never have a wine cup in their hands, they are often depicted with a stylized florescence representing a plant that they have picked or gathered, for which the prototype is the ivy, the wild vine that was hybridized into the grape.

## Plucking Plants in the Cave

The Korykian Cave was named for the nymph Korykia, whose name etymologically derives from the *kórykos* or 'food sack', employable for a similar purpose, which is to say, the nymph of the Cave was also enacting the rituals of plant gathering, just as Kreousa back in the Cave at Athens. It is, of course, unlikely to find herbs growing in a cave, and the cave as an entrance to the cosmic axis is instead the locale for the entranced Mystery experience accessed by the entheogen.

The Parnassian *kórykos* sack was reportedly filled with honey and water. It was supposedly upon 'honey' that the women in the Cave fed like bees to access their entranced state. The honey-filled sack does not indicate that the women drank fermented honey as mead, which is a weak drink in any case, limited like wine in the percentage of alcohol grown by natural fermentation, and totally incapable of inducing the extreme derangement attested for the Thyiades, especially in the very limited capacity of the *kórykos* to supply a whole troupe of women.[148] Honey is metaphoric of a drink more ancient than the wine, analogous to nectar; and it

---

148 Carl A.P. Ruck, Blaise Daniel Staples, José Alfredo González Celdrán, and Mark Alwin Hoffman, *The Hidden World: Survival of Pagan Shamanic Themes in European Fairytales* (Durham, NC: Carolina Academic Press, 2006), 294-307.

provides the basic verb in Greek for drunkenness.[149] Bees themselves were thought to be generated like flies from the leathern carcass or '*kórykos* sack' of a bull. According to Virgil, bees swarm out of the bull hides, whereupon the entrails left behind became liquid.[150]

The nymph Korykia bore Apollo a son called Lykoros, the 'mountain wolf'. He was the leader of the wolf pack that journeyed from Lycia to find the Cave on Mount Parnassus. There was a similar cave, so-named, in Cilician Lycia. Lycia herself was a water nymph at Delphi, associated with the Castalian Spring, which is to say, she, too, was a mermaid or fish-serpent maiden.

## *Chrysokomes* Apollo

Xouthos is named for the color of the bee, in the spectrum between yellow (*xánthos*) and 'fiery' red (*pyrrós*), which is to say tawny or golden. Golden hair characterizes Apollo, so that the epithet of *Chrysokomes* ('Golden-hair') alone could designate the god. It was as such golden effulgence that the deity materialized to Kreousa in the Cave of the Long Rocks at Athens, mimicking the color of the crocus that she plucked.

If Xouthos participated in the *thiasos* of bee-maidens in the Parnassian Cave where be begot Ion, he could have done so only in the persona of the pre-Olympian wolf god or as Bacchus, an obliging stand-in for his brother Apollo caught in an embarrassing situation. Hermes in the play is cast in a similar role, helping his Olympian brother avoid the scandalous consequences of his chthonic involvements in ecstatic shamanic herbal rituals conducted in sacred caves.[151]

It is likely, moreover, that the maenad or Thyiad that Xouthos encountered in the Korykian Cave was none other than Kreousa, participating as queen in the Athenian delegation to the *thiasos*. Thus, Ion, in the typical pattern of the monomyth, had two

---

149 Plato, *Symposium*, 203b.
150 Vergil, *Georgics*, 4.538 *et seq.*
151 Euripides, *Ion*, 72-73: 'so that the sexual affair of Apollo be (kept) hidden'.

fathers, who are opposite projections of the same identity. The mother should be only one figure, but with two possibilities.

## The Cave of Triphonios

As the mortal claimant to the fatherhood, moreover, Xouthos, when he makes his entrance in the tragedy, has just returned, like someone presumed dead, from his descent into the oracular cave of the Trophonion, where he learned that neither he nor his wife would go home from Delphi childless.[152] The oracle should not be lying. Ion is indeed the child of them both. He will be recognized as the patrilineal son of Xouthos, although secretly revealed as the matrilineal son of Kreousa. In both versions of his identity, he was indeed a son conceived in drunkenness.

The remains of the Trophonion shrine are in the modern town of Livadia, the town just before Delphi as the pilgrim approaches the sanctuary on the road from Thebes and the Boeotian plain. The consultation of the oracle involved a descent through a chasm into the netherworld and the consulter was usually rendered deranged and disoriented for a considerable time afterward, sometimes found wandering far from the site with no recollection of how he got there.

Thus, as in the monomyth, the mortal claimant to paternity is not only mortal, but also a man with definite chthonic symbolism, in this case actually risen from a state of intense intoxication experienced in a horrendous subterranean chamber. It would have been in such a demented state of mind that Xouthos, as the antithesis of the Olympian Apollo, would have participated in the rites of the Thyiades. Significantly, the Cave of Trophonios was also associated with a swarm of bees, and the consulter carried a honey cake to fend off the serpents that infested the terrifying cavern.[153]

By some accounts, Trophonios was a son of Apollo, as Ion and Asklepios, the patron of drug-men or doctors. Together with his brother, Trophonios built the first temple of Apollo at Delphi,

---

152 *Ibid.*, 407-409.
153 Aristophanes, *Clouds*, 506.

which in those days was a beehive, up at the Korykian Cave. To reward them for their effort, the god let them live only a few days. It was in memory of them that the homily was coined: 'Whom the gods love dies young'. The original beehive was commemorated in Classical times in the *tholos* temple of the *Pronoia* sanctuary dedicated to Athena.

## Ion's Other Name

Ion is given his name in the episode of mistaken pederasty as Xouthos emerges from the Temple. Pederasty was symbolic of intensified maleness in engendering a truly spiritual son, to the exclusion of the female's role in the incarnation of spirit in flesh. Hence, despite the burlesque humor, the theme is appropriate in ascribing Ion to his patrilineal genealogy. Ion is the first man Xouthos meets upon 'going' out from the Temple,[154] hence apparently named as the masculine participle of the verb to go, *ion* (from *iénai*), the same participle that in the neuter supplies the word in modern scientific nomenclature for the moving particle formed from an atom or atomic molecule produced by the loss or gain of its electrical charge, either positive or negative. It is a perfect name for Ion as a son in transition from matriliny to patriliny. Ion is the 'Mover', a rather silly name that fits the circumstances of its assignment. As for his supposed mother, it must have been Earth, the mother of Erichthonios, as Ion suggests; to which Xouthos dryly replies, 'The ground doesn't bear children'.[155]

Apparently however, Xouthos has chanced upon Ion's true name as the eponymous founder of the Ionian peoples, since Hermes already refers to Ion by that name in the prologue.[156] The homonymous true name is indeed someone autochthonous, sprung from the ground like a plant, which ordinarily cannot move. The true name is derived from the verb to minister drugs, *ia-esthai*.

---

[154] Euripides, *Ion*, 535.
[155] *Ibid.*, 542. Melissa Mueller, "Athens in a Basket: Naming, Objects, and Identity in Euripides' *Ion*": 365-402, in *Arethusa*, vol. 43, no. 3 (Fall, 2010).
[156] Euripides, *Ion*, 74-75.

The Ionians in their own dialect could be called *Iáones*, 'Iaonians', without the contraction of the adjacent vowels as in the Athenian Ionic dialectal version as Ionians. This is their true name.

## Viola Boy

As such, Ion belongs to the same group of mythological figures named for the 'drug' or entheogen, such as Iason (or Jason in the Medea myth) and the cow-maiden Io and the flower-maiden Iole, all derived from a more ancient root that began with the lost digamma consonant for the w/v sound, as in *(V)iole* as the 'violet' or 'viola', the fairy flower also called pansy, from the French for 'thought' (*pensée*), traditionally anthropomorphized into the little thought-inducing creatures because of the apparent face suggested by the markings of its petals.[157] Oedipus' mother Iokaste probably belongs to this same violet complex. The role of the violet as the vision-altering botanical agent in Shakespeare's *Midsummer Night's Dream* demonstrates the longevity of this metaphor, probably fostered by Gnostic traditions and secret societies persisting into the Renaissance. The same linguistic *(v)ia-* root yields the druggist or doctor as *iatrós*, as someone who manipulates the 'toxins' and drug-smeared 'arrows', called as the homonymous *iós*. The sacred naming of Iamos, the mythical founder of the shamanic priesthood at the sanctuary of Olympia mentioned above, is the most extensive presentation of this metaphoric motif.[158] Ion's true name is Iáon, contracted to Ion.

Violet is the color of the eyes and hair of the Muses who inspired the colonization of the Ionian Islands, and Ionian maidens scattered violets in rituals honoring their eponymous founder.[159] Neither violets nor crocuses grow in caves, such as the Cave of the

---

157 Ruck *et al.*, *Hidden World*, 204-207.
158 Pindar, *Olympia*, 6.57 *et seq.*
159 Carl A.P. Ruck, "On the Sacred Names of Iamos and Ion: Ethnobotanical Referents in the Hero's Parentage": 235-252, in *Classical Journal*, vol. 71, no. 3 (1976). The rite persisted into Roman times as the Rosalia with funereal significance, in which the scattering of violets could be substituted for the offering of roses.

Athenian Long Rocks where Kreousa conceived and subsequently exposed her son Ion. The two flowers are both surrogates for a fungal growth, probably the sacred *Amanita muscaria*.[160] Mushrooms don't grow in caves either, but the cave was the locale for drug-induced mystical transport as early as the Paleolithic era, and the motif achieved its paradigmatic elaboration in Plato's Myth of the Cave.[161]

The Greek violet is not purple (*porphyra*, a color applied without meaning in the Homeric poems, but subsequently designating the purple-crimson dye derived from sea urchins), but reddish-yellow or *xouthós*, like the color of iodine, which was named after it (*ioeídes*, 'ion-looking') when discovered in the early nineteenth century; its highly addictive chemical compound is called 'violin'. This is the color of Kreousa's husband Xoúthos. Frescoes from Knossos and ancient Santorini depict maidens like Kreousa and a blue monkey gathering crocus flowers; and in the Homeric poems the color describes the saffron-red color of the dawn.

The monkeys are vervet (*Chlorocebus pygerythrus*[162]), a silver gray to green monkey, with a black-marked face, but a vivid blue scrotum for the males, the vividness of the blueness intensifying with ascending social rank. The blueness of the entire monkey in the Minoan frescos seems to indicate a chthonic environment and cultic significance. They were considered humorous burlesque immitations of human activity, and hence had a funereal symbolism, like the grotesque creatures like the dwarfish little beings that materialized in certain Mystery cults, the equivalent of the Celtic gnomes and elves. Such connotations identify the saffron flowers as entheogens.[163]

---

160 Carl A.P. Ruck, "Gods and Plants in the Classical World": 131-143, in R.E. Schultes and Siri von Reis (eds.), *Ethnobotany: Evolution of a Discipline* (Dioscorides/Timber Press: Portland, OR, 1997).

161 Carl A.P. Ruck and Mark A. Hoffman, *Entheogens, Myth, and Human Consciousness* (Berkeley, CA: Ronin Publishing), 35 *et seq*.

162 *Cholor-cebus* ('green-long tail') *pyg-erythrus* ('ass-red'). Egyptian art depicts the monkeys as green.

163 Carl A.P. Ruck, *The Great Gods of Samothrace and the Cult of the Little People* (Berkeley, CA; Regent Press, 2017).

## Saffron Boy

In mythical tradition, Krokos was the boy lover of Hermes, who accidentally killed him in sport; three drops of the lover's blood fell on the stamens or stigmata of the crocus, coloring them. It is the stamen of the crocus that supplies saffron, and hence the flower's metaphoric color is more the color of saffron than the purple or yellow of its petals. The flower's name, moreover, has sexual connotations since it is named for the *króke*, the weft of the loom, the crosswise threads held apart by the comb and through which the shuttle delivers the warp threads back and forth. The 'comb' or *kteís* is the word employed for sacred replicas of the vulva, and the act of weaving has sexual implications, as mentioned above regarding the *arrephóroi* and the weaving of Athena's *péplos*. The shuttle in Greek is called *kerkís*, and by metaphor the *membrum virile* was a *kérkos*. The stamens are the male organs of the flower. The same metaphor is documented for Elizabethan English: "I put my shuttle into her hand and bid her use it at her command. She took it kindly and used it free; so she learned to weave along with me".[164]

The violet flower has similar sexual connotations in myth. Ianthe or 'Violet-flower' (*Io-anthos*) was a Cretan maiden betrothed to Iphis ('Mighty'), a woman raised as a man and eventually metamorphosed into an actual male with the addition of a penis by the help of Isis so that the marriage could be consummated. Isis, of course, is known to have reassembled the dismembered body of Osiris, supplying the lost penis with one of her own design. Ianthe was one of the maidens attending Persephone when she plucked the narcotic narcissus flower that occasioned the sexual abduction by Hades.

## Prismatic Color

Cultures and their languages differ in distinguishing divisions along the trichromatic spectrum of the primary colors red, yellow, and blue. Greek tended to notice the reflective iridescence

---

[164] Ruck and Hoffman, *The Effluents of Deity*, 241-242.

of objects, suggestive of their inner significance, not unlike the glowing transparency characteristic of altered consciousness, called *aiólos* in Greek, 'quick-moving, glowing, changeable of hue', like the scales of a serpent or objects seen in the night. In the *Trachiniae* tragedy, Sophocles appears to link the iridescence of the serpentine shape-shifting River Acheloös (*aiólos drákon*) as suitor of the maiden with the night that despoils the Sun in its sexual embrace (*aióla núx*) and the figure of the enigmatic Iole.[165] Thus the color 'orange' was not distinguished in the spectrum between red and yellow until the discovery of the fruit in the New World, first mentioned in 1512; before that date, it was called *geoluread* or 'yellow-red'. Modern Greek, as several modern languages, adopted a variation of Portugal (*portokáli*) for this color, as the country through which the orange was imported. Ancient Greek similarly did not have a common word for green, the area of the spectrum between yellow and blue. *Prásinos* as the color of the leek was rare in ancient usage, although it developed into the common designation for green in Modern Greek.

The crocuses in the Cretan frescoes are either yellow or white, and the crocuses of the Santorini fresco are reddish-brown. The operative symbol in the myths of Krokos and Ianthe is probably the motif of homoeroticism or implied hermaphroditism and the fact that the essential element in both the crocus and the violet is the male member, hence basically phallic or penis-shaped, like a mushroom. The crocuses that Kreousa picked in the Cave were 'reflecting golden light' from the god who materialized from them 'sparkling with gold as his hair' and she plucked them 'to flower' into the fold of her gown, which is to say, into her lap or groin.[166] The saffron-red-golden color characterizes the sacred mushroom, which is also metaphorically associated with the glowing sun.

---

165 Sophocles, *Trachiniae*, 11, 94.
166 Euripides, *Ion*, 887-890.

## Ionic Column

Since Ion is the eponymous founder of the Ionian tribal group, it is not surprising that his botanical consubstantiality is reflected in the Ionic order of columns. The colonnade surrounding the central *cella* or small inner chamber of a Greek temple is an architectural replica of a forest grove, with the house of the deity at its center. The columns are often ornamented with botanical motifs, and the replacement of the columns with caryatids or nymphs of the nut tree (*káryon*) makes explicit the symbolism that the forest is magically animate with spirits materialized from botanical agents or entheogens. The tree nymphs of the caryatids are anthropomorphisms of the hazelnut tree, which is associated in Celtic lore with the fairy creatures, and the nuts of the tree feed the sacred salmons in the pool of waters at its base with the food of knowledge, which implies obviously, the metaphor of an entheogen. Celtic bardic shamans accessed their inspiration by eating these sacred salmons. The spots on the salmon were thought to represent the number of hazelnuts consumed, suggestive of the spotted caps of the Amanitas, and it is probably this association that is responsible for the naming of the spore-bearing structure on the cap's underside as 'gills' in English, rather than the *lamella*, diminutive of the Latin *lamina* for 'plate'. The gills of the mushroom are a zoomorphism making it into a fish.

Vitruvius (first century BCE) derived the Caryatids from the insignificant Peloponnesian town of Carya (presumably named for its abundance in hazelnut trees) that supposedly sided with the Persians in the invasion of Greece,[167] making the maidens into enslaved females condemned to bear the burden of the roof for eternity,[168] but neither they nor the caryatids of the Siphnian and Cnidian treasuries at Delphi appear to be intended as victims of shame and torture. Similarly, the two caryatids of the inner portal to the Eleusinian sanctuary appear to be priestesses, persons of

---

167 The event is not otherwise documented.
168 Vitruvius, *De architectura*, 1.4.8-5.11. Hugh Plommer, "Vitruvius and the Origin of Caryatids": 97-102, in *The Journal of Hellenic Studies*, vol. 99 (1979).

honorific authority. The occurrence of caryatid columns predated the event of Vitruvius's anecdote, and they are derived from maiden dances around the hazelnut tree.[169] On the porch of the Athenian Erechtheion, the six caryatids commemorate or replace the sisterhoods like the Aglauridai who once attended the primordial version of Athena. The many dedications of *kore* figures on the Acropolis had a similar symbolism.

The temple design, moreover, with its gabled roof is an importation into the Mediterranean environment from more northern climates, where the weight of snow might endanger a flat roof, as customary on other buildings indigenous to southern regions. The particular entheogen would be something at home in a wooded landscape.

As mentioned above, the mushroom with its stipe or trunk lends itself readily to the metaphor of a tree, as well as a pillar supporting the heavens, represented by the psychoactive cap of the Amanita, glowing like the sun. The Ionic order of columns is characterized by a capital apparently inspired by the appearance of the *Amanita muscaria* mushroom. It is one of the few species that springs from an egg-like *volva* ('womb, membranous wrapper'). Its unopened *pileus* (or 'cap') trimmed front and rear reveals the spirals or volutes, like an upside down opened scroll, that define the Ionic order. The trimming also exposes the spore sacks that alternate all around the underside of the *pileus*. The alternating egg and dart design of the moldings that ornament the cushion of the Ionic capital imitates this gill structure. The shaft of the column was left white, but the capital was originally painted red for the spirals or volutes like the cap of the sacred mushroom and the cushion moldings were trimmed in yellow or golden foil.

This style of capital originated in Asia Minor and the Ionian islands in the sixth century BCE, a notable example being the Temple of Hera on Samos (*ca.* 570 BCE). The temples, moreover, were originally square, rather than rectangular, with a pyramidal

---

[169] Joseph Rykwert, *The Dancing Columns: On Order in Architecture* (Cambridge, MA: MIT Press, 1999).

red-tiled pitched roof, making the whole design resemble a mushroom house or a fairy ring. The capitals of the other orders of capitals (Doric, Corinthian) can also be interpreted as simplified geometric designs or more extravagantly botanical variations upon the same fungal archetype.

### Kreousa as the Gorgon Queen Medusa

When Kreousa learns that Xouthos has been awarded Ion as a son, she decides to kill him, with the full approval of her entourage of Athenian women, her companions at the shuttle of the loom,[170] and the old tutor of her father Erechtheus, so that the foreign husband not claim her matrilineal heritage. The dramatic persona of the chorus as weavers is an important element in the play's design. Kreousa has in her possession two precious drops of the Gorgon Medusa's blood, the very ones that Athena first gave to her own serpent child Erichthonios, in separate vials attached to the infant with a golden chain, and inherited by her father Erechtheus. Since Erichthonios is a serpent, the child's toxic gift suggests the motif of milking snakes to access their venom. One drop of the Medusa blood is a deadly poison, the other a cure-all panacea and sustainer of life, an elixir of immortality.

Euripides puns on Ion's name in the exposition of this twofold venom: 'the serpents of the Gorgon's poison-arrow going' (*iós ión*),[171] surely an intentional and oddly phrased juxtaposition of words that leap from the verse and command attention. Obviously, it is extraordinary and not an everyday item of attire that Kreousa wears a necklace or bracelet with two vials of Gorgon's blood, 'an antique instrument of gold work' (*chrysom' . . . palaión órganon*).[172] The old pedagogue is instructed to add the deadly drop in secret into the cup of the young man at the birthday ceremony that his father is celebrating. The murder plot fails because one of the household servants broke the requisite silence just as

---

170 Euripides, *Ion*, 747-748.
171 *Ibid.*, 1015.
172 *Ibid.*, 1030.

the drinks were about to be drunk, and Ion, being well versed in ritual procedures as a servant of the Temple, commanded that the drinks be poured out on the ground and a new round of drinks be poured.

At this juncture, a 'winged revel band of doves' from the god's Temple swooped down upon the poured wine and drank.[173] The metaphor of the revel or *kómos* of doves connotes a bacchant orgy, since the maenads were said to fly like birds, swooping upon their prey,[174] and vase paintings depict them with their arms raised beneath their *péplos* to create the appearance of wings. It should be noted that birds do not customarily drink wine. The 'dove', moreover, is more properly called a carrier pigeon, employed for delivering messages, a theme Christianized as the dove of the Annunciation and the accompanying messenger bird-man, the archangel or 'supreme messenger-angel' Gabriel. The one that drank from the wine that Ion spilled quivered, staggered, screamed in anguish, and died. Since these pigeons nest in the cornice of the god's Temple, they must function in the motif of Ion's monody in the play's opening scene as the agents of the Temple's defilement with their droppings. As such, the defiling pigeons interrupt the paternity celebration and almost cause the disclosure of Apollo's embarrassing role in the scandalous seduction in the Cave of the Long Rocks, something inappropriate to his Olympian persona.

## The Court of the Delphinium

Medea similarly tried to poison Theseus when he arrived in Athens to prevent his recognition as the son of Aegeus, and she had the same motive as Kreousa, namely to preserve the matrilineal inheritance of the supposed kingship for her son Medos. The spot where the cup of poisoned wine was dashed to the ground was enshrined at Athens in the Delphinium, which supposedly was built upon the location of the house of Aegeus.[175] This was dedicated to

---

173 *Ibid.*, 1196-1197.
174 Euripides, *Bacchae*, 748-750.
175 Plutarch, *Theseus*, 12.3.

the Delphic Apollo, implicating the foiled attempt upon the life of Theseus in the same Dionysus and Apollo dichotomy as the myth of Ion. The location of the Delphinium is not known, but it is assumed to have been in the area of the later Temple of Olympian Zeus. It was one of the three courts of law established in the sixth century for prosecuting cases of homicide, specifically justifiable murder, as contrasted with the Areopagos for intentional homicide and the Palladium for accidental homicide, this latter named for the goddess Pallas whom Athena accidentally killed as a displacement of her former identity as a goat-serpent hermaphroditic pre-Olympian goddess. It is unlikely, however, that Aegeus had a house in what would have been the countryside in his day. More probably his house would have been with his Queen on the Acropolis at the site commemorated as the Erechtheion.

**Weaving a New Identity**

The Pythian priestess finally exposes the birth tokens that reveal Kreousa as the mother of Ion. The prophetess must be played by the same actor who had impersonated the role of Xouthos. This is thematically appropriate in that she is authenticating the true identity of the child to whom at Apollo's will she had assigned a false patrimony in her response to Xouthos' consultation. This actor also assumed the roles of the two deities, Hermes of the prologue and Athena of the epilogue. This actor would also have impersonated the roles of the old pedagogue of Erechtheus and Kreousa's servant, both ardent sympathizers with Kreousa's unfortunate plight and hence advocates for matrilineal legitimacy. The Pythoness, moreover, has been the foster mother of Ion, like Athena's role with the serpent child Erichthonios. 'Greetings, mother', Ion says, 'even though you didn't bear me'. To which the prophetess replies, 'Let's call me your mother. I do not dislike the name'.[176] The Pythoness is, of course, named for the python serpent that Apollo slew at the Korykian Cave, which was either the original

---

176 Euripides, *Ion*, 1324-1325.

goddess's consort or the masculine attribute of the hermaphroditic female, the equivalent of Athena's Erechthonios. As such the Delphic prophetess is the analogue of Athena as a pacified version of ultimately the Gorgon Medusa.

Kreousa can correctly identify the tokens unseen, hidden in the basket hamper. There is a piece of weaving, an unfinished exercise from her childhood, a depiction of the Gorgon-head, fringed with serpents, as on the aegis that Athena wears as breastplate.[177] This was what Kreousa had employed as swaddling for the infant. There is also a necklace, as was to be worn by a newborn child in commemoration of Erichthonios, two serpents, the antique piece of gold jewelry. The third item is the wreath of olive from the tree that Athena caused to sprout upon the Acropolis in her contest with Poseidon.

The juxtaposition of the toxic Gorgon's head and the olive is the traditional motif indicating the transmutation of the wild plant into the pacified cultivar. The prototypic wild growth in this paradigm is the sacred mushroom. She had placed the wreath upon her baby's head, and it has lost none of its freshness. The crocus as an ethno-botanical motif has yielded to the olive. The olive as surrogate has replaced the primordial identity of Ion, who wore the wreath emblematic of his new botanical consubstantiality.

As the noblest of the Athenian women, Kreousa had probably woven her childhood practice piece of tapestry as one of the prepubescent *arrephóroi* who wove the new *péplos* for the Polias effigy of the goddess, just as she no doubt would have been the leader of the Athenian delegation to the revel in the Korykian Cave in her maidenhood. The women who attend her as the chorus for this visit to the Delphic sanctuary are her household slaves, specifically, the women who assist her with the task of weaving. They form a sisterhood attendant on their mistress, a relationship of close dependence that probably went back to the Queen's childhood, perhaps even learning the art as disciples of the noble *arrephóros*.

---

177  Ibid., 1412 *et seq.*

They are tourists, happy to view the sights from outside the Temple, humorously content to avoid the fee for entering. As they decipher the images depicted in the bas-reliefs of the *metope* plaques, they recognize myths that they have portrayed in their weavings. The Temple as the house of the god is a sacred enclosure evoking the persona of the deity enthroned within. Hence, it is significant that the mythical themes of the Temple's decoration are equivalent to a tabernacle of woven tapestries. A similar evocation of divine persona was the ritual purpose of the *arrephóroi* weavers. They commemorate and replace the Arachne of the mythical tradition, the spider weaver whose salubrious tapestry depicting the amorous events of the gods, like Apollo's scandalous escapade with Kreousa in the Cave, were distasteful to Athena's Olympian persona.

Nothing remains of the Herakles *metope* from the Archaic Temple (sixth century) except this description by Euripides in the *Ion*. It depicted the hero's harvesting of the heads of the Lernean Hydra with a golden pruning hook (*hárpe*), while Iolaos stands ready to cauterize the wounds with blazing torch.[178] The use of the *hárpe* as weapon makes the episode an analogue of Perseus' harvest of the Gorgon-head. Next they decipher Bellerophon, a doublet of Perseus, mounted on the winged horse Pegasus, (Pegasos) as he slays the three-bodied Chimera. Undoubtedly, these were among the *metopes* extant at the time of Euripides.[179] The playwright chose next to describe the pedimental sculptures of the western façade, of which there are fragmentary remains. These would not have been visible from the eastern entrance to the Temple, which is the imagined set for the play, and probably indicate that Euripides is making a conscious amalgam of themes selected for their symbolism. The pediment sculptures portrayed the Battle

---

178 *Ibid.*, 190-200. On the use of the *hárpe* as instrument, see William N. Bates, "Two Labors of Heracles on a Geometric Fibula': 1-17, in *American Journal of Archaeology: The Journal of the Archaeological Institute of America*, vol. 15 (1911).

179 The French excavators of the site assume that Herakles and Bellerophon must be part of the pedimental sculptures, but these two heroes could have played no role in the Battle of the Giants.

of the Giants, with Athena brandishing the Gorgon-head on her shield against the serpent-man Enkelados, while Zeus hurls his flaming thunderbolt at Mimas, also a serpent-man, and Bacchus combats another son of Earth with his staff.

The common theme in Euripides' symbolic amalgam is the transmutation of the primordial toxins of monsters like the Hydra and the Chimera into weapons for the ascendancy of the Olympian realm over the creatures of Gaia. Thus, the weapon that Bacchus wields is a 'staff not meant for war', that is to say, his *thyrsus*, the herbal container that is stuffed with ivy, the primordial version of the vine. It is surely not without significance that Erichthonios and Erechtheus, as well as Ion, exposed with the antique serpent jewelry, are also serpent-men. Apollo, as an Olympian who slew the Python serpent-man, is housed within a Temple that evokes that transcendent version of his identity. It symbolizes his imposition of masculine dominance over a site that once belonged to Gaia.

## The Birthday Party

The birthday celebration continues the theme of a tabernacle woven with symbolic motifs meant to identify its occupant. The tent would probably have been erected in the sanctuary of Dionysus, nearby to the east, outside the precinct of Apollo, at the base of the twin Phaedriades Cliffs that loom over the sanctuary, here referred to as the two rocks of Dionysus. Within the Dionysian sanctuary was an altar lit with a fire, supposedly at the spot that interred the remains of the god dismembered by the Titans. The ecstatic Thyiades were said to waken the god as *Liknites* here, while the 'Holy Priests' (the *Hosioi*) who attended or managed the Pythoness made a secret (árrheton) offering at the same time within Apollo's Temple.[180] The *líknon* of the god's Mystery epithet was

---

180 Plutarch, *De Iside et Osiride*, 365A. On Dionysus at Delphi, see Paul Ciholas, *The Omphalos and the Cross: Pagans and Christians in Search of a Divine Center* (Macon, GA: Mercer University Press, 2003), chap. 2, "The Legacy of Apollo," 27 *et seq*.

a winnowing basket, in which he materialized as something that had the appearance of a phallus. The winnowing basket ordinarily contains grain. It is no more a bassinet than the covered wicker hamper in which Kreousa abandoned the infant Ion.

Hence Ion's birthday celebration as Xouthos' Dionysian son is a complement to the hamper basket of his identity as the Apollonian son of Kreousa, preserved by his foster mother within the Temple. This Dionysian sanctuary beside the Temple of Apollo is a commemoration of the more distant events enacted much higher up Mount Parnassus at the Korykian Cave. Xouthos leaves Ion in charge of the preparations for the celebration, while he goes off, probably to the Cave, to make an offering to the Birth Goddesses. He expects a long absence at the distant site and, in fact, is not present for the ensuing attempt on Ion's life.

The celebration is the tenth day *dekáte* feast, when a child of wealthy parents received its name and was accepted as its father's legitimate offspring; poorer families performed the feast on the seventh day as the *Amphidromia*, dancing around the household hearth. Before that acceptance, the child was not recognized as a citizen. The later Apaturia would gain the child acceptance into his father's tribal brotherhood. The tabernacle is constructed significantly with sacred tapestries from the Temple treasury, and is immense. The absence of Xouthos allows the possibility for both fathers, in the paradigm of heroic dual paternity, to claim the child. It was meant to accommodate the entire staff of the Temple and the people of the town. To Euripides' audience, the tabernacle would recall the tent of the Persian Xerxes, which had been imitated in the Odeum of Pericles, adjacent to the Theater of Dionysus, where this play was being enacted. As the Odeum or Music Hall, it had a similar symbolism as commemorating the defeat of eastern or Anatolian barbarism.

In its entirety, the tabernacle defines Ion's new identity as a transfer from his matrilineal heritage to his double patrimony from Dionysus/Xouthos and Apollo. The roof pole is draped with weavings originally made by the Amazons, which Herakles took as spoils in his conquest of that Anatolian tribe of fearsomely dominant females. The walls were similarly hung with weavings of foreign workmanship: enemy ships attacking Greeks, and mixed-race creatures, half man and beast, and mounted horsemen hunting stags and lions. Hence, the tapestries, in their new employment, like the adjacent Odeum, symbolize the subjugation of barbarism.

## The Horoscope

The figures depicted in the roof tapestries describe a celestial horoscope, a sky with the constellations that indicate Ion's date of birth. The appearance of the Pleiades, Orion, and the Hyades together characterizes the winter sky, the time of the Thyiades and the delegations of maenads for the Mystery revel on Mount Parnassus. The entrance is hung with some Athenian weavings, depicting Kekrops, coiling his serpent tail amid his daughters. Upon entering the tabernacle, the guests would pass through the matrilineal episode of Kreousa in the Cave of the Long Rocks into a central chamber, cavernous like a cave, signifying the winter rite of the Korykian Cave and transcendence to the empyreal realm of the stars.

When Ion is reconciled with his mother, who had mistakenly attempted to poison him, Kreousa explains that a friend can give a friend his own son to be an heir in the other's house.[181] If Ion were only the son of a god, he would never possess the material heritage of a house and a father's name.[182] Under the kingship of Ion, the matrilineal ruler became empowered, not by his descent from the female, but from his supposed lineage from the father. This allows the Queen's scandalous illegitimate encounter with the god Apollo to remain a secret. As Athena explains in the epilogue, Apollo did not see fit to show up in person for fear that he would incur blame for what happened before.

This is what the god demands of those closest to him, sons

---

181  Euripides, *Ion*, 1535-1536.
182  *Ibid.*, 1541-1543, 1560-1562.

like Trophonios and Asklepios and Ion, or brothers like Hermes and Dionysus, or those heroes like Oedipus, who take on the task of being the god's allies, namely to bear the burden of the god's former pre-Olympian persona.

Thus, when Sophocles' Oedipus reveals his blinded eyes to the chorus, they ask, 'How could you bring yourself to do this, to quench your sight? Which of the deities so exalted you?' To which Oedipus replies, 'This is all Apollo's doing, but no one but myself with my own hand struck out the sight'.[183]

---

183 Sophocles, *Oedipus Tyrannus*, 1327-1331.

# Chapter Six
# The Riddle of the Sphinx

**Jocasta as the Sphinx**

Jocasta recognized that Oedipus must have been the murderer of Laïus before her son figures it out for himself, but instead of telling him, she withheld the solution to the riddle and withdrew to her bridal chamber, where she took the answer to the grave by her suicide in Sophocles' tragedy. 'Oh poor man', she had declared. 'May you never know who you are!'[184] This curse has definite reverberations with the prime Apollonian dictum as inscribed on the god's Delphic Temple: 'Know thyself' (*gnóthi seautón*).[185] The same actor who had played Tiresias, who also knew the answer, now impersonates her role. The succession of an actor's impersonations is an indication of the playwright's intended meaning in constructing his tragedy. When Oedipus broke into the bridal chamber (*prós tá numphiká léche*[186]), sword in hand, he apparently intended to attack and kill her as an enemy, although they have had four children together. The bridal chamber has obvious connotations of a sexual encounter.

**Two Names**

The two versions of the heroic persona, in addition to the double set of parents of the monomyth, also yield the motif of the two names, one for each of the personae, or two ways of interpreting

---

184 Sophocles, *Oedipus Tyrannus*, 1068.
185 γν θι σεαυτόν, Pausanias, *Description of Greece*, 10.24.1, ascribed to a variety of wise men of antiquity.
186 Sophocles, *Oedipus Tyrannus*, 1242-1243.

the same name.[187] In the case of Ion, the parameters of his identity were defined by the fanciful designation as the transitional 'Moving' being, contrasted with the autochthonous child of Earth, with the fixity of his botanical consubstantiality. Oedipus in his ascendant persona as the one who solved the riddle of the Sphinx achieved the honorific title as the one who 'Knows the Foot', namely that many can in fact, as with the false report of the multiple murders, be one. This endows his fugal consubstantial anthropomorphism also with the property of the knowledge essential to its role as an entheogen, an agent inducing transcendent vision.

The riddle that the Sphinx had posed, which wasn't actually recorded in full until late antiquity,[188] was what creature walks on four legs in the morning, two legs in the afternoon, and three legs in the evening.[189] Oedipus had correctly sensed that the answer was man, who crawls as an infant, walks upright in adulthood, and then supports his old age with a cane as a third foot. Some kind of riddle was essential to the mythical traditions about the Sphinx[190] and it was so well known to the audience of Sophocles' tragedy that it needed no statement.[191] As a riddle, it is analogous to the riddling responses delivered by the Delphic prophetess; and the Sphinx, as mentioned above, was an element in the symbolism of the Apollonian sanctuary, with connotations of the bacchant rapture of the Thyiades at the Korykian Cave.

---

187 Carl A.P. Ruck and Mark A. Hoffman, E*ntheogens, Myth, and Human Consciousness* (Berkeley, CA: Ronin Publishing), 121-125.

188 Athenaeus, *Deipnosophistai*, 2nd century CE, citing as his source the mid-fourth-century BCE Asclepiades, *Tragodoumena*, in epic verses perhaps from the *Oedipodeia*, a poem of about 6,600 verses, attributed to an eighth-century BCE Spartan Kinaithon.

189 Perhaps first attested by two words in an inscription on a fragmentary vase, *ca.* 520-510 BCE, Vatican Museum 16.541.

190 The fourth-century BCE tragedian Theodectes presented a different riddle about day and night being two sisters, each bearing the other as her child (fragment 4, Snell).

191 The sixth-century BCE Boeotian poet Korinna, however, had Oedipus kill the Sphinx (and a fox) with a spear (fragment 672 *PMG*), and a few fifth-century vases arm the hero with a spear. The armed hero implies that the Sphinx could also be viewed as a more traditional heroic labor of a monster to be overcome by force, rather than the solving of her riddle.

Oedipus himself as a cripple must have been costumed with such a third leg as his staff. The three-legged human, however, is often depicted in ancient figurines with the swollen phallus as the third leg of the tripod, the dominant foot, and Oedipus in burlesque depictions on vases frequently is portrayed with an erection of comic proportions as he confronts the Sphinx. See, for example, the red-figure vase in the collection of the Boston Museum of Fine Arts that depicts Oedipus as an ithyphallic dactyl with spindly legs, wearing a Phrygian cap, with exaggerated penis and paunch belly, supporting himself with a staff in alignment with his dangling penis and forming a tripod with his two legs, as he confronts the Sphinx perched high on a pile of rocks.[192] The Phrygian cap has connotations of the Zoroastrian mysteries of the Persian elite,[193] and the red cap is a common anthropomorphism of their mushroom sacrament, persisting in European lore as the fairytale of *Rotkäppchen* ('Redcap', *Little Red Riding-Hood*). The English translation, which is earlier than the version preserved by the Grimm brothers, makes the cap into a 'riding hood', with shamanic implications of a metaphysical trip.[194] The anthropomorphism of the little fungal creature with the red cap is so obvious an autosuggestion that the Ojibwa (Anishinaabeg) Native Americans of the Great Lakes region call the *Amanita muscaria* 'redtop' (*ostimisk*) and personify it in their folklore.[195]

---

[192] Campanian red-figure *oinochoe*, *ca*. 350-325 BCE, reputedly from Capri, Museum of Fine Arts, Boston, no. 01-8036. Carl A.P. Ruck and Danny (Blaise) Staples, *The World of Classical Myth: Gods and Goddesses, Heroines and Heroes* (Durham, NC: Carolina Academic Press, 1994), 250. David Walsh, *Distorted Ideals in Greek Vase-Painting: The World of Mythological Burlesque* (Cambridge, UK/New York, NY: Cambridge University Press, 2009), 209, image 83.

[193] Carl A.P. Ruck, Mark A. Hoffman, and José Alfredo González Celdrán, *Mushrooms, Myth, and Mithras* (San Francisco, CA: City Lights Books, 2011), 45-47 *et passim*.

[194] Carl A.P. Ruck, Blaise Daniel Staples, José Alfredo González Celdrán, and Mark Alwin Hoffman, *The Hidden World: Survival of Pagan Shamanic Themes in European Fairytales* (Durham, NC: Carolina Academic Press, 2006), 126 *et seq*.

[195] Keewaydinoquay (Peschal) (with an introduction by R. Gordon Wasson), *The Miskwedo in Anishinaabeg Life* (Verona: Stamperia Valdonega, 1984), from the hand-corrected master proof of the unpublished printing, of which only five copies exist, sequestered from access in the Wasson Archives, Harvard Library.

Lacking in the enumeration, four, two, three, is 'one', the one foot of his own identity. Oedipus as the little red-capped erection is reduced to his basic identity as the personified penis found sprouting on the mountainside. The answer to the new riddle about the murderer of Laïus is not man, but himself, one man, not many as in the false report of the event. Sophocles' tragedy elaborates the motif of the search for the murderer of Laïus as a hunt, tracking down the footprints of the perpetrator, which inevitably lead to his own one essential so-called 'foot'. His other name designates him as this swollen phallic foot. The foot metaphor is an elaborate element in Sophocles' poetic diction.

## The Zoomorphism of the Sphinx

The Sphinx, like the Gorgon Medusa, is a zoomorphism of the primordial entheogen, anthropomorphized as a monstrous manifestation of the Earth goddess. The Greek Theban Sphinx is not derived from the Egyptian Great Sphinx of Giza, despite the African origin of Cadmus (Kadmos) and the claim by some that the Sphinx of Thebes originated from Ethiopia. The Egyptian sphinxes are usually male and not winged, and the Theban is female, with the body of a lion and the wings of an eagle. The Greeks simply named the Egyptian figure, some two thousand years after its creation, after their own mythical version of the creature. They did the same thing with the Pygmies, the dwarfish Ethiopian tribe, who already existed in their mythology as the 'fistful' ('pugilist', from *pymé*, 'fist') of dactyl-men, no taller than a finger.

The zoomorphism of the Greek sphinx as a lioness, recalls the goddess's leonine attendants, as in the Lion Gate of Mycenae, a motif traceable back to Anatolian Çatal Hüyük, from which is extant a terracotta figurine of a corpulent woman, seated while giving birth, with her hands on feline attendants on either side of her throne. As the Anatolian Cybele, a cart pulled by lions draws the goddess. The addition of wings to the Sphinx is indicative of her ecstatic trance, as in the numerous Minoan figurines of the goddess or her priestesses, with ornithological attributes or attended by birds. The Sphinx's eagle wings associate her with Hera, as consort of Zeus, whose ornithological emblem is the eagle. Beyond the exemplars directly traceable to the Anatolian context, the hybridized combination of female with lion and bird attributes occurs as autosuggestion or archetype worldwide. The conjunction of Oedipus' Sphinx with a fox in some accounts associates her with lycanthropy, and the Sphinx is generally described as a maenad or bacchant, which would imply the rituals of mountainside plant gathering. The fox/wolf plant is one of the manifestations of the sacred mushroom.[196]

## Consuming Goddess

As the Great Goddess, not surprisingly, the Sphinx's threat is sexual dominance over males. Unlike the Gorgon Medusa, however, she is usually not portrayed as ugly, making her sexual allure more irresistible. The Medusa was only rendered 'ugly' by Athena to defuse her sexual attractiveness, although there are also ancient depictions of her that present her as still 'beautiful'. Although the Sphinx was supposedly encountered on Mount Phikion[197] (still called Mount Phaga) three kilometers outside Thebes on the ridge that divides the two Boeotian basins at the southeast corner of Lake Copaïs, she could also be found in the city's marketplace or agora, or guarding one of the seven magical gates of the legendary city. The Sphinx configuration was also employed as tomb decoration, indicating that she was not evil, but a guardian figure. Because of her riddling, she could also be associated with Apollo's shrine on Mount Parnassus, so that she is essentially the same thematic configuration that is pacified as the Pythoness priestess who served as Ion's foster mother. In Lycophron's *Alexandra*, Cassandra's whole prophetic vision is accessed by ingesting Apollo's

---

196 Carl A.P. Ruck (ed.), Mark A. Hoffman, Evie Marie Holmberg, Stavros Kiotsekoglou, and Vassil Markov, *Dionysus in Thrace: Ancient Entheogenic Themes in the Mythology and Archaeology of Northern Greece, Bulgaria, and Turkey* (Berkeley, CA: Regent Press, 2014).
197 Phix is Boeotian dialect for 'sphinx'.

*daphne* and is a mimesis of the Sphinx's song.[198]

The Sphinx personified the plague, which consisted in her sexual abduction of the men of the city.[199] Although this could be interpreted as her eating them raw, like a ravenous beast,[200] she is depicted carting them off, carrying them horizontally beneath her with her talons in a position suggestive of aggressive sexual rape.

As a female raptor, she is like the Harpy 'raptors'. These were soul-snatchers, materializing as a whirlwind, carting their victims to the other dimension. In the riddle about the edible tables in Virgil's *Aeneid*[201] that would signal the site for the founding of the Etruscan/Trojan settlement that would lead to the city of Rome, the harpy-tables partake in the folkloric motif of the fairy tables, which are metaphoric for the *Amanita muscaria*, spread with the bits of food represented by the white scabby remnants of the shattered universal veil adhering to the fully extended red cap that is the defining characteristic of this mushroom.[202] The Harpies are the way that the fairies of Celtic lore were manifested in Classical traditions, similar to the figure of Psyche, who actually has butterfly wings like a fairy. Even the Gorgon Medusa, who belongs to this same tradition, could be depicted with butterfly or fairy wings.

As a man-eater, the Sphinx is analogous to the Medusa, whom Freud long ago recognized as a fantasy of the *vagina dentata*, the consuming vulva with teeth.[203] As with the Sphinx, the threat of the Medusa, however, is not emasculation, but inextricable entrapment by the tightened gasp of the oral aperture. In attempting to rid Thebes of the plague in Sophocles' tragedy, Oedipus transfers the symptoms of the plague to the as-yet unknown murderer of the

---

198 Lycophron, *Alexandra*, 7.
199 Aeschylus, *Seven Against Thebes*, 773 et seq.: *harpaxándran*, 'man-snatcher'.
200 Ibid., 539 et seq.: *omósiton*, 'raw-eater'. Cf. Euripides, *Phoenician Women*, 1025.
201 Vergil, *Aeneid*, 3.254-257.
202 Carl A.P. Ruck and Robert Larner, "Virgil's Edible Tables": 387-449, in John Rush (ed.), *Entheogens and the Development of Culture: The Anthropology and Neurobiology of Ecstatic Experience* (San Francisco, CA: North Atlantic Books, 2013).
203 Sigmund Freud, *Das Medusenhaupt* (1922).

king. He curses the culprit or his confederates with the same symptoms of sterility of crops and animals that now visits Thebes, so that the plowland offers them no crops, or children from their women's wombs.[204] Significantly, the choral persona in the tragedy represents the three ages of the Sphinx's riddle, 'fledglings not yet able to fly, others bent with age, and men chosen in their prime'.[205] They are a visual presence throughout the play as Oedipus tracks down the feet to his own single foot. That so-called 'foot' and its intrusion into the primordial goddess, with implications as well of a ritual of shamanic rapture accessed by its fungal botanical analogue, will restore the fertility of the land and the progression of the generations.

## Sexual Conquest

In Aeschylus' *Seven Against Thebes*, each of the attackers at the seven gates is chosen for his emblematic motif as symbolically neutralizing the guardian of the particular gate. Thus, it is Parthenopaios (Parthenopeus) who bears the image of the Sphinx, the 'city's shame', on his shield at the fifth northern gate beside Amphion's tomb, so that the defenders will be required to hurl their spears at this threatening image.[206] Parthenopaios is named as the child of the 'Pierced Virgin', a name suggestive of his countering sexual challenge to the Sphinx; and like Oedipus, he was exposed on a mountain, the Virgin Mount, as an infant. Parthenopaios is not only the son of a 'pierced virgin', but the name better describes him as the one 'who smote the virgin', an honorific title of sexual conquest, like a dragon slayer.

The hybrid monsters in Greek myth are often sexualized. Burlesque depictions of the Sphinx show her being mounted by Oedipus' hunting dog, or with Oedipus himself as a dog, wagging his tail, inevitably implying the motif of lycanthropy. In addition to her other zoomorphic features, the Sphinx was imagined as a

---

204 Sophocles, *Oedipus Tyrannus*, 269-275.
205 *Ibid.*, 15-19.
206 Aeschylus, *Seven Against Thebes*, 526 *et seq.*

bitch, a watchdog,[207] and hence a canine like a fox or a wolf. She can be shown also with vaginal pubic hair. Several vases show satyrs confronting or mounting her, probably derived from satyr plays, where the erections of the goat men are comically insufficient to answer her riddles or satisfy her voracious appetite. The Sphinx could also have a serpent tail or the lower body of a man.[208] She can even be satirized as the demagogue Kleon, whom Aristophanes parodied in the *Knights* comedy as a leather merchant, a purveyor of dildos for the sexual gratification of the anally receptive Demos or populace, with a scrubby beard and ejaculating with a fuller stream than the puny sexual apparatus of the hero Oedipus standing below him.[209] The scholar who commented on this vase painting suggests that it is an example of the situation: 'You show me yours and I'll show you mine!'

The obvious etymology of her name indicates her fundamental sexuality. She is named for the 'sphincter', both anal and vaginal, and the threatened encounter would imprison and consume the male's intruding member, 'strangling' it and making him a part of her so that he can never withdraw. This is the true significance of the consuming vagina with teeth, not castration, but emasculation through total assimilation with the female.[210] It is the same threat that the sorceress Circe posed, until the erection of Odysseus was softened and mollified by the application of the magical plant-drug moly.[211] It is an ambivalent threat, moreover, as indicated by the colloquial profanities descriptive of the perhaps desirable 'tightness' of the sexual sphincters, potentially loosened by overuse.

---

207 Aeschylus, fragment 129, from the satyr play, *Sphinx*, extant in Aristophanes, *Frogs*, 1287, with scholiast. Sophocles, *Oedipus Tyrannus*, 391.
208 Tzetzes, Byzantine scholar, on Lycophron, *Alexandra*, 7.
209 Walsh, *Distorted Ideals in Greek Vase-Painting*, 191-192, 204-212.
210 On the phallic mother, see Otto Rank, *The Trauma of Birth*, 1929. Marcia Ian, *Remembering the Phallic Mother: Psychoanalysis, Modernism, and the Fetish* (Ithaca, NY: Cornell University Press, 1993).
211 Homer, *Odyssey*, 10. Ruck and Staples, *World of Classical Myth*, 125. Richard Walter Hooper, *The Priapus Epigrams from Ancient Rome* (Urbana, IL: University of Illinois Press, 1999), 133, epigram 68.

## The Drunken Sphinx

Thus, in Sophocles' so carefully constructed plot of the *Tyrannus*, there lurks a chronological inconsistency. The sole surviving witness to the murder of Laïus did not immediately reveal the murderer, since, when he arrived back at Thebes, he saw that Oedipus had already become king by his marriage to Jocasta. Presumably, the witness ran immediately back to Thebes, whereas Oedipus had paused long enough to confront the Sphinx, whereby he won Jocasta as his bride; and logically, it would require at least a few days to arrange the nuptial ceremony. Thematically, there is no inconsistency, since Jocasta is the Sphinx, and solving the riddle was synchronous with her sexual gratification and with her pacified transmutation from Great Mother into his bride. Thus, by some accounts, Jocasta witnessed the murder of Laïus, and Oedipus immediately had sex with her.[212] The terror of Oedipus' incestuous union with his mother is that he has returned to the womb that gave him birth.

Typical in the monomyth is the motif of the hero's marriage to an apparently docile and subservient woman whose latent primordial identity tragically emerges as instrumental in his downfall, or more exactly expressed, in his assumption of the descendant or decadent version of his liminal dichotomy.[213] In the case of Oedipus, this is the role he plays as Apollo's ally, the Dionysian child that bears the burden of the Apollonian god's displaced past and pre-Olympian function and identity in rituals of drunken rapture.

In this way, the Sphinx is identical with Jocasta as the maenad who was fantasized as mother and bride in the rituals of plant gathering. It is as such that she must have functioned in the ritualized bout of drunkenness with Laïus whereby she conceived her son. Poetic descriptions of the bacchant revels include the

---

212 George Devereux, "Why Oedipus Killed Laïus: A Note on the Complementary Oedipus Complex in Greek Drama": 132-141, in Wayne R. Dynes and Stephen Donaldson (eds.), *Homosexuality in the Ancient World* (Taylor and Francis, 1992), 133 *et seq.*

213 Carl A.P. Ruck and Mark A. Hoffman, *Entheogens, Myth, and Human Consciousness* (Berkeley, CA: Ronin Publishing), 125 *et seq.*

tending of the infant god in the winnowing cradle and the rending or *sparagmós* of their babies, both of which must be metaphors, since the god can only materialize from another dimension and the women did not take their babies with them on their mountain excursions, nor was the mountainside apt to provide a suitable habitat for the growing of grain. By all accounts, the Sphinx was indeed a maenad. She may even have been sent by Dionysus,[214] or have been even one of the Cadmean maenads along with Agave and her sisters in the troupe that pulled Pentheus to pieces.[215] Both of these traditions merely indicate that the Sphinx was apt to materialize amid the bacchanalian rituals.

### The Daughter of Laïus

Pausanias, who always was interested in his travels in the local versions of the myths, records that the Sphinx was actually the illegitimate daughter of Laïus, and that she had numerous brothers, conceived like her from the king's concubines. One of these extra-marital affairs is responsible for the name of Euryganeia ('Widely-glittering') as a doublet of Jocasta.[216] That is to say that Jocasta and the Sphinx represent the same thematic motif. It was Laïus who had entrusted his illegitimate daughter with the riddle. As an illegitimate daughter, the Sphinx would have had no acknowledged father, but only a mother.

Apollo had first taught the riddle to Cadmus and its answer, known only to the succeeding kings of Thebes, empowered the true ruler of the city.[217] Hence, as we have uncovered as the mythic motif, it is knowledge of the sacred fungal sacrament and its consubstantial anthropomorphism as the 'king' in a secret rite of shamanic rapture with the Sphinx that conferred legitimacy on the city's ruler. The solution of the riddle confers the crown matrimonial to the victor, in the transition, like Ion, to patriliny. The

---

214 Scholiast on Hesiod, *Theogony*, 326.
215 Scholiast on Euripides, *Phoenician Women*, 45.
216 Pausanias, *Description of Greece*, 9.5.10, citing the *Oedipodeia*.
217 *Ibid.*, 9.26.3.

antiquity of the riddle, traceable back to the founder Cadmus, implicates the motif of the 'sown men' or Spartoi in the paradigm. These were the indigenous people who sprouted from the plowland that Cadmus sowed with the toxic fangs of the serpent guardian and consort of the Goddess water nymph at the site where the city of Thebes was founded. Cadmus threw a stone in their midst, so that an internecine strife arose, from which only five survived. To one of these most noble representatives of the autochthony (a pentad or fistful of fungal fingerlings) Cadmus gave his maenadic daughter Agave in marriage.

The many unsuccessful claimants who attempted to solve the Sphinx's riddle were the sons of Laïus, but not the child of Jocasta. This was the essential qualifying characteristic, a matriarchal son who might enact the transition to patriarchy. Laïus obviously did not refrain from sex, but only from conceiving a child from the Queen, since that son would replace him. As for the Queen, he, of course, did sleep with her, but avoided conception through sodomy. No one but the Queen's son could succeed him in the supposed kingship, like Ion at Athens.

### The Rapture of the Golden Steed

Thus, Laïus was credited with the invention of sodomy to avoid begetting a son from Jocasta.[218] He supposedly discovered the ruse when he fell in love with Chrysippos (Chrysippus, 'Golden Steed'), the bastard son of Pelops, whom he was tutoring as an athlete for the Nemean Games in honor of the god Poseidon. Some claimed that the episode placed a curse on the dynastic house, and that Hera sent the Sphinx as punishment. It wasn't homoeroticism, however, or pederasty that was the cause of the curse. Pelops himself had experienced such an honorific sexual abduction by Poseidon, a point of pride among his empowered

---

218 Lois Bragg, *Oedipus Borealis: The Aberrant Body in Old Icelandic Myth* (Cranbury, NJ: Associated University Presses/Fairleigh Dickinson University Press, 2004), 42 *et seq.* K.J. Dover, "Greek Homosexuality and Initiation": 127-146, in Wayne R. Dynes and Stephen Donaldson (eds.), *Homosexuality in the Ancient World* (New York and London: Garland Publishing, 1992).

descendants, and it was metaphoric for his shamanic initiation.[219] In Pindar's *First Olympian Ode*, the abduction is presented as a parallel to Zeus's sexual abduction of the Trojan prince Ganymedes, who thereafter served on Olympus as the servant pouring out the sacred drink of nectar for the gods. His task among the deities indicates his association with a magical food that conferred divinity. It was as Poseidon's protégée that Pelops ran the race with Oenoaüs for the marriage to Hippodamia at Olympia, which we have seen was transitional for the reassignment of the sanctuary from Hera, or more exactly her primordial female predecessor, to the Olympian father.

Thus, some accounts claim that Atreus and Thyestes, the legitimate sons of Pelops killed Chrysippos because they feared he might displace them as their father's heir.[220] Some accounts even implicate their mother Hippodamia in the murder and for the same reason. To this same motif of initiatory empowerment belongs the tradition that not only was Jocasta present at the murder of Laïus, but that Oedipus was a rival of his father as a lover of Chrysippos, the 'Boy with the Golden Horse'. The name is suggestive of the shamanic rapture, as Laïus and his 'swollen-footed' son, whom Laïus once again maimed with his chariot wheel, jointly confronted the demands of the Sphinx Jocasta at the symbolic narrow mountain pass, which, in fact, is not narrow at all. Some accounts place the site at a town outside Thebes called Potniai, the 'Ladies', named after Demeter and her holy daughter Persephone or Kore, implying that the murder of Laïus involved the motif of the religion of the two goddesses.[221] As rival lovers of Chrysippos, the quarrel of father and son was over possession of the spirit of the golden steed. Pegasus, a similar magical horse, emerged from the severed neck when Perseus harvested the Medusa mushroom.

The motif of Oedipus and the Sphinx Jocasta is the same as

---

219 Pindar, *Olympia One*. Andrew Calimach, *Lover's Legends: The Gay Greek Myths* (New Rochelle, NY: Haiduk Press, 2002).
220 Thucydides, 1.9; Hellanikos, *FGrH* 4 F, 147; Hyginus, *Fabulae*, 85.
221 Pausanias, *Description of Greece*, 9.8.1.

that of Ion, as the son of the Medusa Kreousa. The difference is that Oedipus, as the son conceived in drunkenness, will be revealed as the transitional child of both parents, whereas Ion is Kreousa's son and only the son of Xouthos by false report, although it was probably Kreousa that he encountered in the drunkenness of the Korykian Cave, which would make him an exact analogue. Oedipus's replacement of his murdered father and his marriage to his bacchant mother, however, do not effectively confirm the shift to patriarchy, which is left unresolved at Thebes. He himself reverts to the matriarchal primacy, as ratified by his placement in the Grove of the sisterhood of the Erinyes at his burial at Colonus; and the unresolved problem of the rival claimants to the throne of Thebes will be played out in the controversy of his brothers and sons by Jocasta, Polyneices and Eteocles and in the War of the Seven at the Gates of Thebes, and its repetition in the second War of the *Epigonoi*, or 'Offspring', fought by the sons of the Seven.

**The Sacrosanct Body**

Oedipus becomes a sacrosanct pawn in the battle for legitimacy. At the end of the *Tyrannus* he does not, as many misremember the plot, go immediately into exile as the mythical scapegoat, the bearer of the city's sins. Instead, Kreon insists that they must first again seek guidance from Apollo. Oedipus' body, which is the embodiment of the anthropomorphized empowering sacrament, is claimed by his rival sons and heirs, and in Euripides' *Phoenician Women*, he has been confined at Thebes in an underground chamber. By some accounts, Oedipus was given an honored burial with funeral contests at Thebes, which were the eponymous etiology for a Theban celebration of athletic games.[222] The burial site was outside the city in a sanctuary of the goddess Demeter.

In Sophocles' *Coloneus* tragedy, with its obvious Athenian prejudice, Theseus, in his traditional theme of settler or 'burier', will ratify a covenant with the old and filthy Oedipus, according

---

[222] Homer, *Iliad*, 23.678-80; Hesiod, *Catalogue of Women*, fragment 192 M-W = 24 Loeb.

him an honored burial as an eternal ally to the city's perpetuated ascendancy through the vicissitudes of time and shifting alliances. The dishonored Erinyes threaten the same plague of sterility that visited Thebes,[223] unless honored and pacified as Eumenides, as here at their Athenian Grove at Colonus, within sight of the hill of Demeter, where his body was cleansed for burial.[224] The hill of Demeter again implies the religion of the two goddesses, and significantly there was also a sanctuary of the Erinyes at the Theban Potniai.[225]

By his burial at Colonus, Oedipus is reunited with the sisterhood of the pacified chthonic goddess. Oedipus is holy, inspiring the same dread as the Erinyes. He is twice called an Erinys in his curse directed to his son Polyneices,[226] but by careful ritual tending, he, like the fearsome goddesses, can become a beneficial ally. Oedipus was also buried on the Hill of the Areopagos.[227] Sophocles presents the final moment of the hero's death as a mystery event, uniting the chthonic and celestial realms along the blinding flash of lightning that passes through the Grove of the Eumenides; and the terrifying Oedipus, like them, becomes a well-wisher for the city's future prosperity.

---

223 Aeschylus, *Eumenides*. 809 et seq.
224 Sophocles, *Oedipus Coloneus*, 1600.
225 Euripides, *Orestes*, 317-318; *Phoenician Women*, 1124-1125.
226 Sophocles, *Oedipus Coloneus*, 1299, 1434.
227 Pausanias, *Description of Greece*, 1.18.6-7.

# Chapter Seven
# The Problem with Thebes

### The Purity of Bloodlines

Oedipus' daughter Antigone, like the Sphinx, is also his sister. Her name is a transparent etymological personification of her role as the 'Stoppage of Birthing'. As a pacified version of the Sphinx-Jocasta, she had taken upon herself the role of nourishing her old and constantly hungry brother-father like a surrogate mother's baby. Sophocles even costumed his persona as someone needing never-ending nourishment, dipping into a miserable food sack he carries as an element in his theatrical portrayal.[228] Although we are aware of the food sack only when Polyneices mentions it late in the play, it would have been visibly present ever since the opening verse of the play. The basic theme of the tragedy is the transfer of Oedipus into the care of Theseus and Athens by his burial, which will extend the tending of the hero's sustenance beyond the grave through offerings upon his tomb. Antigone is paired with her sister Ismene, named for one of the rivers of Thebes. Ismeme's role has been to maintain constant contact through the years with Apollo at the Delphic oracle. Thus, she performs the other function of the original sister-mother-Sphinx as the purveyor of riddles. Ismene, by a folkloric pseudo-etymology, suggests derivation from *[w]ismé*, 'knowledge, cognate with 'wisdom'.[229] Oedipus now does nothing that is not in accord with the Delphic priestess.

---

228 Sophocles, *Oedipus Coloneus*, 1262-1263: 'he carries the nourishment (*threptéria*) for his miserable belly'.
229 Hesychius (fifth-sixth-century CE lexographer), *s.v. isme*.

## THE SON CONCEIVED IN DRUNKENNESS

In Sophocles' *Antigone* tragedy, Antigone insists on uniting her warring brothers in burial, even to the point of forfeiting the infusion of alien bloodlines in the person of her intended spouse, Haimon, the son of Kreon, who is the brother of Jocasta and empowered as regent by his matrilineal connection with her in the interregnum following her suicide. In Euripides' *Phoenician Women*, he has the same function, even though Jocasta is still alive and Oedipus remains in Thebes, secluded in some underground chamber. Kreon is not really a name, but an office or rank. It is a masculine verbal present participle meaning 'Ruler', the equivalent to the feminine Kreousa, as the designation of Ion's mother's role at Athens. Antigone explains her justification for defying Kreon's edict about separating the rival brothers, burying Eteocles, and not only leaving Polyneices unburied, but also even unburying him once Antigone had buried him. Antigone's justification, as she explains it, is that the same commingling of bloodlines that occurred in Polyneices can never be reproduced, with Oedipus and Jocasta now dead, the same commingling that she herself has.[230] Her sister Ismene, of course, has that same commingling, but Kreon's edict has the result of disjoining her from her brothers and sister, although she may have defied the prohibition in secret. The disjoining of bloodlines is an appropriate symbolism for the period of transitional interregnum. Antigone refuses to accept her participation, and thus Kreon's edict has the additional result of disjoining Antigone not only from her dead brother Polyneices, but also from her living sister Ismene.

As for Haimon, whose name means 'Blood', he is abandoned at the altar. When he finds Antigone already dead in her underground chamber, where Kreon, who unburies the dead, buried her while still living, he is left with no one with whom to share his bloodline. He is, of course, Antigone's maternal cousin and offers another opportunity to unite the bloodlines of her mother and father. He kills himself, spilling his rejected blood; as Sophocles

---

230 Sophocles, *Antigone*, 911-912.

puns, 'Blood bloodied himself' (*Haímon . . . haimássetai*) 'by his own hand' (*autócheir*),[231] pouring out his blood upon the corpse of his intended bride.[232] The pun is extraordinary and is certainly intended to emphasize the meaning of Haimon's name. This same Haimon in another tradition had previously been one of the victims of the Sphinx.[233] Although in Euripides' *Antigone*, the heroine is already dead when Haimon spilled out his blood upon the corpse, it was a union in the traditional motif of a marriage to death, and by other accounts resulted in the birth of a son.[234] These variant accounts indicate that Antigone was a thematic analogue of Jocasta and the Sphinx. Kreon's wife Eurydice kills herself to join her son in the underworld.

## To the Left of Laïus

The name Laïus (Λάϊος, *Láios*) is derived from the word for 'left', *laevus* in Latin, with loss of the Greek digamma or 'w'. His father Labdacus (Labdakos) was named for the letter lambda, which in Boeotian dialectal form was *ladba*. Amphion had a lame daughter whose nickname was Labda,[235] supposedly deriding her deformity. Nicknames often took the form of an alphabetical sign.[236] It would appear that the foot deformity and lame gait that characterized Oedipus' swollen penis was a dynastic feature of the Labdacid males. The letter lambda is also suggestive of the shape of the compass (*diabétes*), which was an obscene metaphor for an anally receptive male, descriptive of a stance with legs spread apart, with the further implication of 'penetration' (*dia-baínein* 'passing throught'), as well as an obscene metaphor for a 'bent

---

231 *Idid.*, 1175.
232 *Ibid.*, 1236-1243.
233 Cinaethon, *Oedipodea*.
234 Hyginus, *Fabulae*, 72.
235 Herodotus, 5.92.
236 Pierre Henri Larcher, *Notes on Herodotus: Historical and Critical Remarks on the Nine Books of the History of Herodotus*, translated from the French (London: John R. Priestly, 1829, from the French of Paris: Musier, 1786). For Labdakos as 'lame', see the twelfth-thirteenth-century CE *Etymologium magnum*.

prick/ruler', for similar employment.[237]

The etymolgies of the Labdacids were elaborated in Claude Levi-Strauss's 'structural' analysis of the Oedipus myth, where the foot deformities are classified as characteristic of autochony,[238] that the creatures that sprout from the ground like plants have difficulty walking: "In mythology it is a universal character of men born from the earth that at the moment they emerge from the depth, they either cannot walk or do it clumsily."[239] That is simply because they are indeed botanical.[240]

In the Ion myth, the fanciful interpretation of his name that assigns him a father as 'Moving' away from plant-like fixity toward the eponymous tribe of Ionians is indicative of his transitional role in establishing male dominant paternal culture. The same symbolic motif of a botanical child moving toward patrilineal acceptance occurs with the hero Iamos of Lake Stymphalos, who waded into the river to call for acceptance by his dual male lineage in bastardry from both Poseidon and Apollo, whereby he became the eponymous founder of the brotherhood of Iamid shamans at the sanctuary of Olympia.[241] The name of Iamos has the same botanical drug etymology as that of the hero Ion.

## Promethean Fire

No botanical growth lends itself so readily to anthopomorphism as the mushroom, suggesting as well the whole metaphoric

---

[237] Aristophanes, *Clouds*, 178; *Birds*, 1003. The lambda shape was applied to the siphon in late (2nd century CE) Greek, which supplied the medical term for diabetes (1560s CE) as characterized by excessive urination.

[238] Claude Lévi-Strauss, *Structural Anthropology* (New York, NY: Doubleday Anchor Books, 1963, 1967).

[239] Claude Lévi-Strauss, *Tristes Tropiques* (Paris: Librairie Plon, 1955, translated as *A World on the Wane*, John Russell, 1961, and as *Tristes Tropiques*, John and Doreen Weightman, New York, NY: Athenaeum, 1973), 91.

[240] Carl A.P. Ruck, "On the Sacred Names of Iamos and Ion: Ethnobotanical Referents in the Hero's Parentage": 235-252, in *Classical Journal*, vol. 71, no. 3 (1976).

[241] Carl A.P. Ruck, Blaise Daniel Staples, and Clark Heinrich, *The Apples of Apollo: Pagan and Christian Mysteries of the Eucharist* (Durham, NC: Carolina Academic Press, 2000), 46-51.

complex that we have been uncovering of penis, foot, cap/hat, warrior shield, magical table, stool, engraved tablet, scroll of knowledge, tree, ecstatic ornithological flight, taurine manifestations, acquatic analogues, lightning bolt insemination, and hermaphroditic self-penetration. The complex can be amplified by adding fire and spirit via the mushroom's association with Prometheus, the creator of man. This is the same total panoply of metaphoric identities inasmuch as Prometheus stole fire from the Hephaestean volcanic crucible of alchemical transmutation, hidden in the narthex container of the root-cutters; and the Promethean herb was employed by Medea to anoint Jason to protect him in his quest of the Golden Fleece from the fire-breathing bulls that he yoked to sow the other half of the fangs from the Cadmean serpent. The anointment gave him his name as Iason, the 'toxically anointed' hero. The motif continued into Christendom. The Hellenistic Greeks Hellenized the name of Jesus (Joshua) as Jason.[242] Jesus is the 'anointed' as Christ named for the chrism.

The Promethean herb grew with a double stem on the mountainside from the spilled blood of the tormented Titan, or more exactly, from his *ichor*, the rarified fluid that flowed in the veins of the gods.[243] Prometheus was the son of Iapetos, a name with the transparaent etymology as someone 'who flies with the agency of the drug-plant', descriptive of a shaman. Prometheus himself has a name that designates him as the embodiment of 'clairvoyant knowledge', an expectable metaphor for the personification of a psychoactive sacament. The color of the Promethean herb was that of the crocus of the Korycian Cave, obviously identifying it as the flower that occasioned the conception of Ion both in the Cave of the Long Rocks at Athens and its analogue on Mount Parnassus where Xouthos consorted with the Delphic maenadic female who was probably no other than the unwedded Kreousa of Athens. This was the sort of mythical lore that would have delighted a Hellenistic scholarly poet like Apollonius of Rhodes. When Medea cut its root

---

242 *Ibid.*, 143-234.
243 Apollonius *Rhodius, Argonautica*, 3.844 *et seq.*

on the slopes of the volcanic mountain in the Caucasus, the plant flowed with the sap of the oak, indicating that it must have grown in symbiosis to the sacred tree of Druidism, and it bellowed like a bull or mooed like a cow, indicating a botanical zoomorphism commonly associated with the sprouting of mushrooms.

In Greek tradition, mushrooms bellow like bulls as they sprout from the ground.[244] It is the sound that Agave heard in Euripides' *Bacchae* tragedy as she wakes the other women for the mountain revel.[245] The motif is probably influenced by the pun upon 'bellowing' (*mykemata*) and 'mushroom' (*mykes*). It should be noted also that the Gorgons 'mooed' as the cows[246] that are the mate of the bull, and that this same bellowing was the sound of the thunder,[247] whose accompanying lightning flash was the commonly accepted origin for the fruiting mushrooms.[248] 'Mushroom' in English is ultimately derived from this same 'mooing' sound' (Greek *myá-ein*, via Latin *muss-are*, Late Latin *mussarion*, introduced into English as early as the sixteenth century).

The double stem of the Promethean herb is a riddle, since only one plant grows with a double stem, a mushroom, the *Amanita muscaria,* whose 'trunk' or stipe prolongs itself in two directions, up and down, in effect a double stem, specifically a 'twin' sten, not a branching stem, growing from its mid point, like conjoined twins, as it separates the base from the cap to produce the characteristic dumbbell configuration, with the shattered 'egg' (obviously laid by some bird) split or hatched into two segments, above and below.[249] The torment of Prometheus is metaphoric for

---

244 Aristias (fifth-century BCE tragedian), frag. 6 (727, Nauck, *TGrF*), probably from his *Perseus* tragedy, quoted in Athenaeus, *Deipnosophistae*, 2.60B: *mukaísi d' oréchthei tó léinon pédon; rhóchthei*, 'rattle, swell, roar'.
245 Euripides, *Bacchae*, 689-691.
246 Eustathius, on *Iliad* 2.498; Stephanus of Byzantium *s.v. Mykale, Mukenai*.
247 Aristophanes, *Clouds*, 291-298.
248 R. Gordon Wasson, "Lightningbolt and Mushrooms": 83-94, in Wasson *et al., Persephone's Quest.*
249 Ruck *et al., The Apples of Apollo*, 87-142. Carl A.P. Ruck and Mark A. Hoffman, *The Effluents of Deity* (Durham, NC: Carolina Academic Press, 2012), 278-283.

the ordeal of shamanic initiation. The eagle or vulture that daily gnaws upon his liver, the organ that figures in the hepatoscopy of the prophetic haruspex, probably is interchangeable with the raven as identifying the Promethean liver with the metaphor of raven's bread for the sacred mushroom. This association occurs worldwide, influenced by the bird's fondness for ingesting the mushroom. An analogue is the eagle as the thunderbird in indigenous North American tradition, and its association with the *Amanita muscaria* mushroom.

It should be pointed out that Lévi-Strauss supported the fungal researches of R. Gordon Wasson. Like Joseph Campbell, he was also a friend. Both Lévi-Strauss and Campbell, however, came to an awareness of the role of psychoactive sacraments or entheogens too late to influence their own definitive contributions to the study of mythology.

In Levi-Strauss's paradigm, this 'structure' of autochthony is contrasted with the Sphinx and the Cadmean serpent, which are classified as denials of autochtony, the oppositional dichotmous 'structure' required for this method of mythical analysis. The family relationships, are further categorized as the over-valuing of family relationships (Cadmus and his sister Europa; Oedipus and Jocasta; Antigone and Polyneices) and the under-valuing of family relationships (the fraternal internecine strife of the Spartoi, Oedipus' murder of Laïus; and the warring brothers Eteocles and Polyneices). The particular selection of the defining categories in a structural analysis, however, is always somewhat arbitrary. The Sphinx and the Cadmean serpent, for example, are forced into the required opposition of autochthony denied, even though the sown fangs of the serpent sprout as the autochthonous tribe, presumably possible only by slaying the serpent as opposing that event. Jocasta as the Sphinx, moreover, would place the monster in the category of over-valued blood exclusiveness.

### Shamanic Rapture

The drunkenness of Laïus has no role in the analysis, and the monsters are not seen as paradigms of shamanic rapture and zoomorphisms of the psychoactive sacrament. Drunkenness, especially at Thebes, with its heavy involvement in the traditions of maenadism and the Mystery cult of the Kabeiroi, cannot be seen as a convivial bout of conubial tipsiness between Laïus and his Queen Jocasta that unfortunately engendered a Labdacid son with the dynastic defining birth defect of lameness characteristic of plants.

Moreover, Lévi-Strauss's explanation of the function of the myth as an attempt to transition from the belief that mankind is autochthonous to the knowledge that humans are actually born from the union of man and woman (which could not have been a secret to the myth-makers) does not account for the motif of the supposedly foreign founder and the controversy about maternal versus paternal descent and nomenclature. Cadmus is only supposedly 'foreign', because in the mystery traditions he was also indigenous, surfacing vertically from a netherworld dimension, probably out of the muck of Lake Copaïs, famous for its eels, the likely candidate for the idenity of the indigenous serpent who was guardian consort of the water Lady Thebe at the aboriginal magical spring.[250] Thus in the accounts that record the destruction or unfounding of the city of Thebes, Cadmus reverts to his serpent identity,[251] and the spring of Thebe with the giant snake is equated with the Delphic Castalian spring,[252] making the serpent analogous to the Python of the Korycian Cave. Similarly, Medea of Colchis at the far end of the Black Sea was also indigenous to Corinth, where her sacrifice of her two sons by Jason in Euripides' tragedy

---

250 Carl A.P. Ruck, "The Regression of Cadmean Thebes": 212 *et seq.*, in R. Gordon Wasson, Stella Kramrisch, Jonathan Ott, and Carl A.P. Ruck, *Persephone's Quest: Entheogens and the Origins of Religion* (New Haven, CT: Yale University Press, 1986).
251 Euripides, *Bacchae*, 1330 *et seq.*, reconstructed from the twelfth-century Byzantine *Christus Patiens*, once attributed to Gregory the Great; a tradition known to Ovid, *Metamorphoses*, 3.96-98.
252 Ovid, *loc. cit*; Pseudo-Hyginus (second century CE), *Fabulae*, 6 and 178.

was a mythologized version of a Corinthian ritual of initiatory dedication of children to serve for a period of sequestration in the temple of the goddess.

With the psychoanalytical addition of patricide and matricide and the supposed invention of homoeroticism,[253] both for the ravishing boy of the golden steed and as practiced or suppressed between father and son,[254] the interpretation of the myth goes far afield from the episode of marital seduction in drunkenness.

## Chthonios

There may be another etymology for the left-sided Läïus/ Läïos. It would be as a Doric (Boeotian) dialectal variant of *léïon*, the 'plowland' or its 'crop', replacing the *eta* with the Doric *alpha*. This would explain the antepenultimate accent and the diaeresis on the iota, making the word trisyllabic, whereas the Greek word for 'left' is disyllabic, accented on the ultimate without the diaeresis, *laiós*. This other etymology would have meaning as associating him with the crop of autochthonous sown men that emerged from the field that Cadmus sowed with the serpent's fangs. The five original Theban Spartoi were Echion ('Viperous'), Chthonios ('Chthonic'), Hyperenor ('Overweening' or 'Superman'), Oudaios ('Earthy'), and Peloros ('Monstrous'). Although there are five survivors from the internecine strife of the Spartoi, the number is probably influenced by the motif of the pentad of dactyls or fistful of fingerling creatures. Apart from Echion, as the father of Pentheus, the Theban genealogy centers upon Chthonios as the matriarchal autochthonous lineage in contrast to that of the patriarchal foreigner Cadmus.

Both Jocasta and Läïus are descended from Chthonios, one of these Spartoi; they are cousins four or five time removed. In the case of Läïus, his relationship to the lineage of Chthonios is

---

253 Cameron Shelley and Paul Thagard, "Mythology and Analogy": 152-186, in David R. Olson and Nancy Torrance (eds.), *Modes of Thought: Explorations in Culture and Cognition* (Cambridge, UK: Cambridge University Press, 1996).

254 George Devereux, "Why Oedipus Killed Laius": 132-141, in *International Journal of Psychoanalysis*, vol. 34 (1953).

solely through his grandmother, who was the mate of Polydoros, the only son of Cadmus, and hence he represents the directly male Cadmean lineage, that will be brought back into contact with the Chthonios line for the second time in his marriage to Jocasta.

The lineage of Jocasta, however, as a sixth-generation descendent of Chthonios, involves the tradition of the second founding of Thebes, through Antiope's sexual encounter with Zeus disguised as a satyr, and her twin sons Amphion and Zethos. This divine inception is a doublet of Zeus's (maenadic) insemination of the Cadmean daughter Semele via the thunderbolt to engender the god Dionysus, inasmuch as the disguise as a satyr implies that Zeus and Antiope were participating in the maenadic revel and that hence the twin sons were conceived in drunkenness.[255] Antiope, no less than Jocasta, was drunk when she conceived her sons.

Twin sons are a better mythic motif than a single son since the dichotomous identities of twins can been separated into oppositional recipients, whereas a single son like Oedipus must bear the dichotomy as opposite potentials. The dissimilar Amphion and Zethos, moreover, are analogous to Jocasta's warring sons Eteocles and Polyneices. The two foundings of Thebes, by Cadmus and by Antiope's twins, were rationalized by ascribing the citadel of the Cadmean acropolis to Cadmus, and the encircling fortification walls to Antiope's twins. The warring sons and half-brothers of Oedipus will confront each other at the magical seven gates established in the encircling walls constructed by the two sons of Antiope. The internecine strife of Eteocles and Polyneices repeats the original reciprocal brotherly annihilation of the Spartoi.

### The Grove on Mount Kithairon

The torment of Antiope and her rescue by her sons, moreover, implicate the motif of the ecstatic mountain revel and the ritual *sparagmós* or 'rendering apart of the animal-human victim'. Her

---

[255] Arthur Bernard Cook, *Zeus: A Study in Ancient Religion* (1914-1925), vol. 1, 735.

tormentor Dirce (Dirke), a daughter-in-law of Chthonios and wife of his son Lykos, tied her to a wild mountain bull intending to rend her apart. Needless to say, this would be a dangerous and difficult event for a woman to manage in reality, even with assistants, and it more probably is a metaphor. She did this in the very same spot on Mount Kithairon where all these maenadic events have taken place: the *sparagmós* of Pentheus, equally implausible for women to manage with their bare hands, and the similar rendering of Actaeon by his hounds as wolves, as well as the exposure of the infant Oedipus. The wolf manifestation was a thematic metaphor for the women of the maenadic revel, who metamorphosed as wolves or foxes. Antiope's twins Amphion and Zethos from the encounter with the satyr Zeus were also exposed to die here on the mountain, but like Oedipus, they, too, were rescued by a herdsman and raised as his sons. Pentheus' mother Agave and Actaeon's mother Autonoë were also buried in this same place on Mount Kithairon.

Dirce had unexpectedly chanced upon Antiope there, arriving to take part in a maenadic revel, for she was a notorious devotée of the god. Antiope must have been there for a similar purpose, and it was probably in this same sacred grove that she had previously experienced her sexual encounter with Zeus disguised as a satyr. It seems to be traditional that the child conceived in drunkenness was exposed in the same place where he had been conceived. Dirce's name appears to describe her as 'sighted or a seer', derived from the verb *dérk-esthai*, 'to have accute sight', and in botanical lore, she lent her name to a plant that was associated with the great sorceress Circe and was identified as the psychoactive datura.[256] That is to say, that Dirce was named as a maenad associated with wild psychoactive plants. The same etymology from 'sight'

---

[256] Dioscorides, 3.119; 4.72, also identified as various umbelliferous plants similar to wild carrot and Queen Anne's lace, which probably implies the toxic hemlock and the now extinct magical plant known as silphium, 3.72. It is unlikely that the great popularity and demand for silphium actually led to its extinction; more probably, the plant is unidentifiable because it wasn't so much a plant as a mixture like curry.

underlies the giant seprent as a *drákon* (cognate with 'dragon'), so-named for its staring eyes. Antiope, whose name is a transparent 'opposite persona' of her tormentor, plays a role like Semele in the divine engendering of Dionysus as transitional to viticulture.

In historical times, the sanctuary on Mount Kithairon was where the most ancient cult statue of the god Dionysus was stored and annually escorted down from the mountainside into the city of Athens for the commencement of the festivals of drama. This acceptance of the god into the city ritually enacted the opposite potential of the rejection of the cult as mythologized in the tradition of the Theban Pentheus.[257]

Semele's conception is thematically linked with her sister Agave's union with Echion (the Serpent-man of the Spartoi) to produce the Dionysian anti-persona, her son Pentheus. Pentheus, as the suffering antithesis of ecstatic joy, is easily recognizable as the alternate persona of the god (the agony by which the ecstasy is measured), making the Pentheus and Dionysus duo into the same configuration as the dissimilar twins, Amphion and Zethos, and the warring Oedipean brothers Eteocles and Polyneices. The oppositional pair consisting of the cousins Pentheus and Dionysus is explicity defined in Euripides' *Bacchae* as two different mind-altering drugs producing opposite mental experiences.[258]

The Oedipus myth thus represents a second attempt to mediate the union with an autochthonous inhabitant of the Theban site, bringing together the direct Cadmean patriarchal lineage of Polydoros with two infusions of female lineage descended from the autochthonous Chthonios, namely his two granddaughters, Antiope and Nykteïs, the latter the wife of the Cadmean Polydoros and the former Antiope, who represents the second infusion of Zeus into the lineage. The first infusion produced Dionysus, which yielded no further Theban descendents.

---

[257] Carl A.P. Ruck, "Democracy and the Dionysian Agenda": 343-385, in John A. Rush (ed.), *Entheogens and the Development of Culture: The Anthropology and Neurobiology of Ecstatic Experience* (Berkeley, CA: Atlantic Books, 2013).
[258] Euripides, *Bacchae*, 326-327. Carl A.P. Ruck, "The Mad King and the God": 198-200, in Wasson *et al.*, *Persephone's Quest*.

## Regency of the Wolf

Twice in Laïus' descent, the patriarchy shifted to Jocasta's side of the dynasty. His father Labdakos was only a child when Polydoros died, and his maternal grandfather Nykteus, who was son of the autochthonous Chthonios, took over as regent. Polydoros was his son-in-law, the husband of Nykteïs, who has no name other than as the daughter of her father Nykteus. When Nykteus died, his brother Lykos, took over as regent. Lykos is named simply as 'Wolf'. When Labdakos finally took control, he ruled only briefly, leaving his son Laïus again too young to rule, so that Lykos again took over as regent, followed by the supposed joint rulership of his neice Antiope's two sons. The joint rulership obviously leaves the leadership undecided. Surely this is implausible as anything but mythologized history, representing not actual events, but symbolic motifs. The wolf-man Lykos spans three generations of disrupted lineage and is probably an inherited title or role, rather than a person. He was still operative in the generation before the Trojan War, which was chronologically four generations after his first regency.

The dynastic lineage at Thebes is extremely complex, resulting from a later scholarly attempt to homogenize and reconcile a variety of family and local traditions into a coherent line of descent. The problem is further complicated by the fact that many of the persons involved are indistinguishable from dieties of various rank in the divine hierarchy, inasmuch as the actual drama, if it occurred at all in any real sense, was enacted by rulers who authenticated their right to sovereignty by their shamanic assumption of divine personae. In addition, the mythical traditions have undergone allegorical exegesis, as evidenced by the etymologically obvious names of some of the figures. This is inevitable in a culture where knowledge is received as the remembrance of ancient orally transmitted stories, encoding supposed meanings for a New Age waiting for discovery.

Many events, moreover, are backdated as mythologized history. Cadmus, as a Phoenican/Egyptian was credited with introducing a system of writing, supposedly the Greek alphabetic signs which are adaptations of the Phoenician/Levantine consonants. Cadmus would have dated from the mid-second millennium BCE, but the Phoenician writing dates from the end of the second millennium and Greek alphabetic writing first occurs toward the end of the eighth century. The writing system of Cadmus would have been something like the supposed Pelasgian writing attributed to Linus in the mid-second millennium, and that was something that could be read off of the markings on the decapitated head of his prophetic brother Orpheus. Such an imaginary writing system still existed among the Thracian/Dacians at the time of the Roman Emperor Trajan and in actual fact it was read as an inspired intrepretation of the scabby remnants adhering to the expanded cap of the *Amanita muscaria* mushroom.[259]

At Athens, the lineage similarly displays several instances of disjuncture and renewed attempts to fabricate a definite continuous male bloodline from misunderstood traditions of matrilinear descent. Thus at Athens, both Ion and later Theseus, who are unrelated, enact the same transition to patrilineal empowerment. The Theban mythologized dynasty is further complicated by the mystery tradition of the Kabeiroi, in which Cadmus plays a major role, and by the fact that the city lies at the base of the great sacred mountain of Parnassus, which functioned as the 'volcanic' cosmic axis ritualized in the symbolism of the Korykian Cave, the hot springs of Thermopylae at its northern base, and the establishment of the Delphic oracle.

These Chthonian regents on Jocasta's side of the genealogy, moreover, have ominous names suggestive of their maenadic and Apollonian connotations. Nykteus, is named for the 'Nightman', and Lykos is simply the 'Wolf', the two brothers being the Chthonian sons by a mother who has no identity except the name

---

[259] Carl A.P. Ruck (ed.), Mark A. Hoffman, Evie Marie Holmberg, Stavros Kiotsekoglou, and Vassil Markov, *Dionysus in Thrace: Ancient Entheogenic Themes in the Mythology and Archaeology of Northern Greece, Bulgaria, and Turkey* (Berkeley, CA: Regent Press, 2014).

Klonia, which indicates that she was a 'twig' broken off of some plant (*klón*). The sacred twig implies the maenadic revel as a *bákkhos* or thyrsus.[260]

The wolf is easily recognizable as associated with Apollo in his pre-Olympian manifestation,[261] equivalent to Dionysus in his maenadic role as manifestations of the intoxicants from the age before viticulture. Nykteus, the brother of Lykos, is named for the 'Night', which has similar Apollonian connotations of the god before his assimilation into the Olympian hierarchy. Apollo's lycanthropic involvement as a wolf-god (*lykos*) was given a false etymology, not derived from the 'wolf', but from the 'light' of the sun and its solar illumination. *Lykios* was fancifully associated with the Latin *lux* for 'light' and Greek *leukós* for 'white', and Apollo's epithet is explained as derived from 'the sun shinning and making everything white'.[262] The god's tenuous claim to the light of the day, however, is reflected in the word for the dangerous marginal time of the dawn and the twilight as the 'wolf-light' (*lykóphos*). Similarly, the ominous time when werewolves are abroad, the 'wolf-walk' (*lykábas*), is forced to mean the 'path of the sun' and glossed as a period of time, perhaps a year.[263] The completion of a cycle of time probably implies the offering of a human victim, necessary for the renewal of time.

The mother of Nykteus' daughters Nykteïs and Antiope was a fountain nymph, which is to say a mermaid, named either Kelaino, the 'Black', or Polyxo, a name ascribed to various water nymphs and a notorious maenad, in the entourage of the god. The ubiquitous motif of the fountain nymph who empowers her lord cannot be divorced from its fairytale paradigm as it surfaced throughout Europe in the medieval period and Renaissance as the

---

260 Ibid.
261 Daniel E. Gershenson, *Apollo the Wolf God* (*Journal of Indo-European Monograph Series*, no. 8, Ann Arbor, MI: University of Michigan, Institute for the Study of Man, 1991).
262 Antipater of Tarsus (second-century BCE Stoic philosopher), 3.249.
263 David Dawson, *Allegorical Readers and Cultural Revision in Ancient Alexandria* (Berkeley/Los Angeles, CA: University of California Press, 1992), 43.

fountain nymph Melusina, traceable back to Egeria, the nymph who was consort and counselor of the legendary King Numa of Rome,[264] and still more anciently, the tale of the nymph of Scythia and Herakles as the founding hero of the Scythian tribesmen, ultimately, like all these water nymphs of either fountains or the sea, identifiable throughout its long history as the Gorgon Medusa as an anthropomorphism of the sacred mushroom.[265]

Kreon, who assumes control of Thebes after the Oedipus debacle, is merely a participial designation, and he is another instance of the matriarchal place-marker and regency interim. Thus his son who sacrifices himself for the benefit of the city is named Menoeceus or 'House Abide' and he is not the first occurrence of a figure so named in the dynastic lineage, presumably named after his paternal grandfather, who was also the maternal grandfather of Oedipus. Herakles' wife in the controversy with the Lykos regent is Megara, a daughter of Kreon, and a sister of two brothers, both named 'Blood' or Haimon and another called 'House Abide'.

## Amphion and Zethos

As typical with the twins inseminated by a god, only one of Antiope's offspring from the encounter with Zeus was actually the god's son.[266] This was Amphion. He was the musician, which has Apollonian connotations, but as a displacement the god's more sinister pre-Olympian manifestation, inasmuch as the twanging of the lyre's strings was seen as an entrancing transmutation replacing the deadly toxins shot by the strung bow.[267]

His twin Zethos was a hunter and herdsman and resulted from the supposed insemination by Epopeus, the king of Sicyon, to

---

264 Plutarch, *Numa Pompilius*.
265 Ruck and González Celdrán, "Melusina of Plaincourault": 309-379, in Carl A.P. Ruck, Blaise Daniel Staples, José Alfredo González Celdrán, and Mark Alwin Hoffman, *The Hidden World: Survival of Pagan Shamanic Themes in European Fairytales* (Durham, NC: Carolina Academic Press, 2006).
266 Carl A.P. Ruck and Mark Hoffman, *Mushrooms, Myth, and Human Consciousness* (Berkeley, CA: Ronin Publishing, 2013), 104-118.
267 Pindar, *Pythia I*.

whom Antiope supposedly had fled after the maenadic revel with the satyr Zeus, although others claimed that it was actually her own father the Nightman Nykteus who begot that version of the twins. Obviously, the double inseminations must haved occurred similtaneous with each other and represent the dual potential of the inseminator, as indicated equally by the fact that Zeus did this in the persona of a satyr.

Epopeus, therefore, represents the same configuration as the the satyr and Nykteus. Epopeus is named for the hoopoe bird (épops, as the 'watcher'), but the hoopoe at Sicyon plays the same role as the raven.[268] This is an item of arcane mythical lore recorded by the third-century BCE Hellenistic poet Callimachus in his *Aetia*, a scholarly compendium dealing with the foundation of cities and obscure religious ceremonies and unique local traditions chosen for their oddity. This probably implicates the motif of the *Amanita muscaria* as metaphorically 'raven's bread', inasmuch as Sisyphus created the primordial or autochthonous tribesmen of Sicyon out of mushrooms.[269] Here we have it made explicit that creatures like the autochthonous Spartoi are fungal. A predecessor of the hoopoe as king of Sicyon was, in fact, named Korax or 'Raven'.[270] The town was formerly called Ephyra or 'Red'. As thematically typical, the foundation myth of Sicyon-Corinth transmutes the wild toxic plant into the olive and its patronness Athena as the pacified version of the former Medusa zoomorphism.[271] Amphion and Zethos together built the fortification walls of Thebes, with Zethos carrying the stones, while Amphion played the lyre; or the stones may have moved into position of their own accord in harmony with the music.

Zethos took the indigneous fountain nymph Thebe as bride,

---

268 Callimachus, *Aitia*, fragment SH 238; Noel Robertson, "Callimachus' Tale of Sicyon ('SH' 238)": 57-79, in *Phoenix* vol. 53 no. 1/2 (spring, 1999).

269 Ovid, *Metamorphoses*, 7. 392-393: "Here, tradition says, that in earliest times, human bodies sprang from fungi, swollen by rain." Compare, Apollodorus, *Bibliotheke*, 1.9.3.

270 Pausanias, *Description of Greece*, 2.6.5.

271 *Ibid.*, 2.11.1.

after whom the city was named or renamed, in the plurality of her sisterhood, Thebes, an anglicized plural representing the Greek *Thebai*. Amphion, who was Jocasta's grandfather, took as his wife Niobe, the sister of Pelops, better known for the destruction of her children by the toxic arrows of Apollo and Artemis. This means that Jocasta is descended on the female side from a woman usually recognized as a version of the Anatolian goddess and a notorious enemy of Apollo in his evolution into an Olympian identity. Not surprisingly, therefore, it is just such an anti-Delphic role that Jocasta plays as a doublet for the Sphinx in Sophocles' *Oedipus* tragedy. Jocasta is obviously transitional, potentially associated either with the pacified toxins of her greatgrandfather Amphion's lyre or its antithesis in the form of his wife Niobe's grief for her intoxicated fourteen children, one of whom was Jocasta's grandfather, even though he should have died as an child.

### The Marriage of Cadmus and Harmonia

Laïus finally assumed control only after the death of the Chthonian wolf regents and his marriage to Jocasta. The repeated regency of the two sons of the autochthonous Chthonios, Lykos and Nykteus, instead of the Labdacids, Labdakos and Laïus, delays the final ascendancy of an heir descended from the union of Cadmus and Harmonia, the foundation myth, in which the bride, a daughter of Ares and Aphrodite—War and Love—is transparently symbolic of the hoped-for 'harmony' between the realms and the stability of the evolving male dominance of the Olympian family. As such, the Olympian gods attended the marriage feast, signifying the stabilizing of the realm of male dominance.

They did this only twice, the second being the marriage of Thetis to Peleus. This latter event is even more obvious in its symbolism, inasmuch as Eris or 'Strife' was expressly excluded among the guests, and the marriage itself was a ruse to prevent Zeus from begetting a superlative son from the bride, a son like the hero Achilles who might have replaced him. Significantly, the hoped for harmony is disrupted by the 'Apple of Discord' thrown into their midst, the event that will lead to the epic War at Troy.

The 'Apple' was one of the Golden Apples of the Hesperides, hence synonymous with the homonymous Golden Fleece (both *mélon*) and utlimately identifiable as the mushroom that Perseus harvested as the Gorgon Medusa.[272] This indicates that the whole controversy hopefully settled by the marriages still centers upon control of the magical plant or entheogen and the dichotomous traditions of shamanism as either empyreal or chthonic in its orientation, involving the dominance of either male or female deities.

Chthonios, moreover, had another name, a topographic designation as Hyreius, eponymous of Hyria in Boeotia, formerly named in the feminine purality as the 'sisterhood of the beehive'. With this name, he is known as the father of Orion, a myth that implicates the bull carcass, the Korykian Cave on Parnassus, and the insemination of divine urine in the shamanic paradigm. The urine, after which Orion was named, suggests the common association of the *Amanita muscaria* and its psychoactive urinous metabolite,[273] represented also in the naming of mistletoe as the 'urine twig'; and the bull carcass is metaphoric for the dried fungal cap which is rehydrated in the preparation of the shamanic potion.

## The Divine Mother

The first attempt to incorporate the Spartoi or autochthonous inhabitants in the founding of the city of Cadmus failed, in the death of Pentheus, the son of Echion, as an enemy of his cousin Dionysus. The four daughters of Cadmus also had a troubled involvement with the god. Semele died in conceiving him, and her three sisters formed the leaders of the first bacchant revel at Thebes, with Agave as the head of the ritual trinity. She led the *sparagmós* of her son Pentheus. Autonoë was the mother of Actaeon, torn to pieces by his hunting hounds reverting to wolves.

Ino, the third of the Cadmean sisters, served as the wet nurse of the infant god. The role of wet nurse implicates her in the mythical

---

272 Ruck *et al.*, *Apples of Apollo*, 119-128.
273 *Ibid.*, 74-77.

## THE SON CONCEIVED IN DRUNKENNESS

paradigm of Hecate, the postmenopausal crone who is patroness of herbalism and witchcraft and who reunites in her single divine persona the other two phases of womanhood as maiden and mother.[274] As such, she functioned as the titular ancestor presiding over the sisterhoods of maenads in historical times, representing the triumphant union or totality of femaleness in her typical portrayal as three identical maidens, back to back, and branishing the implements of a mystery initiation. The maenads traditionaly divided into three such groups.[275]

Autonoë's husband was Aristaeus, not a name, but a cult epithet as the 'Best', and he was recognized in antiquity as a version of Apollo in his pastoral role as protector of flocks and patron of beekeepers, as well as mead and and the lore of medicinal or psychoactive herbs. Aristaeus knew the secret of breeding bees from the carcass of a dead bull.[276] We have already seen that the pastoral version of Apollo is implicated in the supposed begetting of the mountain infant child, and the superlative title of 'best' is a euonymous optimistic avoidance of naming him at his true value as just the opposite, as in interpreting the wolf as signifying the light. Thus, some traditions cited Aristaeus as the father of Hecate.[277] Artemis had a similar euonymous persona as Callisto, the 'fairest', who became the etiology for the goddess's familiar as a bear. Aristaeus finally disappeared after he was initiated into the Dionysian mysteries in Thrace.[278]

Aristaeus aided his sister-in-law Ino in caring for the infant Dionysus,[279] and he was also involved with the god in his adulthood in a contest of intoxicants, in which mead was deemed inferior to the god's gift of wine.[280] He thus is emblematic of the wild precedents to viticulture. His marriage to Autonoë suited

---

274 Ruck and Hoffman, *Entheogens, Myth, and Human Consciousness*, 136-146.
275 Euripides, *Bacchae*, 680.
276 Vergil, *Georgics*, 4.281-558.
277 Pherecydes (mid-fifth century BCE),
278 Pausanias, *Description of Greece*, 10.17.3; Diodorus Siculus, 4.81.1.
279 Oppian (third century CE), *Cynegetica*, 4.265 *et seq.*
280 Nonnus (fifth century CE), *Dionysiaca* 13.253 *et seq.*, 19.225 *et seq.*

her for the role of abducted maiden in the trinity of the maenadic daughters of Cadmus since Aristaeus was implicated in the myth of Orpheus and Eurydice. He was pusuing Eurydice when she was bitten by the serpent and descended to the netherworld, and in Boeotian depictions, he was portrayed with wings like an abucting Boread (son of of the wind Boreas), as in the myth of Oreithyia.

Ino's role as wet nurse and titular leader of the maenads brings us back to one final version of the son conceived in drunkenness. This detail emerges only in the fifth-century CE colossal Dionysian epic of Nonnus, a Hellenic Egyptian Christian, who despite the lateness of his date belongs to the tradition of scholarly polymaths and records more ancient items otherwise lost.

### The Milk of the White Goddess

Ino was the second wife of Athamas, whose first wife was Nephele, a 'Cloud' nymph, from whom he had the twins Phrixus and Helle. Nephele is better known as the deceptive lookalike of Hera, whom Ixion raped to beget the race of centaurs. They sprouted from the mountainside as zoomorphic hybrid anthropomorphisms after a fall of rain from their mother. Centaurs, moreover, were traditionally reputed for their drunken behavior and arcane knowledge of plants and toxins.[281] Phrixus and his twin sister perhaps had a similar identity as the children of Athamas. For reasons never explained, Nephele and Athamas tired of each other and divorced, or perhaps she died.

Ino entered the bridal chamber of her husband Athamas with an entire Dionysian revel and conceived two sons of her own from the king:

> After the bridals of Nephele of the earlier marriages, maiden Ino went with revels to the bridal chamber of Athamas. She bore Learchus ... and Melicertes.[282]

---

281 Ruck *et al., The Apples of Apollo*, 89-98.
282 Ibid., 5.556 *et seq.*

Learchus was apparently named after the Phoenician Melqart, the lord of the city of Tyre, a name like the probable meaning of Learchus as the 'leader of the people'. They were probably twins. Melqart was identified as the Tyrian Herakles, but Melicertes was given the false Greek etymology as a 'Honey-eater'.

Ino plotted to usurp the right of primogeniture away from Nephele's children in favor of her own sons by right of matrilineal descent. She secretly roasted all the seeds of grain in Boeotia so that they would not sprout, and when a embassy was sent to Delphi to seek a remedy for the resultant barren crop, she bribed the messengers to report that Phrixus, the first-born son of Athamas, should be offered as sacrifice. In orchestrating the plague of barrenness, Ino is another version of the Sphinx.

The opposite of roasting the seeds before planting would be to soak them in water so that they geminate before planting. This produces malt, the germinated grain, usually barley, that is then dried or roasted and used as the basis for fermenting malt liquors like beer. Ino had another hermetic name as 'Malt', *Byné*.[283]

The myth encodes an opposition between wild and cultivated plants, inasmuch as the roasting of the seeds before their planting is a perversion of cultivation, and the escape of Phixus represents the countervailing motif of reconciliation with primitivism in the form of the wild plant denoted by the so-called Golden Ram. The ram materialized at the moment of the intended sacrifice and transported Phrixus and his twin Helle, who had joined him for the sacrifice, to another reality, although the sister did not make it all the way to their final destination, but she fell from the ram as it swam through the narrow passage of the Hellespont that connects the Aegean to the Propontis or Sea of Marmara. It received its name as the Hellespont from Helle ('Helle's Sea'). The Sea of Marmara is narrowed again at its eastern end at the Bosphorus/Bosporus straits. Its name as the 'Cow-crossing' (*boús póros*) was ascribed to the cow maiden Io's passage through the straits as she

---

283 Lycophron, *Alexandra*, 107.

she fled in estrus prodded by the cow-fly who was the ghost of her former tender Argos.[284] Phrixus was apparently consubstantial with the ram of the sacrifice since he is named as 'Fleecy'. The fleece itself would end up hung on the tree in Medea's far-eastern grove, homonymous with the Golden 'Apple' on the tree in the far-western grove of the Hesperides.

In retaliation for Ino's nursing of the infant Dionysus, Hera drove Athamas mad so that he slew his son Learchus, mistaking him for a ram. The delusion obviously makes this murder an analogue for the sacrifice of Nephele's son Phrixus as the ram of the Golden Fleece. When Athamas then took off in pursuit of Ino and his other son Melicertes, Ino threw herself with the boy, or perhaps both her sons,[285] into the sea. She became the white goddess Leucothea, and the boy was renamed Palaemon, the 'Wrestler', in which persona as the Tyrean Herakles he presided over the athletic contests of the Nemean Games. Although in linear chronology, the death of Learchus and the transformation of Melicertes into Palaemon must have occurred after the nursing of the infant Dionysus, it is with the same breast that nurtured her dead sons that Ino suckled the god.[286] As an alternative to the transcendence occasioned by the leap into the sea, it was also said that Ino, like Medea with the ruse of the rejuvenated ram, boiled up Melicertes in a cauldron and then jumped with the cauldron into the sea.[287]

As a sea nymph and Queen of the Sea,[288] Ino is equivalent to Amphitrite, the mate of Poseidon, hence a mermaid and ultimately a pacified version of the Medusa Queen. Thus, Sisyphus found Palaemon washed ashore beneath a pine tree and had him removed to Corinth as the etiological myth for the Nemean

---

284  Aeschylus, *Prometheus*, 749 *et seq.*
285  Euripides, *Medea*, 1289.
286  Nonnus, *Dionysiaca*, 5.556 *et seq.*: 'To both she gave one common breast, Palaemon and Dionysus'.
287  Eustathius (twelfth century CE), on Homer p. 1543; Plutarch, *Symposium*, 5.3; Ovid, *Metamorphoses*, 4.505, 520.
288  Alcman, frag. 83.

sanctuary. As a wrestler, Palaemon is a version of Dionysus.[289] Palaemon was depicted as a triton, which is to say, a merman. Both Leucothea and Palaemon were deities invoked for fair voyage. They were assimilated into Roman religion as Mater Matuta, the nursing mother, and her son Portunus, the lord of harbors. It is understandable that the pacified or transmuted mermaid monster should preside over fair sailing.

Leucothea is probably a doublet for Galatea, who is named either as 'Milky-white' (from *gála*, 'milk') or 'Calm-seas' (from *galéne*, 'stillness of the sea'), which is to say, she is named for both. Galatea was wooed by the Cyclops Polyphemus (a fungal anthropomorphism of the 'One-eye' creature) and was the mother of the eponymous king of Galatia.

Despite her transformation into the White Goddess, Ino by some accounts continued roaming the mountains as the leader of the bacchant troupes, with her sons still alive. Even though Athamas was now married to Themisto and had children by her, he sent secretly for his former maenadic wife. By this version, Themisto resolved to usurp the right of primogeniture for her own children. She ordered her slave to dress her own children in white and the sons of Ino in back, so that she would know which ones to slay. The slave was actually Ino in disguise. Ino switched the color code so that Themisto murdered her own children.

Ino's repeated involvement in similar incidents of child sacrifice or transmutation and her perpetual roaming as a leader of the bacchant revel is obviously a mythologized history that betrays the ritualized fantasies of maenadic herbalism and identifies the son conceived in drunkenness as the botanical agency for the shamanic rapture.

---

289   Pentheus taunts Dionysus in Euripides' *Bacchae* as a wrestler only with words, and not manly enough to match him, 455, 491. In the myth of the Thracian Sithon and his daughter Pallene, Dionysus wooed the maiden in a wrestling match, Nonnus, *Dionysiaca*, 48.90-280.

## The Necklace of Harmonia

The Theban heritage of the Cadmean lineage almost ended with the internecine murder of the sons of Oedipus in the war of the Seven Against Thebes. Polyneices had enlisted the support of King Adrastus of Argos from another branch of the Cadmean line descended through the cow-maiden Io, who was a daughter of the River Inachos and hence probably another version of the water nymphs like the Gorgon sisterhood. Through descent from Io, Cadmus was her greatgrandson and a brother not only of Europa, but also of Belus or the Canaanite Ba'al, Beelzebub, the 'Lord of the Flies'. Polyneices also enlisted the unwilling participation of the seer Amphiaraüs by bribing his wife with the cursed necklace of Harmonia. It had been fashioned by Hephaestus, who presented it to Harmonia, the child of his wife Aphrodite's sexual affair with Ares out of wedlock. It made women irrestistably beautiful. It had been worn by Semele on the very night that she conceived Dionysus and it had passed on to Jocasta, which might explain why Laïus could not refrain from the drunken conception of their son. The wife of Amiphiaraüs had the transparent name of Eriphyle, which means 'Strife in the Tribal Family'. The necklace still existed as a pious forgery in the second century CE, originally a dedication deposited at Delphi.[290] Some knew that it actually had been first employed when Zeus seduced Europa as a bull.[291]

The sons of the original seven in the war against Thebes returned ten years later as the 'descendants' or *Epigonoi*. This is probably a mythical motif, rather than actual history, since it took two generations also to finish the Trojan War. Thersander, the son of Polyneices, bribed the same Eriphyle this time to send her son Alcmaeon, offering her the robe of Harmonia as the ploy. He was the first as the leader of the Argive allies through the gates and killed Eteocles' son Laodamas. The leadership of Thebes then passed to Thersander. The provenance of the robe was disputed in

---

290 Pausanias, *Description of Greece*, 9.41.2.
291 Apollodorus, *Bibliotheke*, 3.4.2, citing the fifth-century BCE mythographer Pherecydes of Leros.

antiquity. It may have been the original net that Hephaestus had cast over Aphrodite and Ares to catch them *in flagrante delicto* as adulterous lovers, dishonoring the matrimonial vow that was supposed to have bound her to him as his wife. Nonnus in his fifth-century CE epic on Dionysus, knew that Aphrodite was wearing it when she goaded her daughter Harmonia into the estrus of the wild intoxicated revel of desire for Cadmus which was the origin of the House of Cadmus at Thebes.[292]

---

292 Nonnus, *Dionysiaca*, 3.373-4.292.

# Chapter Eight
# The Hero's Weapon of Choice

## Tools of the Trade

The hero in Greek mythology is often characterized by a weapon that is not an ordinary armament of warfare, but indicative instead of the shamanic nature of the hero's task, involving the role of a psychoactive sacrament or entheogen. Perseus employs a pruning hook, and both Herakles and Theseus use a club. Herakles, in addition, is portrayed as an archer whose arrows are anointed with the toxins derived from the monsters he overcomes in the pursuance of his career of heroism. Similarly, both Perseus and Theseus subsequently employ the token head of their defeated monster as a weapon. In one episode of his heroic career, Herakles even employs a shovel against his opponent.

## The Pruning Hook of Perseus

Perseus[293] received his defining pruning hook or hárpe from either Athena[294] or Hermes.[295] The curved *hárpe*, with its protruding straight barb or notch, is sometimes replaced with a sickle (*drépanon*) and equated with the very same implement that

---

293 Ulrike Kenens, "Greek Mythography at Work: The Story of Perseus from Pherecydes to Tzetes": 147-166, in *Greek, Roman, and Byzantine Studies*, vol. 52 (2012).
294 Nonnus, *Dionysiaca*, 24.270 *et seq.*; 30.264 *et seq.*
295 Apollodorus, *Bibliotheke*, 2.4.2.

Kronos (Cronus) had used to castrate his father Ouranos (Uranus).[296] This was the cosmic event that initiated the separation of the male realm from its immersion in the vulva of Gaia.

It has obvious analogues in the threat posed by the overly retentive sphincter of the Sphinx and the immobilizing power of the Medusa, which can turn the hero into a phallic pillar of stone imprisoned within her cave, either literal or figurative. The sorceress Circe posed the same threat of inseparability to Odysseus until it was mediated by the magical intervention of the moly plant. This plant was identified at some point in its long tradition as the *haoma* sacrament of the Zoroastrian Persians and known to the Greeks as ómomi (*[h]ómomi*).[297] This was the same sacrament as the Vedic Soma, which R. Gordon Wasson identified as the *Amanita muscaria* mushroom.[298] It was the psychoactive sacrament of the wolf fraternities of warriors throughout Europe, extending back to the ancient Achaemenid Persians and surfacing among the Dacians at the time of the Roman Emperor Trajan and among the medieval Nordic peoples as the berserkers.[299] This sacrament was a mushroom, which figures throughout its long involvement in folkloric traditions as the perfect mediator between dichotomous structural oppositions.[300]

---

296 Aeschylus, *Phorcides* (ca. 490-460 BCE), fragment 262 i-vi, *TrGF*. The *Phorcides* was the satyr play from the *Perseus* tetralogy. The Phorcides were the triad of sisters of the Gorgons. They are also known as the Graeae or 'Grey Ladies', old women with a single eye.

297 Plutarch, *De Iside et Osiride*, 46 (369d-3669e).

298 R. Gordon Wasson, *Soma: Divine Mushroom of Immortality* (New York, NY: Harcourt Brace Jovanovich, 1972).

299 Carl A.P. Ruck (ed.), Mark A. Hoffman, Evie Marie Holmberg, Stavros Kiotsekoglou, and Vassil Markov, *Dionysus in Thrace: Ancient Entheogenic Themes in the Mythology and Archaeology of Northern Greece, Bulgaria, and Turkey* (Berkeley, CA: Regent Press, 2014).

300 Vladimir Nikolaevič Toporov, "On the Semiotics of Mythological Conceptions about Mushrooms": 295-357, in *Semiotica*, vol. 53 no. 4 (1985), translated from the Russian by Stephen Rudy. Carl A.P. Ruck, "Fungus Redivivus: New Light on the Mushroom Controversy": 351-381, addendum in republication of John Allegro, *Sacred Mushroom and the Cross: a study of the nature and origins of Christianity within the fertility cults of the ancient Near East*, with an introduction by Allegro's daughter Judy Brown (Los Angeles, CA: Gnostic Media Research and Publishing, 2010).

To make the weapon more appropriate for a warrior, modern scholars, aware of the oddity, sometimes call the item a scimitar, the curved Persian sword. The scimitar, however, is less curved (5 to 15 degrees from tip-to-tip) than a sickle (semicircular) or pruning hook (a full 90 degree turn), and the significant detail is simply that neither the pruning hook nor the sickle is an ordinary weapon of war. They are agricultural tools.

The scimitar, which is of Central Asian origin, was called *sampséra* in Greek and not mentioned until the first century CE.[301] The word is Indo-European and is represented in Greek as the *xíphos*, simply a straight sword. The armies of Darius and Xerxes did not employ the scimitar, and it wasn't introduced into the Persian armory until the twelfth to sixteenth century CE. The scimitar is intended for slashing, whereas the sword is plunged into the opponent.

## Mithraism

The *hárpe*, however, as a ritual implement, was also associated with the Persian Zoroastrian Mithras. It was the emblem of the fifth degree in the sevenfold stages of initiation, when the candidate was elevated to the rank of Persian or *Perses*, with whom the hero Perseus is largely interchangeable.[302] Perseus, in fact, had a son Perses, who became the fonder of the Achaemenid dynasty. Here, too, it is an unlikely weapon with which Mithras was supposed to have slaughtered the cosmic bull. A cosmic bull, of course, is no ordinary bull, but is a metaphor. Mithras is depicted as plunging the *hárpe* down into the neck or shoulder of the bull, but only the barb could enter, impeded from plunging deeper by the outer curved rim of the hook, which is not even sharpened to a cutting edge. It would be totally insufficient for its task in slaughtering an actual bull, inflicting only a slight puncture.

---

301 Josephus, *Antiquities of the Jews*, 20.2.3.
302 David Ulansey, *The Origins of the Mithraic Mysteries: Cosmology and Salvation in the Ancient World* (New York, NY: Oxford University Press, 1989), 36 *et seq*.

Hence artists, apparently not privy to the symbolism, sometimes portray both Perseus and Mithras with a straight sword, but this is contrary to the tradition.

Emblematic as well of this fifth stage of the Mithraic initiation is the scythe, which is merely a sickle, fitted with a long handle for reaping fields while standing upright. The pruning hook occurs again amid the emblems of the final seventh stage of Father or *Pater*, without the barb, where it is accompanied by the Persian or Phrygian cap, the divining rod, and what is either a ring or more probably a disembodied eye, symbolic of mystical vision.[303] Perseus also is usually attired with the Phrygian cap, and the Pater's rod indicates expertise as a magician or shaman, particularly as a dowsing rod for finding water, as in the water miracle of Mithraism. The head wearing a Persian cap is an anthropomorphism of a mushroom, especially associated with visionary experience in Orphism as it developed into a theological system in sixth-century BCE Greece through contact with Persian Zoroastrianism.[304]

This final stage of the Mithraic initiation was celebrated as a communal feast upon a Eucharist of cosmic bread equated to the carcass of the slaughtered bull, served upon a table spread with the bull hide and shared between *Sol*, the Sun, and his adoptive son, the *Heliodromos* or solar charioteer. The so-called bull slaughtered with the *hárpe* was the substance of this bread, which makes clear that the bull was metaphoric for something more appropriately pruned with the *hárpe* or harvested with the *drépanon*, a botanical item that had metaphoric bull manifestations.

The initial stage was the *Corax* or Raven, and it was the raven that delivered the command to slaughter the bull and who served as attendant at the final banquet. Inevitably, this identified the food of the Eucharistic banquet as 'raven's bread', the common metaphor of the *Amanita muscaria* as the food of the raven and its

---

303 Carl A.P. Ruck, Mark Hoffman, and José Alfredo González Celdrán, *Mushrooms, Myth, and Mithras: The Drug Cult that Civilized Europe* (San Francisco, CA: City Lights Books, 2011), 132-134.
304 Ruck *et al.*, *Dionysus in Thrace*.

analogous birds like the eagle, vulture, and the hoopoe. The initial stage of the Raven symbolized the entrapment of empyreal fire in the wetness of incarnated matter, and the final visionary banquet released this fiery soul back to the empyrean. The symbolism is a transparent embodiment of the common motif of the origin of mushrooms from the entrapment of the empyreal fire that strikes the earth in the fall of the lightning bolt.

### The Container for the Pruned Monster

Perseus also had a special container into which he placed the Gorgon head after harvesting it. This was a *kíbisis*.[305] Since the Gorgon head was toxic, this special container was required to safely house it.[306] The *kíbisis* is depicted as early as the seventh century BCE,[307] and perhaps mentioned in a papyrus scrap of Alcaeus from *ca.* 600.[308]

As an item of mythological or sacred usage, it is obviously something specially linked to the Perseus myth. No one else employed a *kíbisis*. A heroic version of it on the Hesiodic *Shield of Herakles* (eighth-seventh century BCE) is composed of silver with golden tassels, but since this a depiction upon a metal shield, it merely indicates a coloration by an overlay of silver and gold by the craftsman's art.[309] The real object was never composed of gold and silver.

The *kíbisis* was ordinarily something like a knapsack or leathern purse or wallet, a kind of *péra* ordinarily used for carrying food or temporary provisions. It was a kind of portable larder, a lunch basket or survival pack.[310] Probably this was the sort of sack that Oedipus was carrying for the 'nourishment' (*threptéria*) of his

---

305 Hesiod, *Shield of Herakles*, 224; Pherecydes, 11 J; Pindar, frag. 254; Callimachus, frag. 177.
306 Daniel Ogden, *Perseus* (New York, NY: Routledge, 2008), 44.
307 *Lexicon Iconographicum Mythologiae Classicae (LIMC)* Perseus, no. 117.
308 Frag. 255, Campbell = *Incerti Auctoris*, frag. 30, Voigt.
309 Hesiod, *Shield of Herakles*, 224-226.
310 A.Y. Campbell, "The Boy, the Grapes, and the Foxes": 90-102, in *The Classical Quarterly*, vol. 25, no. 2 (April, 1931).

miserable belly in Sophocles' *Coloneus* tragedy.³¹¹ It is a dialectal word, Cypriote or Aetolian (north coast of the Gulf of Corinth), a rare word with variant spellings as *kíbba* and *kúbesos* and *kubesía*.

A desperate attempt to provide an etymology for the *kíbisis* (viz., *keísthai ekeí éstheta*, 'to lay clothing therein') makes it into a suitcase for apparel.³¹² This is wrong, obviously, and the *kíbisis* in ordinary usage was intended for something edible. It is more probably etymologically related to *kibotós* and similar words as a container, box, vessel, cup, chest, or seed capsule. This last definition is particularly interesting since the *kíbisis* in some sense was indeed a seed capsule.

Since the *kíbisis* of Perseus contains not only something edible, but also harvested as a sacred item, it is a kind of Mystery hamper or *kíste* (Latin, *cista mystica*), which takes its name from the rockrose rosehip capsule (*kísthos*), which is a possible etymological derivative,³¹³ especially since the Gorgons are to be found in the Rockrose Plain of *Kisthénes*.³¹⁴ This was the Garden of the Hesperides, traditionally located on either shore at the straits of Gibraltar. The rockrose was also known as Ladon,³¹⁵ which is the name of the serpent that guards the tree there of the Golden Apples. The *kíbisis* was meant to receive the magical 'apples' of that tree in the rockrose realm of *Kisthénes*, located at the narrow straits to the vast Atlantic Sea beyond, and a counterpoise to the analogous straits of the Hellespont and Bosporus that open to the broad Pontic Sea. Both signify the journey to an alternate dimension of reality, one accessed by the so-called 'apple' and the other by the homonymous Golden Fleece of the ram that transported Phrixus and Helle. Only Phrixus with the Ram made it to Colchis

---

311 Sophocles, *Oedipus Coloneus*, 1262-1263.
312 *Apollodorus: The Library of Greek Mythology*, Robin Hard, trans. (Oxford: Oxford University Press, 1997), 172.
313 Carl A.P. Ruck, Blaise Daniel Staples, and Clark Heinrich, *The Apples of Apollo: Pagan and Christian Mysteries of the Eucharist* (Durham, NC: Carolina Academic Press, 2000), 51 *et seq*.
314 Aeschylus, *Prometheus*, 792-800.
315 Dioscorides, 1.97; Pliny, *Natural History*, 26.47.

at the far eastern end, with Helle falling into the sea at the Hellespont as sacrificial victim.

As usually depicted the *kíbisis* has no cover or top closure like a *kibotós*, but gapes open. This not only allows the viewer to glimpse the toxic head carried inside, but also indicates its true utility, once we recognize the reality behind the hero's employment of a pruning or harvesting tool. Like the *hárpe/drépanon* instrument, the *kíbisis*, as we might suspect, is an agricultural implement. Depictions of Perseus with the *kíbisis* show it either slung on a strap over the shoulder or hanging as a sash from the arm.[316]

Modern analogues of the *kíbisis* exist. It is a harvester's bag, gaping open to allow the plucked fruit or gathered herbs to be dropped down or scooped inside with ease. Just as in heroic times, today it can be hung from a strap around the neck or across the shoulder, allowing the picker to use both hands to cut the fruit from the tree to drop into the gaping bag, or it can be slung as a sash from the left arm, freeing the other hand to pluck the herbs from the ground across into the open receptacle. As such, the *kíbisis* belongs to the same category of herbalist utensils as the Dionysian thyrsus and narthex, but specifically linked to the tale of Perseus and the botanical identity of the toxic Gorgon head as a magical fruit or metaphoric apple, and its involvement in Mystery rituals. The substitution of a scythe/sickle for the pruning hook probably indicates that some hermetic traditions were aware that the mushroom apples had a complement in the psychoactive fungal ergot that infests the grain crop. Both the wild mushroom and its cultivated fungal analogues as the yeasts of vinous ferments and the ergot parasitic on crops of grain were involved in the rituals of Mystery religion initiations.

## Baby Bunting

The *kíbisis* was specifically linked to the harvested head of the Gorgon Queen. The heroes who confronted her and her numerous

---

316 *LIMC*, Perseus, as a shoulder bag, nos. 29, 48a, 100, `104, 112, 113, 137, 141, 145, 161, 170, 171, 192; as sash hanging from the arm, nos. 31, 159.

analogous monsters were ultimately her sons and lovers. They had difficulty both in separating from her at birthing and then again in sexual congress. Perseus repeatedly is confined with his mother at birthing, and Oedipus as lover found his way back to the womb that gave him birth. Like Medusa/Sphinx, they, too, were botanical anthropomorphisms or zoomorphic hybrids, often associated with the implement of their ritual gathering, like the head of the Theban Pentheus placed atop the root-cutters' thyrsus/narthex,[317] or the container in which they were abandoned as infants, like Oedipus and Ion.

A version of a leathern food pouch or *péra* as a Mystery bag is depicted in the famous fifth-century BCE Thessalian bas-relief of two identical females, perhaps Demeter and her daughter Persephone, holding mushrooms that they have apparently removed from the empty sack that one of them holds in her other hand.[318] The mushrooms are identified simply as presumably 'flowers' since until recently a mushroom, despite the obvious similarity, would have seemed implausible and without meaningful context. A similar dismissal of an obvious mushroom as a 'flower' occurs in the museum description of the scene on a fifth-century BCE red-figure *hydria* from ancient Thracian Ainos (modern Enez, Turkey), which depicts the mixing of a sacred potion.[319] On the Pharsalos relief, a second sack held by the other female is perhaps partially preserved at the bottom broken edge of the marble slab. It was probably part of an altar for an Orphic cave initiation.[320]

The *péra* belongs to the metaphoric complex of the botanical infant found abandoned on the mountainside. The hero Paris of Troy was exposed like Oedipus as an ill-fated son and supposedly took his name from this wallet pouch.[321] The *péra* from which

---

317 Euripides, *Bacchae*, 1170.
318 Louvre Museum, *Paris*, no. 701, from Pharsalos, Thessaly, northern Greece, known as the 'Exaltation of the Flower'.
319 Museum of Edirne, ancient Adrianopolis, uncovered in the 2011 excavation of the necropolis of Ainos.
320 Ruck *et al., Dionysus in Thrace.*
321 Scholiast on Euripides' *Andromache*, 294.

Paris received his name, however, would need to have been considerably bigger to accommodate an actual infant. Similarly, the rockrose hampers in which Erichthonios, the serpent foster son of Athena, and Kreousa's son Ion were exposed are sizable enough to hold an infant, despite their name as the rosehip seed capsule.[322] It should be pointed out, however, that the rose does not in any way supply reeds suitable for weaving into the basketwork of the Mystery hamper.

Ordinarily, however, the unwanted infant was supposedly exposed to die on the mountainside in a *chytra* or *chytros*. This was a large ceramic stewpot, although the ordinary size of the *chytra* was also not sufficient to accommodate an infant.[323] It was not really suitable for such employment and probably not readily available in such an ungainly requisite size. No exemplar of adequate capacity survives. Surely there would have been some other container more easily obtainable. The narrowing neck, moreover, would make it awkward to stuff or jam an entire infant forcibly into its enclosure, certainly not without inflicting damage to the child. It, too, apparently had a symbolic significance. The monumental seventh-century *píthos/ámphora* (a yard and a half tall) found at Eleusis in 1954 served as the funeral coffin for a boy. It depicts the Gorgons with stewpots or cauldrons for head. On the neck the vase, the blinding of Polyphemus is depicted, with one tear dripping from his single eye, a droplet in the shape of a mushroom.[324] *Grecas* ('Greek motifs') abound in the vase depiction. These whirling geometric designs are indicative of the onslaught of visionary experience, defined as depictions of the eye viewing the entopic coursing of fluids within its own functioning. They are traceable back to similar designs in prehistoric cave paintings worldwide.

---

322 Erichthonios in the rockrose hamper, with lid beside it, Attic red-figure *pelike*, by the Erichthonios painter, from Nola, Classical period, Würzburg H 4803.
323 E.g., British Museum AN51363001, 5$^{th}$-4$^{th}$ century BCE, rim 9.2 cm., diameter 14.2 cm. (max.), height 10.3 cm.
324 Museum of Eleusis, Greece.

As a ritual vessel, the stewpot *chytros* lent its name to the third and final day of the Dionysian February Anthesteria festival, which celebrated a communal feast and drunken revel with the dead as revenant spirits.[325] The *chytroi* of the final day contained a boiled porridge of seeds and was offered as a sendoff for the ghosts, back to the otherworld. The porridge was apparently not intended for consumption, but poured into the sacred swamp of Dionysus that was considered an entrance to the otherworld, and, in particular, the Eleusinian gateway to the chthonic realm. The etymology for the vessel basically indicates that it was not meant for stewing, but for 'pouring' (*ché-ein*), as in the second day of the Anthesteria festival, which was called the Choes for the 'pitchers' from which the wine was drunk. 'To put someone in a stewpot' was synonymous with the verb 'to kill'.[326] It meant something like the English phrase 'to cook one's goose'.[327]

Aeschylus told the tale of Oedipus' abandonment that way, in a stewpot, in his *Laïus* tragedy.[328] Aeschylus' *Laïus* was the lost first play in his *Oedipus* trilogy completed by the extant *Seven Against Thebes*, for which his lost *Sphinx* was the fourth and final satyr play. There was a strong tradition, known as a commonplace to Aristotle, that Aeschylus, while acting in one of his plays, was accused of profaning some Mystery secret, and that he was attacked by the angry crowd and sought asylum at the altar of Dionysus. At the trial, he exonerated himself by testifying that the error was an inadvertent stumble upon some item of prohibited knowledge since he had not been initiated. He was supposedly excused, based on his honorable military service at the battle of Marathon.[329]

The playwright came from the village of Eleusis and many consider it unlikely that he had not been initiated, nor is it certain

---

325 Ruck *et al.*, *The Apples of Apollo*, 3-14, 235-253.
326 Aristophanes, *Wasps*, 289.
327 First attested 1845, of unknown origin.
328 Aeschylus, *Laïus*, scholiast on Aristophanes' *Wasps*, 289.
329 Aristotle, *Nicomachean Ethics*, 1111a 8-10 (book 3.1.9); further elaborated by Proclus (fifth-century CE Neo-Platonist) and Clement of Alexandria (2${}^{nd}$ century CE).

that the Eleusinian secret was what he was suspected of divulging. The playwright's oath in Aristophanes' *Frogs*, 'namely that 'I swear by Demeter who nourished me that I am worthy of your mysteries', [330] is taken by some to indicate that he had indeed been initiated. However, the oath is in the context of the subsequent oaths of his competitor Euripides by a host of new-fangled audacious deities, and since this is a comedy, the oath of Aeschylus may actually be a reference to the tradition of his indictment for impiety, suggesting, from the obscene viewpoint of comedy, that both tragedians were pious frauds. Otherwise the episode is without comic thrust. The reason that Dionysus chooses to resurrect Aeschylus rather than Euripides in the comedy is, in fact, determined by the reputation of his old-time bravery as a Marathon hero.

Based on two fragments from Aeschylus' *Oedipus* tragedy,[331] which perhaps narrate the same events of Oedipus' miraculous death that are extant in Sophocles' *Coloneus*, it is assumed that the reason for the accusation of impious profanation was theological.[332] The fact that Sophocles had no trouble with his description of the event, however, indicates the opposite. It is more likely that it was something more specific like the botanical identity of the item exposed in the stewpot.

Sophocles, in his lost *Priam* tragedy, appears to have used this same *chytra* to expose the Trojan king's unwanted son Paris on Mount Ida,[333] where the herdsman picked him up and took him home in the *péra* wallet that supplied the etymology for his name. Before being found and rescued, the infant had been nursed by a bear, making him metaphorically a cub, with its implications of the motif of the hibernating bear and perhaps the wolf fraternities, since the bear and wolf are interchangeable in this symbolism. The berserkers are named as 'bear shirts'. Inevitably, in any

---

330 Aristophanes, *Frogs*, 886-887.
331 Aeschylus frags. 386, 387 (S. Radt).
332 Andreas Markantonatos, *Tragic Narrative: A Narratological Study of Sophocles' Oedipus at Colonus* (Berlin: Walter de Gruyter, 2002), 200.
333 Sophocles, frag. 532.

case, Paris would be implicated in the motif of the Phrygian cap since he was ordinarily depicted wearing the native red cap, which is one of the most obvious manifestations of the fungal anthropomorphism. The cap was styled upon the fox head and the fox is interchangeable with both the wolf and the dog as canines. The head wearing a Phrygian cap and emerging from a flower blossom became a common motif in the vase paintings of Magna Graecia and probably is an element of Orphic symbolism identifying the *haoma* sacrament as the rep-capped mushroom.

Aristophanes' *Thesmophoriazousae* parodies the exposure of abandoned infants in the *chytra*. The women are accused of deceiving their husbands with a feigned pregnancy, while an old woman runs in with a purchased supposititious bastard concealed in the *chytra*, allegedly plucked from the mountainside.[334] The climax of the joke may lie in the attempt to convince the deceived husband that the child is truly his by saying, 'Look, his prick is the spitting image of you, an exact impression molded in wax, all curved like the vault of heaven' (*streblón hósper kúttaron*). The 'mushroom' (*mykes*) was a common metaphor for the erect penis,[335] and the fungal anthropomorphism could be viewed as a little warrior protecting himself beneath his uplifted shield,[336] while the psychoactive toxins of the mushroom's cap made it an appropriate metaphor for the vault of the empyreal realm. The *kútattos* of heaven is an odd phrase, since the word actually means the 'encapsulated hard shell', and denoted both the cell of a honeycomb and the male pinecone, and the seedpod of the lotus. A late Byzantine lexicographer glossed it as the acorn, like the *glans penis* ('acorn of the penis').

The joke probably resides in the old woman pseudo-midwife's claim that the prick is an exact impression of the would-be father's penis. She is calling him a gullible asshole. The phrase of the 'vault/shell of heaven' (*t'ouranoú tón kúttaron*) occurs in Aristophanes'

---

334 Aristophanes, *Thesmophoriazousae*, 498-517.
335 Archilochus, glossed in Hesychius, frag. 47, Bergk, *PLG*.
336 *Kaulomykétes*, a fantastic tribe of mushroom warriors, Lucian, *True History*, 1.16.

*Peace*[337] and confirms this interpretation. The comedy begins with two house salves kneading up dung bits to feed a dung beetle, obscenely using one of the slave's phallus as pestle and the other slave's asshole as mortar. They are feeding the dung beetle, as-yet unseen, within the house, to serve as their master's Pegasus[338] to fly to heaven. The master is named Trygaeus, which means he is named after the *trúx*, the *vinum mustum* or must wine, young wine or unfermented grape juice, and the man is clearly mad, a maniac. When he appears onstage, his giant erection has been comically metamorphosed into his dung beetle magical steed, fortified by its diet of kneaded dung bits. The dung beetle or *kántharos* was the favorite sizeable drinking vessel of Dionysus, which was so-named because of its two handles which made it resemble the beetle, whose sanctity, despite its association with dung, stems from Egyptian theology, where the ball of dung represents the solar disk and the beetle was seen as rolling the sun as a sign of resurrection and immortality. When Trygaeus gets to heaven flying on his gigantic erection, Hermes tells him he's docked on the wrong side. The gods aren't there; they're far away, on the other side of the dome of heaven. The fungal stipe appears to penetrate the uplifted underside of the canopy of heaven.

## Golden Mushroom

In addition to the explicit depiction of the decapitated Medusa head as a golden apple from the Tree of the Hesperides,[339] the botanical zoomorphism of the Gorgon head as a mushroom is reflected as well in the local version of the Perseus myth as recorded by the second-century CE Greek traveler Pausanias, who placed the event of the supposed decapitation or harvest at Mycenae.[340] Heobviously doesn't understand the tradition he is relating, but

---

337 Aristophanes, *Peace*, 199.
338 Ibid., 76.
339 Perseus picking the mushroom in the Garden of the Hesperides, amphora, 3rd quarter of the 4th century BCE, Pergamonmuseum: Staatliche Museen zu Berlin, Antiken-Sammlung, inv. no. F. 3022. Ruck *et al.*, *The Apples of Apollo*, figure 9.
340 Pausanias, *Description of Greece*, 2.16.2-6.

according to local informants, Perseus tried to pluck his sword from its sheath and discovered that it had lost its pommel, which was called a 'mushroom' by analogy to its shape. He took this as a sign to found the city at this site. Alternatively, Pausanias had also heard that Perseus was simply thirsty, so he plucked a mushroom (*mykes*) from the ground, whereupon a spring flowed and he decided to name the city Mycenae after it. This is the Persea spring that fed the underground cistern beneath the citadel. Still further, the traveler recalls that there was also a maiden called Mykene mentioned in the *Odyssey*,[341] and that it was she who lent her name to the city.

Pausanias rejects the tradition that this Mykene maiden was the same as the Spartan Sparte, whose name indicates that she must have 'sprouted' from the earth. His rejection, however, indicates that some people were aware that Mykene also was a creature 'sprouted' from the earth, of the same type as the 'Sown-men' or Spartoi of Thebes.[342] Sparte was reputed to be a daughter of the Lacedaemonian River Eurotas. Daughters of rivers are all water nymphs, a motif that implies the widespread mythical complex of the fountain maiden who empowers her lover with dominion and leadership of a people. The Mykene maiden must have been of a similar type since the Persea spring flowed from her encounter with Perseus.

Apart from her etymology as a 'sprout', Sparte takes her name from the broom plant (*Lygeum spartum*) that grows in the dry ground of the Eurotas valley, a grassy reed that provides fibers for baskets and ropes. Its yellow pea-like flowers and seeds, however, contain quinolizidine alkaloids (sparteine, lupinine, thermopsine, etc.), which cause nervous dysfunction and the plant is considered toxic to animals and livestock.[343] The plant figures in indige-

---

341 Homer, *Odyssey*, 2.120.
342 Martin Bernal, *Black Athena: The Linguistic Evidence* (Piscataway, NJ: Rutgers University Press, 2006), 513-514.
343 John W. Daley, H. Martin Garraffo, and Thomas F. Spande, "Amphibian Alkaloids": 186-274, in Arnold Brosse (ed.), *The Alkaloids: Chemistry and Pharmacology V43: Chemistry and Pharmacology* (San Diego, CA: Academic Press, 1993).

nous Mesoamerican ethnobotany and its alkaloids are like those derived from toad venoms. The Spartans must take their name from her. A seventh-century CE etymological dictionary, relying upon the fifth-century Eusebius, derives their other name as Lacedaemonians from a son of Semele, who can be none other than Dionysus.

The citadel of Mycenae was probably already called Mycenae after the plurality of the autochthonous Mykene nymph, by analogy with citadels like Athenai and Thebai (anglicized as plurals, Athens and Thebes), which are feminine plurals of a nymph or goddess. There is no record of Mycenae's name before it was taken over by the Indo-Europeans, but the nearby town of Argos was also called Pelasgia.[344] The lion gate is a Minoan/Pelasgian design and the city existed before the coming of the Indo-Europeans. The tradition of the plucked *mykes* represents a renaming, imposing an Indo-European pseudo-etymology upon a Pelasgian or pre-Greek word. The ultimate identity of this Mykene/Sparte was probably the Queen or Medusa of the Gorgon Sisterhood. Perseus' re-founding of the city marked the transition to patriarchy.

## Golden Pluck

Taken together these local historical variants are a garbled version of the harvested Medusa head as a mushroom, from whose severed neck emerged the magical or transcendent horse named Pegasus for the inspiring springs that flowed wherever he touched ground, which is to say, magical water or a psychoactive potion. This discovery of a spring, moreover, is analogous to the water miracle of Mithraism and the similar water miracle attributed to Moses.[345] The sword with the missing mushroom pommel/penis indicates the sexual nature of the encounter with the great Queen monster. Mithras, in fact, was depicted emerging from a rock at the moment of his birth, holding the sword with which he cuts himself free from his entrapment in matter. Not only did the

---

344  Aeschylus, *Prometheus*, 860.
345  *Exodus*, 17.9.

water horse emerge from the decapitated head, but also a transcendent hero, who is analogous to Perseus as the victor, liberated from confinement in the female's womb. This persona was named Chrysaor (Khrysaor). As the 'Golden Pluck', he is both the harvested fruit and the metamorphism of the *hárpe* or sacred knife into the 'Golden Tool'. An *áor*, as in *Chrys-aor*, is a weapon or sword only as something pulled from the 'scabbard hung or suspended on the belt' (*aor-tér*), like the sword with the missing mushroom pommel.

The earliest depiction of Chrysaor is as a youth on the pediment of the sixth-century BCE Temple of Artemis on the island of Corfu, where he appears with his horse brother Pegasus, but he could also be shown winged himself like his twin Pegasus and half-boar, like the pig manifestation of his Gorgon mother, who has a pig's tusks, nose, and ears. The association of the pig with the goddess is well documented as an appropriate offering to the Eleusinian goddesses. It derives from the fact that the boar is sexually roused by the pheromone of human women as well as sows. The metaphor of the 'piglet' as the female genitalia is the basis for the obscene routine in Aristophanes' *Acharnians* comedy, where poverty has driven the farmer to offer his own daughters for sale as pigs.[346]

Chrysaor was placed among the stars appropriately as the constellation of the Great Boar, which later became the Sword of Orion. He was probably identical with the Erymanthian Boar, which figured as one the twelve Labors of Herakles. Chrysaor was the father of the cattle lord Geryon, who was another of the great hero's Labors. Both Orion, who is named for the divine 'urine' that inseminated him from a bull hide, and the Cattle of Geryon are mythical episodes replete with fungal motifs.[347]

---

346 Aristophanes, *Acharnians*, 729 *et seq.*
347 Ruck *et al.*, *The Apples of Apollo*, 74-79; Carl A.P. Ruck, Blaise Daniel Staples, José Alfredo González Celdrán, and Mark Alwin Hoffman, *The Hidden World: Survival of Pagan Shamanic Themes in European Fairytales* (Durham, NC: Carolina Academic Press, 2006), 256-268.

## Salamander

The oldest known representation of the decapitation of the Medusa is extant on as a ceramic bas-relief on the neck of an early seventh-century BCE large Boeotian *pithos* from Thebes.[348] It survived intact because it was placed in a tomb, which probably indicates a sacral theme or function, like the great Eleusinian urn of the Gorgons with cauldron heads. Above the body of the Medusa, who is depicted as a female centaur, is a salamander, aligned with the similarly four-footed equine body below. The salamander has defied interpretation or justification, but the Gorgon Queen is clearly intended to represent an analogue of the amphibian creature.

The hero Perseus is using a straight knife or sword to saw away or cut off the head of the maiden, who is depicted without the hideousness of her monstrous transformation, said to have been visited upon her by the goddess Athena as a way of lessening her power over men.[349] An oblong *kíbisis* hangs from a strap around the hero's neck, ready to receive his culled harvest. Behind him is a decorative symmetrical double vine motif, rising like a tree, banded together at four regular intervals by an upward oriented triple leaf design, with a fifth larger one at the top, *inverted* and directed downward. The design is probably a stylized tree, perhaps the tree of the Hesperid Garden. Behind the Medusa and the salamander is a single tall sprout or reed that curves at the level of the salamander and turns downward, terminating in a triple leaf motif, like an arrow pointing at the hind quarters of the equine female. The reed sprout perhaps suggests the Sparte figure.

The equine manifestation of the Medusa is natural enough for a creature that was the mate of Poseidon, who is a horseman, and pregnant with the superlative horse-child Pegasus and his 'golden-pluck' brother Chrysaor. Like the amphibian salamander, the Medusa was also aquatic, born of sea creatures, and sometimes

---

348 Boeotian relief *ámphora* from Thebes, *ca.* 670 BCE, Louvre, Paris, CA 795. Kathryn Topper, "Maidens, Fillies, and the Death of Medusa on a Seventh-Century Pithos": 109-119, in *Journal of Hellenic Studies*, vol. 130 (2010).
349 Ovid, *Metamorphoses*, 4.770 *et seq.*; Apollodorus, *Bibliotheke*, 2.46.

depicted with a fish bottom,[350] a tradition that survives through Byzantine lore into modern times of her as a mermaid, the sister of Alexander the Great.[351]

The salamander is named from the Greek *salamándra*, a word of uncertain origin, probably assimilated from some Eastern language, whence through Latin it entered the European languages. Certain salamanders are toxic to the touch, through dermal secretions of psychoactive toxins, more commonly associated with toads and frogs,[352] and found also in certain mushrooms, whence their common folkloric fungal nomenclature as toadstools.[353] A salamander could just as easily sit upon such a toad's throne. Although potentially dangerous, the toxins have also been viewed as a mode of access for psychoactive experience, either alone or in combination with other ingredients, as in the manufacture of salamander brandy in the Balkans today.[354]

## Cold Fire

The commonest European salamander is the 'fire salamander' (*Salamandra salamandra*). It is distributed throughout Europe from northern France and Germany to the Mediterranean, and it is well established throughout the Balkans and Greece. The main

---

350 Scythian Gorgon, as the nymph of Scythia, golden belt ornament. Gorgon Medusa with double serpent bottom, bronze urn handle, British Museum, like the handle on the Vix Krater, Chatillon-sur-Seine, Burgundy, *ca.* 500 BCE. On the fairy mermaid Melusina and the Gorgon, see Carl A.P. Ruck and José Alfredo González Celdrán, "Melusina of Plaincourault": 309-379, in Ruck *et al., The Hidden World*.

351 Judika Illes, *The Encyclopedia of Spirits: The Ultimate Guide to the Magic of Fairies, Genies, Demons, Ghosts, Gods, and Goddesse*s (New York, NY: Harper Collins, 2009), 448-449.

352 Valentina Pavlovna Wasson and R. Gordon Wasson, *Russia, Mushrooms, and History* (New York, NY: Pantheon, 1957). 65-214

353 Jonathan Ott, *Pharmacotheon: Entheogenic Drugs, their Plant Sources and History* (Kennewick, WA: Natural Products Co., 1996),177-181.

354 Miha Kozorog, "Salamander Brandy: A 'Psychedelic Drink' between Media Myth and Practice of Home Alcoholic Distillation in Slovenia": 63-71, in *Anthropology of East Europe Review*, vol. 21, no. 1 (2003). The author found the psychedelic properties mythical, but see below on Pliny's description of the aphrodisiac preparation from salamander.

toxin is samandrin, a steroidal alkaloid causing muscle convulsions, elevated blood pressure, and hyperventilation. The newt (Greek *saúra*) is like the salamanders. The toxic dermal secretions make them unpalatable to predators. Various newt species of *Taricha* are found in Europe, producing tetrodotoxin (TTX), which is like the toxicity of the puffer fish, which is cautiously consumed today for the pleasurable effect of the potentially deadly poison.[355]

Salamanders commonly hibernate in fallen logs, from which they emerge when the wood is thrown on the fire, giving rise to the belief that they were born from fire and were impervious to its effect and could even extinguish the flames with the coldness of their bodies,[356] hence the common name as the 'fire salamander'. This became a commonplace in the medieval bestiaries, where salamanders are depicted in this role.[357] They thus participate in the mythological motif of the phoenix as emblematic of resurrection. Their association with magical plants is indicated in *Exodus Rabbah* 15.28 (midrash or Jewish rabbinical exegesis, late antiquity to medieval period) that claims that Yahweh showed the salamander to Moses in the burning bush. The salamander may have been a symbol for animal-derived drugs in general.[358]

It was the Persian magi or Zoroastrian priests, moreover, who were responsible, as Pliny claims, for the tradition that the salamander was so cold that it could extinguish fire, a property that several ancient and medieval skeptics proved false by experimentation with the poor creature, thrown upon the flames. Since the salamander, as we now suspect, is a zoomorphism of the toadstool and the *haoma* sacrament, the myth is transparently

---

[355] Osamu Arakawa, Deng-Fwu Hwang, Shigeto Taniyama, and Tomohiro Takatani, "Toxins of Pufferfish that Cause Human Intoxication": 227-244, in A. Ishimatsu and H-J Lie (eds.), *Coastal Environmental and Ecosystem Issues of the East China Sea* (TERRAPUB and Nagasaki University Press, 2010).

[356] Aristotle, *Historia animalium*, 5.19; Pliny, *Natural History*, 29.23.

[357] E.g., mid-thirteenth-century bestiary, Bodleian Library 602, fol. 027v, which conflates the salamander with the harmless chameleon and sees its imperviousness to flames as a model of Christian martyrdom.

[358] D.C.A. Hillman, "The Salamander as a Drug in Nicander's Writings": 93-96, in *Pharmacy in History*, vol. 43, (2001).

an aspect of the fungal entheogen of Mithraism and its Vedic analogue as Soma. The fall of spiritual fire as the lightning bolt is seen as the death of celestial illumination in its incarnation in the cold extinguishing wetness of the mushroom. The final Eucharist of the cosmic raven's bread served upon the table spread with the slaughtered bull's hide released this fire back to the empyrean.

It was commonly thought in antiquity that serpents and salamanders acquired their toxins by ingesting toxic plants[359] and that conversely they would transfer their toxins to plants by contamination.[360] Not only were reptiles, scorpions, and the like associated with the motif of botanical toxins, but the activity of bees and other insects with the flowers from which the insects most obviously must derive both the venom of their sting and their honey afforded visual proof of the validity of this notion. The nectar gathered from psychoactive flowers, in fact, produces intoxicating honey.[361] Bees fed the eponymous founder of the brotherhood of prophetic shamans at Olympia, according to the myth, with the psychoactive honey of their stings amid a profusion of flowers.[362] Thus 'honey' as in the honey drink of mead does not refer to fermented sugar water, but is metaphoric for much more potent psychoactive potions.[363]

---

359 Vergil, *Aeneid*, 2.471: *coluber mala gramina pastus*: 'a viper that has grazed on evil grasses'. Serpents don't eat plants.

360 Nicander, *Alexipharmaka*, 521 *et seq*.; Pliny, *Natural History*, 9.5.

361 Xenophon, *Anabasis*, 4.8.18-21, on honey from the Pontic rhododendron (oleander): 'The effect upon the soldiers who tasted the combs was, that they all went for the nonce quite off their heads, and suffered from vomiting and diarrhea, with a total inability to stand steady on their legs. A small dose produced a condition not unlike violent drunkenness, a large one an attack very like a fit of madness, and some dropped down, apparently at death's door. So, they lay, hundreds of them, as if there had been a great defeat, a prey to the cruelest despondency. But the next day, none had died; and almost at the same hour of the day at which they had eaten they recovered their senses, and on the third or fourth day got on their legs again like convalescents after a severe course of medical treatment'. Compare Pliny, *Natural History*, 21.77.

362 Carl A.P. Ruck, "On the Sacred Names of Iamos and Ion: Ethnobotanical Referents in the Hero's Parentage": 235-252, in *Classical Journal*, vol. 71, no. 3 (1976).

363 Ruck *et al.*, *The Hidden World*, 294-306.

## For Love of a Salamander

The first-century BCE Greek writer on pharmacology,[364] whom Pliny the Elder quotes,[365] claimed that a concoction of salamander, properly prepared and preserved in honey, was an effective aphrodisiac. Psychoactive preparations are often claimed as aphrodisiacs because the pleasurable experience easily induces sexual desire, whereas a true aphrodisiac acts directly upon the genitalia. The reputation of Spanish fly (*Lytta vesicatoria*) as an aphrodisiac derives from the toxin *cantharidin*, which is like strychnine and acts as an irritant on the genitourinary tract.

The newt is equated with the Delphic serpent or Python in the famous Praxiteles sculpture of Apollo as the 'Newt-killer' *(Sauroktonos)*,[366] although it would be difficult to distinguish the newt from a salamander.[367] The myth of Askalaphos implicates the Eleusinian potion as well with these toxic botanical lizards. When Demeter arrived at the future sanctuary of the Eleusinian Mystery in search of her abducted daughter, Misme (a primordial version of Persephone) gave the goddess a drink of barley water, which she drank with such greediness that Misme's son Askalaphos laughed, whereupon the goddess splashed the remainder of the drink upon the boy, causing him to metamorphose into a salamander, *stellio*, named for the spots of barley grouts that 'star' his skin.[368]

This myth of the lizard boy identifies the scabs that spot the cap of the Amanita mushroom as the speckled skin that characterizes the salamander and these other similar toxic creatures. The

---

364 Late first-century BCE African Sextius Niger, written in Greek with the title *Peri Hyles*, 'On Medical" Substances'.

365 Pliny, *Natural History*, 29.23.76: *Sextius venerem accendi cibo earum, si detractis interaneis et pedibus et capite in melle serventur, tradit negatque restingui ignem ab iis*. 'Sextius says that venery (sex) is ignited by ingesting them if the entrails, feet, and head are removed and they are preserved in honey; he also says that fire is not extinguished by them'.

366 *Ibid.*, 34.69-70.

367 Apollo *Sauroktonos*, life-size youthful Apollo leaning against a tree trunk, about to kill a lizard, several copies in bronze and marble of lost original, *ca.* 350 BCE. Marble copy, Louvre Museum, Paris; bronze version claimed to be at least partially original, Cleveland Museum of Art.

368 Ovid, *Metamorphoses*, 5.460 *et seq.*

same association was made with the warts of the toads and frogs. Since the toad worldwide, moreover, is metaphoric for the vulva, it hints at the vision that cheered Demeter when the little mushroom dwarf Iambe exposed her genitals in her obscene dance before the goddess.[369] Askalaphos (the 'owl' of Athena) is a verbal version of Asklepios as the physician son of Apollo.[370]

Similarly, the salamander speckled with the grouts of barley fits perfectly the symbolism of the Eleusinian Mystery. The mushroom was the sacrament of the Lesser Mystery, which commemorated the abduction of Persephone. The sacrament was not shared with the candidates for the initiation, but reserved for the titular Queen of Athens, the wife of the king archon, the man of noble lineage who continued the sacral function of governance into the time of plebian democratic rule. The public probably did not know the identity of the sacrament, only that the Queen performed some secret rite of shamanism in a special temple opened on that one day alone and involving the sexual metaphor of the bull. The very ancient temple was called the 'Bull Stall' (*boukoleíon*).[371] Her shamanic rapture with the god coincided with the feast of the Anthesteria, which ended with the final day of the 'stewpot' offerings.

The sacrament of the Greater Mystery was an ergot potion, a fungal growth upon the grouts of barley, from which a psychoactive agent like LSD was prepared. The ergot is recognizable to the unaided eye as a mushroom when the infested kernels of grain sprout into the fruiting stage. The Mystery celebrated the incorporation of the wild seedless mushroom of the Lesser ceremony into the grand plan of cultivation, in which the mushroom seems to have acquired a seed. The initiates journeyed in the spirit to the otherworld to affirm a covenant of reciprocal rights of visitation and friendship with the lord and queen of the netherworld. They

---

369 Carl A.P. Ruck, *Sacred Mushrooms of the Goddess: Secrets of Eleusis* (Berkeley, CA: Ronin Publishing, 2006), 169-170.
370 Michael C. Astour, *Hellenosemitica: An Ethnic and Cultural Study in West Semitic Impact on Mycenaean Greece* (Leiden: Brill, 1967), 299-322.
371 Aristotle, *Athenian Constitution*, 3.5.

resurfaced in the great hall of initiation at the same moment that the goddess gave birth to her son as the mediator between the realms of life and death.[372] The same pattern was enacted in the simple act of planting the seed so that it might be risen in the growth of the cultivated grain.

The association of the salamander with fire was a theme developed in alchemy, where the elements were encoded as animals from the bestiary tradition.[373] The alchemist was depicted burning the salamander in the crucible at the base of the volcano, the forge of its namesake Vulcan.[374] The salamander, moreover, was conflated with the harmless chameleon. Its ability to change color was the very essence of the alchemical work. The Rosicrucians and other occult groups adopted the salamander as emblematic of spiritual transcendence, along with the myth of Melusina as a hybrid creature. In the early nineteenth century, the Scottish poet Charles Mackay told a version of the tale of Melusina/Medusa as *Salamandrine*, the great love of a man for a salamander. The nineteenth- and twentieth-century occult society that hid its identity under the alchemical persona of Fulcanelli ('Little Vulcan') proposed a blatantly erroneous etymology for salamander, deriving it from Latin *sal* ('salt') and *mandra* 'manger', and hinted that it was the Christ Child of the incarnation, spiritual fire made flesh.[375]

---

372 Ruck, *Sacred Mushrooms of the Goddess*.

373 MS Bodleian 602, fol. 027v was incorrectly cited as an alchemical text, Chris Bennett, Lynn Osburn, and Judy Osburn, *Green Gold and the Tree of Life: Marijuana in Magic and Religion* (Frazier Park, CA: Access Unlimited, 1995), and followed by Giorgio Samorini, "'Mushroom Trees' in Christian Art": 87-108, in *Eleusis: Journal of Psychedelic Plants and Compounds*, new series no. 1 (1998), and subsequent commentators. The manuscript is, in fact, a bestiary (Thomas Hatsis, personal communication, ascertained by autopsy). The image as published on the web, moreover, is deceptive in falsifying the colors. The image is, however, intriguing because the man who has eaten the fruit of the tree is holding it upright by its stem, and although the tree and the fruit are blue, he appears to have eaten the likeness of the entire adjacent tree.

374 *Museum hermeticum* (Frankfort a. M., 1678), vol. vii: Lambspringk, *De lapide philosophico figurae et emblemata*, 337-372.

375 Ruck and Hoffman, *The Effluents of Deity*, 53-54.

THE SON CONCEIVED IN DRUNKENNESS

# Chapter Nine
# The Pruned Olive

### The Conquest of Primitivism

The olive tree is the preeminent Greek plant that requires the application of the pruning hook.[376] Without the annual intervention of the human who prunes it, the olive would in its natural state send up numerous shoots from its roots, producing a useless thicket, which does not fruit. The olive generally fruits on the previous year's new growth,[377] and hence requires constant tending. Thematically in Greek botany, it is the prototypic triumph of cultivation, emblematic of mankind's mastery over discord and primitivism. As such, it was awarded as the victor's wreath in the games at Olympia, and it survives into modern times as the olive branch of peace, enshrined in the insignia of the United Nations.

The olive shares this distinction as a symbolic cultivar with the grapevine of the god Dionysus. It similarly fruits only on new growth; and in the rituals of the god's more primitive persona as Bacchus, its pre-hybridized antecedent was symbolized as ivy and similar toxic trailing plants, like bryony and smilax. The ivy and its diminutive berries were reputedly maddening in their natural state, whereas the luscious bunches of grapes and the leaves of the vine are both quite edible. Upon the juice of the pressed fruit, however, a sophisticated intoxicant could be grown as a

---

376 Theophrastus, *Historia plantarum*, 2.7.2. Signe Isager and Jens Erik Skydsgaard, *Ancient Greek Agriculture: An Introduction* (London: Routledge, 1992, 1995), 19 *et seq.*
377 Theophrastus, *Historia plantarum*, 1.14.1.

similar triumph of civilization.[378] Bryony (wild cucumber) and smilax (bindweed or wild morning glory), like the ivy, resemble the vine and its clusters of grapes, and they, too, are toxic in their natural state. Both are sources of tropane and other alkaloid toxins, and the latter is a source of lysergic acid amide (LSA), closely related to LSD and identical with the main psychoactive chemical found in the morning glories employed in indigenous Mesoamerican shamanism as the sacrament called *ololiuqui*. European folklore indicates awareness of these intoxicants in the medieval pharmacopeia.[379]

The grape as the liquid foodstuff and the barley as the dry were commonly linked and contrasted as the parallel gifts of Dionysus and Demeter.[380] In the cultivation of the grains, the primitive grass, analogous to the ivy, was seen as the reportedly intoxicating *Lolium temulentum*, which spread as a common weed in fields of grain and endangered the planted crop not only by competition for space, but also by contamination with its infestation of ergot (*Claviceps purpurea*).[381] As with wine from the grape, however, a similar psychoactive agent could be accessed from barley through the secret procedure for isolating it from the total complex of deadly ergotoxins.

## The Wild Olive and the Cultivated

The wild olive and the domesticated were contrasted as a mythical motif. The wild olive (Greek *kótinos, élaios*, Latin *Olea*

---

378 Carl A.P. Ruck, "The Wild and the Cultivated: Wine in Euripides' *Bacchae*": 179-223, in Wasson *et al.*, *Persephone's Quest*. Ruck, *Sacred Mushrooms of the Goddess*, 85-100.

379 Carl A.P. Ruck (ed.), Mark A. Hoffman, Evie Marie Holmberg, Stavros Kiotsekoglou, and Vassil Markov, *Dionysus in Thrace: Ancient Entheogenic Themes in the Mythology and Archaeology of Northern Greece, Bulgaria, and Turkey* (Berkeley, CA: Regent Press, 2014).

380 Euripides, *Bacchae*, 274-283.

381 Carl A.P. Ruck, "Documentation": 85-136, in R. Gordon Wasson, Albert Hofmann, and Carl A.P. Ruck, *The Road to Eleusis: Unveiling the Secret of the Mysteries* (New York, NY, and London: Harcourt Brace Jovanovich, Inc., 1978, reprinted expanded editions 1998, 2008, Spanish, German, and Greek translations).

*oleaster*) produces more fruits, but of lesser size than the domesticated *Olea europea* (Greek, *eláa*, *elaía*, whence *oliva* in Latin),[382] but it was noted in antiquity that no amount of pruning could actually convert the wild into the domesticated,[383] or if such a change spontaneously occurred in either direction, it was considered a miraculous event.[384]

The olive that was enshrined in the courtyard of the Erechtheum on the Athenian Acropolis was the domesticated *eláa*,[385] a memorial of the goddess Athena's victory over Poseidon for possession of the land of Attica. Olives derived from it in Athens were called *moríai* (from *meíresthai*, 'separate, part from') and placed under the protection of Zeus Morios. They were planted in sanctuaries, as distinct from the ones called *ídiai*, which were those held in private possession. At Olympia, however, the olive grove that supplied the wreaths for the victorious athletes was the wild *kótinos*,[386] supposedly planted there when the hero Herakles returned from his quest for the Golden Antler of the Ceryneian Hind.[387]

## The Deer Hunt

This deer inhabited the central highlands and mountains of the Peloponnesus, but it led an elusive hunt and the hero had to chase it all the way through Thrace to the mythical lands beyond, which were known as the realm of the Hyperboreans in the steppes of central Asia, a destination supposedly reached by several Greek travelers in what can only be termed a shamanic rapture.[388] The

---

382 Theophrastus, *Historia plantarum*, 1.4.1; 3.2.1.
383 *Ibid.*, 2.2.12.
384 *Ibid.*, 2.3.1.
385 Herodotus, 8.55.
386 Theophrastus, *Historia plantarum*, 4.13.2.
387 Pausanias, *Description of Greece*, 5.7.7.
388 Carl A.P. Ruck, "The Offerings from the Hyperboreans": 225-256, in R. Gordon Wasson, Stella Kramrisch, Jonathan Ott, and Carl A.P. Ruck, *Persephone's Quest: Entheogens and the Origins of Religion* (New Haven, CT: Yale University Press, 1986).

grove at Olympia, known as the Altis,[389] therefore, symbolized the primordial zoomorphism of the plant as a magical deer, with its implication of the motif of the deer hunt and mystical vision. This would surface in medieval European hagiography in the tales of the second-century Saint Eustace and the seventh-century Saint Hubert, both of whom while on the hunt saw the Crucified Christ between the antlers of a deer.

Since the Ceryneian deer was a female with horns and submissive to the harness as a draft animal, it must have actually been a reindeer,[390] not native to the Mediterranean and hence appropriately found in the central Asiatic plateau beyond the Himalayan barrier, from which Boreas, the north wind was thought to blow. Only the doe of the reindeer bears antlers and only reindeer are submissive to the harness. The paradise beyond the northern wind was the land of the Hyperboreans, memorialized as the original home of the migrating Indo-Europeans. The fondness of reindeer for grazing on the psychoactive *Amanita muscaria* mushroom is well known[391] and documented in Siberian shamanism, where the deer functions as the animal familiar and ecstatic transport. The role of the mushroom in these rituals is depicted in ancient second-millennium BCE petroglyphs of the deer hunt and fungal anthropomorphisms on cliffs above the Pegtymel River.[392]

The deer hunt is analogous to the hunt for the sacred mushroom. In Mithraism, among the iconographic themes are depictions of the hero-god hunting deer, which would be an extraneous item to the corpus of symbolism, were it not for its significance as an herbal metaphor. The flesh of animals that ingest psychoactive plants becomes itself psychoactive. All deer, not just the

---

389 *Altis* is a dialectal corruption of *álsos* or 'grove'.
390 Robert Graves, *The Greek Myths* (Harmondsworth, UK: Penguin Books, 1955, frequently reprinted), vol. 2, 112.
391 R. Gordon Wasson, *Soma: Divine Mushroom of Immortality* (New York, NY: Harcourt Brace Jovanovich, Inc., 1968), 75-76, 161-162
392 Nikolaï Nikolaevich Dikov, *Mysteries in the Rocks of Ancient Chukotka: Petroglyphs of Pegtymel* (U.S. Department of the Interior, National Park Service, Shared Beringian Heritage Program, 1999). M.A. Kiriyak, *Early Art of the Northern Far East: The Stone Age* (U.S. Government Printing Office, 2007), 39-264.

reindeer, and other animals as well eat mushrooms.[393] In European lore, deer are linked with mushrooms, often with implications of eroticism, implying their psychoactive properties. The pun on venery (Venus, i.e., sex) and the hunt (Latin *venari*) runs through the Romance languages.[394] Deer meat is called venison in English, introduced from Norman as early as the eleventh century.

## Arboreal Hosts

Although the *Amanita muscaria* is more commonly associated with the oak, the pine, and the birch as its mycorrhizal hosts (the mutually beneficial symbiotic association of the mycelium of a fungus with the roots of certain plants), its range is wider, and it has been sighted with the cedars of Lebanon, and although in Greece it abounds along with *Psilocybes* in the forests of Mount Olympus and elsewhere, it also appears to be linked to the olive.[395] Pliny records that all that were left in his day of the mythical golden grove of the Hesperides were some wild olives and an altar dedicated to Herakles.[396] The eastern analogue to the Hesperid grove in the west was the tree hung with the Golden Fleece in the Jason and Medea myth. As mentioned before, the word for 'apple' and 'fleece' (*mélon*) is a homonym in Greek. It seems well agreed that the Fleece was hung on an oak,[397] but the anointing of Jason with the chrism after which he is named as the 'Anointed Drug-man'

---

393 Leonard Lee Rue, III, *The Deer Hunter's Encyclopedia* (Guilford, CT: 2000), Lyons Press), 96-97.
394 Valentina Pavlovna Wasson and R. Gordon Wasson, *Mushrooms Russia and History* (New York, NY: Pantheon Books,1957, 2 vols.), 173-176.
395 Wasson Archives, Harvard Library: N. Angelis, Greek newspaper *Eleftheria*, 1962: "On the pine trees and on the sacred olive there grow some big red mushrooms with a terrible poison.... The shepherds wonder: how does it come about that the olive produces bad mushrooms". Donald E. Teeter, *Amanita Muscaria: Herb of Immortality*, chap. 11 (Ambrosia Society). Confirmed by personal communications.
396 Pliny, *Natural History*, 5.3: *exstat . . . nec praeter oleastros aliud ex narrato illo aurifero nemore*. 'There's nothing left of that fabled gold-bearing grove except wild olives'.
397 Apollodorus, *Bibliotheke*, 1.9.1; 1.9.16. Apollonius Rhodius, *Argonautica*, 2.406, 1268-1270; 4.123; 4.162.

involves the blood or *ichor* of the tormented Prometheus as a fungal analogue, the riddle of the plant with a double stem. The Fleece itself, moreover, was not so much golden as 'red like the sun',[398] and the cap of *Amanita muscaria*, with its common metaphor of a solar disk.

Druids are named as the priests or 'brotherhood' of the oak (*drús*). The red mushrooms that grow at the base of the tree as its fruit are linked thematically with the fungal growth of the parasitic mistletoe that hangs from the branches, both similarly thought to be caused by the fall of the lightning bolt. Mistletoe in English is named as the 'urine twig'. The Druids called it *ixos, (w)ixos* or *(w)ixia* in Greek, whence its Latin botanical nomenclature as *Viscum album*. Mistletoe contains betaphenylethylamine (PEA) and tyramine, the former an endogenous amphetamine and the latter found also in ergot and certain psychoactive toads and cephalopods, like the stinging squid. The effects of the two chemicals are popularly referred to as the chocolate or love chemical and the cheese syndrome. Like the salamander added to the brandy, mistletoe is an ingredient in a Balkan liqueur called *rakija*, like Greek *ouzo*.

## The Olive as Pacified Toxin

In depictions of the hero's encounter with his opponent, it is almost universally a motif that the olive is shown growing at the site, usually exactly at the spot or through the defeated monster. The mastery over the monster transmutes its toxins into the cultivated olive. This makes perfect sense in view of Perseus' employment of the *hárpe* as his weapon of choice. He is not simply harvesting the botanical zoomorphism, but also pruning it into a cultivated metamorphosis. Chronologically, Perseus was the first of the heroes and set the pattern for those who would follow.

The magisterial exemplar of this motif of the olive's transmutation is the epic tradition about the bed of Odysseus. The whole generic theme of the 'homecomings' in the Homeric oral narratives

---

398 Apollonius Rhodius, *Argonautica*, 4.123.

is called the *nóstos*, which in Greek means the return to the perceiving mind or *noús*, the 'awakening' from the shaman's dream world.[399] To certify that it is indeed Odysseus who has returned home, and not some delusion that only looks like him, his wife Penelope poses the final test, the secret of the bed. She claims that it has been moved, but he knows the truth. The bed is immoveable. He constructed a special bed. At the level of the second floor of his house, he pruned an olive tree to serve as a leg of the bed. After all the toxins of his journey of heroism, he finally reached the island of the maiden Nausicaä, where he collapsed into a thicket of wild olive, to awaken the next morning to the sounds of the princess and her attendants washing clothes in the river. In the paradisiacal, and still unreal, court of her father, he recalls the tale of his journeys and then refuses to stay on the isle with the girl who could have been his wife in the otherworld. He falls asleep on the magical ship that the islanders offer for his return, and wakes up back in his home island of Ithaca, to validate his true awakening by the knowledge of the pruned olive that is his bed.

The bed is where normally one undergoes the diurnal alteration of consciousness. Odysseus' bed of olive is a perfect example of the transmutation of the soporific trance-inducing toxins into the awakening consciousness. Since the Homeric poems are transcriptions of an oral tradition reaching back perhaps millennia, the extended treatment of the theme of the olive demonstrations how deeply imbedded the motif was in the traditions of Greek mythology and religion.

## The Secret Offering

The transmutation of the fungus into the domesticated olive[400] was commemorated as a ritual on the island of Delos. Each year among the offerings of first fruits sent to the sanctuary from the

---

399 Douglas Frame, "The Origins of Greek NOUS," dissertation Harvard University, 1971, published as *Myth of the Return in Early Greek Epic* (New Haven, CT: Yale University Press, 1978).
400 The Delian olive was the domesticated tree, Herodotus, 4.34.

various Greek cities, there was a secret offering, carefully preserved and hidden in straw and transmitted from town to town along a specifically designated route traceable back to what was supposed to be the mythical land of the Hyperboreans. In all likelihood, this was a fungal specimen. The route is not the most direct pathway and appears to be a mythologized history preserving the memory of the actual spread of the Indo-European migrants into the Greek lands.[401]

Supposedly the first Hyperborean ambassadors with the secret specimen to the island, where the god and his twin sister were reborn into their Olympian personae as children of Zeus, died and were buried as honored sacrificial victims in the sanctuary. They supposedly visited when human sacrifice was still practiced at the site. The olive that replaced the primordial sacred fungal sacrament was later ritually involved in a sham enactment of the original human sacrifices. Each city sent with its gift of first fruits a troupe of male and female pubescent children of noble lineage, who danced about the holy tree. They were not sacrificed, but only mimetically flagellated as they chewed upon pieces of bark from the olive. The olive replaced whatever toxic potion in previous times would have prepared them to acquiesce peacefully to their role as human victims.

The rite commemorated Theseus' defeat of the Minotaur of the Cretan labyrinth,[402] formerly a similar site for human offerings, and the winding of the line dance (*géranos*, imitating the winding of a serpent) of the children with linked hands, around the sacred olive on Delos choreographically reproduced the design of the deadly labyrinth. The line dance is still traditional in Greek choreography and it is a perpetuation of a funeral dance.[403] Nothing

---

401 Carl A.P. Ruck, "The Offerings from the Hyperboreans": 225-256, in Wasson et al., *Persephone's Quest*.
402 Plutarch, *Theseus*, 21.
403 Lillian Lawler, *The Dance in Ancient Greece* (Iowa City, IA: University of Iowa Press, 1964). "The Geranos Dance—A New Interpretation": 112-130, in *Transactions and Proceedings of the American Philological Association*, vol. 77 (1946).

was allowed to remind the god of his former role as recipient of human victims in Minoan religion during this rite. In Athens, the very ship that Theseus had first employed to sail to Crete was still extant in the Classical period from a millennium earlier, carefully preserved and repeatedly restored, and it was used to transport the Athenian dancers to the island. By chance, the annual ritual coincided with the trial of Socrates and since the ship was delayed by storms, the philosopher was not immediately executed after his condemnation, but lingered in prison until its return, allowing time for the conversations recorded in Plato's *Crito* and *Phaedo* dialogues.

THE SON CONCEIVED IN DRUNKENNESS

# Chapter Ten
# The Club of Herakles

### The Olive of Nemea

We are admonished that 'some ingenuity was wasted in determining where [Herakles] cut the club,'[404] as if it were a matter of no import, except for scholarly pedantry. Nevertheless, it is generally agreed that he acquired it at Nemea (named as the *némos* or 'grove') and that it was pruned from the trunk of a wild olive, probably with the aid of the goddess Athena.[405] Since the confrontation with the Nemean Lion is counted as the hero's initial Labor, it set the pattern for the ensuing encounters, where whenever possible the opponent is seen transmuted into the olive tree. The club is traditionally depicted with the knobs representing the scars from the pruned branches. Apart from its symbolism, a club is a suspiciously inappropriate weapon of choice for the great hero.

The hero's victory over the Lion was claimed as the etiology for the athletic games celebrated at the site from the sixth century on.[406] In the quadrennial cycle of pan-Hellenic contests, they were performed along with the Isthmian Games[407] in the years before and after the Olympic Games, with the Pythian Games at Delphi in the third year of each Olympiad, the four year period from one Olympic Game to the next that supplied one of the standard

---

404 H.J. Rose, *A Handbook of Greek Mythology* (New York, NY: Dutton and Co., 1959), 212.
405 Apollodorus, *Bibliotheke*, 2.4.11.
406 Inaugurated in 573 BCE, nearly a millennium after the supposed time of Herakles.
407 Probably inaugurated in 582 BCE.

chronologies or calendars of the Classical world, starting from 776 BCE.

## A Crown of Parsley

The victors at Nemea received a crown of wild celery leaves (*sélinon*, *Apium graveolens*), an umbelliferous plant resembling Queen Ann's lace. The wild celery is a marsh plant, as distinguished from the cultivated *Petroselinum sativum* or 'cultivated rock-celery', from which English 'parsley' is derived. The early first-century CE Roman Aulus Cornelius Celsus listed the plant as a painkiller in his pharmaceutical encyclopedia, a use to which it is still put in ayurvedic and herbal medicine.

The Nemean Lion was a difficult beast to conquer since nothing was strong enough to rip its pelt except one of its own claws, and the animal was elusive, withdrawing further and further into its cave; and as the hero pursued it, an ever-deepening narcosis fell upon him. He is depicted with the conquered lion, just coming back to his senses outside the cave, as one of the fifth-century *metopes* from the Temple of Zeus at Olympia. In view of the narcotic effect of the Lion, we should expect that 'celery' is a psychoactive agent that has been transmuted into the cultivated olive, as usually depicted in vase paintings of the episode. Not only does the hero henceforth wield the club as his weapon of choice, but he also acquires the beast's symbolic invulnerability by wearing its pelt as his headgear. In effect, he becomes a lion.

Another and earlier etiology for the Nemean Games involves the infant Opheltes.[408] He was the little prince of Nemea, son of the 'wolf' king Lycurgus (or Lykos) and his wife Eurydice. It had been foretold that the baby should never touch the ground until he had learned to walk. He is named as a 'serpent' (óphis). His wet-nurse put him down in a marshy bed of celery, while she pointed out a spring to the six generals who were marching against Thebes as allies of Polyneices, the son of Oedipus, in his contest with

---

[408] Corinne Ondine Pache, *Baby and Child Heroes in Ancient Greece* (Urbana, IL: University of Illinois Press, 2004), 95-134.

his brother Eteocles. Some accounts claimed that the baby was crowned with violets, picking flowers and gathering honey, as he lay on his bed of celery. This makes the scene an analogue of the naming of Iamos of Stymphalos, who founded the Iamid dynasty of prophets at Olympia. In any case, the serpent boy Opheltes fell into a fatal narcosis, strangled by a giant serpent that was guardian of the marsh. The serpent smothered him, snuffed out his breath. The infant became the brightest or alpha star Regulus, named as the 'little prince', in the constellation of the Lion. The Greek *basilískos* is both a 'little king' and a 'basilisk' or serpent.

The shaman Amphiaraüs interpreted his death as a sign that their expedition against Thebes was doomed to fail and he renamed the infant Archemoros, the 'Forerunner of Death'. His accidental death masks this truer role as a human offering at the site. The games were instituted as his funeral memorial. Celery was traditionally worn as wreaths by mourners and hung on tombs. It was considered lethal. Homilies claimed that a wreath of celery would end the life of someone gravely ill or that all that someone near death needed was the celery.

## Deadly Hemlock

Obviously, a mild painkiller or anodyne like celery must mask a plant more worthy of the Nemean Lion, especially since Herakles always employs his conquered monster to poison his arrows. An arrow toxin is required. Another umbelliferous plant of the *Apiaceae* (also called *Umbelliferae*) family is a much more potent psychoactive agent. This is the poison hemlock, *Conium maculatum* (and related *Cicuta* species). Its employment as a lethal potion for capital punishment is evidence of its involvement in religious symbolism. When crushed, it has a rank odor, like that of *Apium graveolens*, or 'rank-smelling' *sélinon*, often compared to parsnips, which smell like parsley. A common name for water hemlock is false parsley. Like the *sélinon*, it grows in wet ground, like the marshy spring where the infant snake-king was gathering celery. (The North American hemlock tree (*Tsuga* species) is unrelated to the toxic herb and named so since the eighteenth century merely by resemblance of its leaves to the marsh plant.)

The toxicity of hemlock is greatly diminished by drying. The most prominent of its chemicals is coniine, which is similar in structure and pharmacological properties to nicotine. The effect upon the body is like curare, producing a numbing muscular paralysis ascending, resulting in fatal suffocation when it reaches the pulmonary muscles. Plato's description of the death of Socrates in the *Phaedo* makes clear that the dosage was critical since the philosopher was instructed to drink the entire cup, with none to be spared for a final libation to the gods. Thus, hemlock was also employed as a medical pharmaceutical.

There is evidence that hemlock was employed for its visionary or hallucinogenic potential as early as the Neolithic period.[409] It was similarly used as a recreational intoxicant in Classical antiquity, often as an additive to wine.[410] The second-century BCE Nicander describes men staggering through the streets in a hemlock stupor, obviously not survivors from a botched execution.[411] It was a psychoactive ingredient in a flying ointment first described by the Bavarian physician Johannes Hartlieb in 1456,[412] reportedly used by European witches and supposedly capable of inducing lycanthropy. Lycurgus (Lykos), the father of the infant Opheltes, bears a name indicative of his involvement in the wolf cult.

## Lycanthropy

By some accounts, it was not the Nemean Lion that figured as the initial Labor of Herakles, but his conquest of the dog Kerberos (Cerberus). This version of the hero's sequence of Labors allowed

---

409 Kath Gourlay, *The Independent*, Edinburgh, Scotland, Sunday, 2 September 2001.
410 D.C.A. Hillman, *The Chemical Muse: Drug Use and the Roots of Western Civilization* (New York, NY: Thomas Dunne Books/ St. Martin's Press, 2008), 80, 158-159.
411 Nicander, *Alexipharmaca*, 186-194.
412 Johannes Hartlieb, *Das Puch aller verboten Kunst, Ungelaubens und der Zaubrey* (Augsberg, 1465).

the Kerberos episode to provide a rational motive for the hero's subsequent tasks in the service of Eurystheus as expiation for the murder of his own wife and sons in a delusionary madness induced by the conquered monster.[413] In the *metope* sequence on the Temple of Zeus at Olympia, Kerberos figures as eleventh, allowing the Cleansing of the Stables of Augeias to supply the final episode as the etiological foundational myth for the sanctuary.

Vase paintings typically show Herakles confronting the dog in the underworld, with the olive sprouting through the axis of the ferocious three-headed canine.[414] He wields the dog as his weapon, along with his club, as he presents his catch to Eurystheus.[415] It is a contest between recipients of the toxic beast, as the victor Herakles intimidates Eurystheus, who cowers down into a giant *píthos* or funeral/wine urn. The Eleusinian coffin *píthos* with the stewpot-headed Gorgons indicates that it was probably such a giant urn that was used for the exposure of the abandoned infants in reality. Herakles is transferring the toxicity of the beast to his defeated opponent. This, too, is a thematic motif. The same intimidation and urn lair is depicted with the presentation of the Erymanthean Boar.[416]

To seek refuge in a *píthos* urn is an unlikely event and clearly indicates a thematic motif suggesting both the toxic additives to the wine (i.e., the *píthos* as a wine vat) and the transfer of the lethal intoxication (the *píthos* as a grave marker) from Herakles as the intended victim to his opponent Eurystheus. Herakles performs his sequence of Labors to regain the Olympian patrimony that Hera had usurped for her chosen candidate Eurystheus. She had

---

413 Apollodorus, *Bibliotheke*, 2.4.12.
414 Amphora, attributed to the Andokides Painter and the Lysippides painter, *ca.* 520-510 BCE, Musée du Louvre. Paris, Louvre F204.
415 Eurystheus hiding in a bronze *píthos* jar, *ca.* 525-530, Musée du Louvre, Paris, Louvre E701.
416 Herakles presenting the boar to Eurystheus, with Iolaos holding the club, Attic amphora, *ca.* 540-520 BCE, University of Mississippi Museums, 1977.63. Amphora, attributed to the near Group E, archaic, British Museum, London B213. Also depicted thus in the *metope* sequence of the Temple of Zeus at Olympia.

hastened the gestation of Eurystheus and delayed that of Herakles so that her favorite would be born on the appointed day instead of Zeus's candidate Herakles.[417]

Euripides made the Kerberos episode the last of the hero's labors in his *Herakles* tragedy. Herakles has just returned from his netherworld encounter with the chthonic hound of Hades, to find that his wife and family are about to be killed by the Theban interim regent Lykos, whose name, of course, means quite simply 'Wolf' and who is probably costumed with a wolf headgear. Amphitryon says: 'If I were young and still had control of my body, I would take this sword and bloody *this guy's tawny locks*, so that he would flee my weapon beyond the Atlantic pillars in cowardice'.[418] Lykos' hair would be a gratuitous mention, were it not in-all-probability an aspect of his ever-present appearance wearing a wolf mask. As such, it is a major theme in the tragedy. It contrasts with Herakles, who wears his similarly *tawny* lion headgear.[419]

## Herakles as Wolf

The same actor plays both Lykos and Herakles.[420] This is not an unfortunate inconvenience of dramaturgy, as some critics have implied, but an intended aspect of the choreographed performance as determined by the tragedian in constructing his drama and employing the particular talents of the three actors in his troupe of performers. It was also something noticeable to the audience, since a prize was awarded in the contest to the best actor, so that the viewers must inevitably have followed the actors through their succession of 'masks' or impersonated personae. Euripides, far from obscuring the doubled role, brings Lykos back on stage for a brief extraneous interlude, after the actor had already changed into his Herakles gear, simply to emphasize the shared

---

417  Homer, *Iliad*, 19.95 *et seq.*
418  Euripides, *Herakles*, 232-235.
419  *Ibid.*, 359-363, 465-466.
420  Thalia Papadopoulou, *Heracles and Euripidean Tragedy* (Cambridge, UK: Cambridge University Press, 2005), 9-57.

personae. Lykos exits at verse 347, enters as Herakles at verse 523, exits at verse 636, reenters briefly as Lykos at verse 701 to 733, and finally reappears after the madness as Herakles at verse 1088. It is an extraordinary feat of dramatic virtuosity for the actor to impersonate the main villain as well as the hero. A similar tour de force required the same actor to play both Herakles and his wife in Sophocles' *Trachiniae*.

In his madness, Herakles enacts the very same murders that Lykos had intended, hallucinating that he is performing yet one more task for Eurystheus. It is a full hallucinatory scenario, since he even stops to bivouac in Megara for the night, inasmuch as the journey from Thebes to Mycenae would require two day's travel.[421] This is a schizophrenic delusion in which thinking he is still Herakles he has become Lykos.[422] It is a clear incidence of lycanthropy.[423]

## Rabies

The madness is caused by the figure called Madness. That is an insufficient translation of her name. The persona is named Lyssa, played probably by the same actor who had impersonated the wife Megara and who will return as Theseus.[424] All three sympathize with the hero's downfall, and thus represent a coherent dramatic theme in the play's enactment. Lyssa, however, is not just any sort of madness; she is specifically rabies. Herakles, in fact, even foams at the mouth in his madness, which is a typical symptom of the virus that spreads from rabid beasts to humans, making them similarly aggressive and wild: 'He was no longer himself, but his bloodshot eyes rolled back, *he drooled foam* upon his thick beard'.[425]

---

421 Euripides, *Herakles*, 954-957.
422 Carl A.P. Ruck, "Duality and the Madness of Herakles": 53-76, in *Arethusa*, vol. 9 (1976).
423 Carl A.P. Ruck, Blaise Daniel Staples, José Alfredo González Celdrán, and Mark Alwin Hoffman, *The Hidden World: Survival of Pagan Shamanic Themes in European Fairytales* (Durham, NC: Carolina Academic Press, 2006), 87-124.
424 Lyssa could also be played by the Lykos-Herakles actor, but with less thematic justification.
425 Euripides, *Herakles*, 931-934.

Lyssa and the rabid affliction in Greek is actually a she-wolf, derived from the *lyk-* root for 'wolf', plus a feminine forming *-ia* suffix, yielding *lyssa*. She was probably costumed with a wolf's headdress, as depicted on a red-figure vase of the death of Actaeon in the Boston Museum of Fine Arts, where she leads the hunter's hounds against their master. The depiction is thought to represent her stage costume in the lost *Toxotides* ('The Sisterhood of Archers') tragedy of Aeschylus.[426] She turns domestic dogs backwards in evolution to the wolf. Such a relationship of dog and wolf as an ancient Greek notion is documented by the exclusion of all canines from the sacred island of Delos,[427] which was originally shown to the pregnant mother of Apollo and his twin sister Artemis by a pack of wolves from the Anatolian Lycia.[428] The exclusion was meant to isolate Apollo from contamination with his more sinister, pre-Olympian identity. Similarly, no burials, after the first embassy from the Hyperboreans, were allowed on the sacred island. The Lykos actor probably wore a similar lupine headgear.

As Euripides describes the action of the rapid Lyssa in the play, she is a hunter leading her hounds[429] in a chase against the hero's children,[430] goading her horses, with eyes blazing like a Gorgon, the hundred serpents shrieking in a bacchanalian orgy gone wrong, not graced with *thyrsus*, nor the libation of the Dionysian wine.[431] The viewers would have readily recognized this as the encounter with visionary madness without the requisite etiquette of ritual.

---

426 Attic red-figure vase, *ca.* 440, probably a depiction of Lyssa's appearance onstage in Aeschylus's *Toxotides*, Arthur Dale Trendall and Thomas Bertram Lonsdale Webster, *Illustrations of Greek Drama* (London: Phaidon, 1971), 62.
427 Hyginus, *Fabulae*, 247.
428 Antoninus Liberalis, *Metamorphoseon Synagoge*, 35; Aelian, *De natura animalium*, 4.4.
429 Ibid., 860.
430 Ibid., 898.
431 Ibid., 880-884, 899, 892-893, 894-895.

## Wolfsbane

We can identify the lycanthropic psychoactive agent, at least thematically. It is aconite (*Aconitum lycoctonum* and species, family *Ranunculaceae*), which the Greeks called 'wolf's-bane' (*lykoktónon*[432]), the same metaphoric name in English. In Greek, it is also an epithet of Apollo. Euphemistically, it could mean that Apollo 'kills the wolf', although in reality, he is the 'wolf that kills'. Although a potentially deadly poison, it has been used since Classical antiquity and elsewhere for its sedative and anesthetic potential. It is easily absorbed through the skin as a local anesthesia, producing an initial tingling, often interpreted as growing a pelt, that can progress to lycanthropic hallucinations, paralysis, and death through pulmonary and cardiac arrest, hence its other Greek name as *akóniton*, 'without a struggle'. This etymology suggests that aconite, like hemlock, was also used ritually to render human victims docile for sacrifice. It is sufficiently lethal to be used as an arrow toxin, and Medea was said to have tried to poison Theseus' wine with it.[433]

It is specifically identified with the dog Kerberos that Herakles dragged up from Hades. From its foaming mouth, specks that fell to the ground sprouted into the aconite plant.[434] The site for Herakles' descent was identified as a Cave of Hades on Cape Taenarum,[435] where the sierra of Mount Taÿgetos terminates at the sea, forming the western limit of the Laconian Gulf, which was Sparta's access to the sea at Gytheion (modern Gythio), reputedly founded by Herakles and Apollo.[436] Orpheus used the same cave entrance in his attempt to retrieve Eurydice.[437] The cave was a sacred site[438] and probably figured in the Spartan rituals of

---

432 Galen, 11.820.
433 Ovid, *Metamorphosis*, 7.404- 407.
434 Ibid., 7.406 et seq.
435 Pausanias, *Description of Greece*, 3.25.5.
436 Ibid., 3.21.8.
437 Vergil, *Georgics*, 4.467.
438 Frederick A. Cooper, *The Temple of Apollo Bassias* (Princeton, NJ: American School of Classical Studies at Athens, 1996), 114.

lycanthropic warrior initiation.⁴³⁹

Aconite can induce visionary experience, depending on the dosage and method of access, and it was added to wine to enhance its inebriating effect.⁴⁴⁰ It was a reputed ingredient in lycanthropic flying ointments,⁴⁴¹ and its many common names suggest its use in heretical Christian rites and warrior initiations: monkshood, friar's cap, soldier's cap; and its involvement in the folkloric motifs of fairies, witchcraft, and the survival of paganism: woman's bane, devil's helmet, *Venuswagon, Wolfskraut*, Odin's hat, hat of Jupiter.

### Divestiture of Mortality

In Euripides' tragedy, the hero's downfall is presented as an ironic apotheosis orchestrated by Hera. She could not destroy the hero until he had completed his sequence of Labors,⁴⁴² which would earn back for him the usurped Olympian patrimony. Now that he has proven his merit, she intends to induct him into the celestial realm. If his victories have indeed warranted his destined immortality, she now will demonstrate that this entails divesting himself of the mortal ties of love and family. Her plot would have succeeded, were it not for the intervention of the goddess Athena, who throws a stone at him, reviving him from his madness just as he was about to kill his mortal father Amphitryon, the one remaining tie to his humanity.

Of the two fathers, Amphitryon had declared himself better than Zeus, who showed no love for his son.⁴⁴³ Unfortunately, love

---

439 Carl A.P. Ruck, "Aristophanes' Parody of Socrates as a Pothead and the Spartan Cult of the Wolf": chap. 4 in J. Harold Ellens (ed.), *Seeking the Sacred with Psychoactive Substances; Chemical Paths to Spirituality and God*, vol. 1, History and Practices (Santa Barbara, CA: ABC-CLIO, 2014).

440 Mannfried Pahlow, *The Healing Plants* (Hauppauge, NY: Barron's Educational Series, 1993), 117.

441 Its medieval use for werewolf metamorphosis was divulged under torture and may reflect the intentions and expectations of the Inquisitors, but it appears to have figured in the flying ointments of witchcraft. Thomas Hatsis, "Medieval Witches and Flying Ointments": chap. 7, in *Psychedelic Press UK*, vol. 2 (2014).

442 Euripides, *Herakles*, 822-832.

443 *Ibid.*, 339-347.

is a human affliction. As the play concludes, Herakles is not destined for the divine apotheosis and transcendence to the empyreal realm from the pyre on Mount Oeta that would have burned away his mortality. Instead, his path will lead to Athens, where the Athenian hero Theseus offers him a tomb as a bond of human affection. The same actor who earlier had impersonated Megara, the wife of Herakles, now plays Theseus. Like Oedipus at Colonus, the body of Herakles is another sacrosanct addition to the metaphysical fundament of Athens as an eternal city.

### Mistress of the Chambers

In her love for her husband and children, Megara had inadvertently enacted the symbolic significance of her persona as the 'Lady of the Megaron Chambers' as she begged from Lykos the favor of going inside to prepare for death, a funeral instead of a massacre, leading her children by their hands into the palace *mégaron*. When they emerge from the Chamber, they will have exchanged their clothing for shrouds, the investiture for death. The etymology of her name would have been inescapable to the viewers in the Theater of Dionysus, since the *mégara* 'chambers' were a cave at the base of the Athenian Acropolis, where women performed a ritual descent symbolic of death as the renewal of the land's fertility.

It would also be inevitable that the name of Megara would recall the sister city of Megara, just beyond Eleusis along the coast toward Corinth. It was named for its Chambers, temples of Demeter.[444] This is the very same city where Herakles bivouacs in his mad delusional journey to Mycenae. Ultimately, the name etymologically describes exactly what Megara does in the tragedy: *megarízein* means 'to perform the chamber rite'.[445]

In the interim, before finalizing the chamber rite in the

---

444 Pausanias, *Description of Greece*, 1.29.5.
445 Jan N. Bremmer, "Demeter in Megara": 23-38, in Attilio Mastrocinque and Concetta Giuffré Scibona (eds.), *Demeter, Isis, and Cybele: Studies in Greek and Roman Religion in Honor of Giulia Sfameni Gasparro* (Stuttgart: Franz Steiner Verlag, 2012).

persona of Theseus as the person who will entomb Herakles, Megara impersonates Lyssa, who reluctantly does what she does only at the behest of the goddess Iris, the rainbow messenger of the gods who is enforcing the will of Hera. Appropriately, although ironic, she is impersonated by the Amphitryon actor, since he and Hera can both claim to have shared a bed with Zeus. In the first verse of the play, he had introduced himself by saying, 'Who does not know the bed-mate (*súllektron*) of Zeus?'

## The Line Dance of Humanity

The linked hands of the old men who danced the chorus similarly enacted this choreographed gesture of human movement toward the tomb, men so old that they tooter on the brink of death, as insubstantial as dreams, able to stand only by reliance on their partners to stabilize the chain of the danced steps of their weakened bodies. This is the same *géranos* funeral dance of the winding serpent as performed annually at the Delian sanctuary of Apollo, whose more sinister identity lurks behind the Lykos persona of this drama.

Theseus completes the symbolic choreographic gesture as he offers his hand,[446] a 'linkage of friends', and leads the old Amphitryon and his mortal and unfortunately beloved son to their burials beneath the land of Attica. In the underworld, when Herakles descended to fetch up the dog Kerberos, he had found Theseus fixed to the rock upon which he sat. He liberated him and freed him for his career of heroism. Theseus, in his ascendancy, is thematically more important as an Athenian, than the Dorian Herakles. Hence the stone of Athena that preserved the mortal father has a higher calling as the stone that Theseus offers as the tomb, repaying his friend for the liberation from the stone in Hades. The motif of the stone was first introduced in the tragedy as the stone monument at which the family of Herakles had sought asylum in the opening scene of the play. The audience would have easily

---

446 Euripides, *Herakles*, 1401-1402.

appreciated this motif, also, since the two etymological meanings of the name of Theseus define the parameters of his heroism, as the 'settled' or the 'settler'. He is frequently depicted confronting an opponent who tries to put a stone on him, while he retaliates by placing a stone upon his monstrous adversary. On the tragic stage, he repeatedly was presented offering burials in Athenian soil.

The line dance, moreover, of mortals linked by love on the serpentine path to death had provided the tragedy's basic thematic enactment. At the beginning of the play, Megara had sought asylum from Lykos at the stone monument erected by Herakles as victor over the chthonic predations of the city's Minyan/Pelasgian neighbors, with her two sons clinging to her robes. When she took them into the palace chamber to dress them in shrouds, she had pulled them along, hand in hand, like ships in tow. When Herakles unexpectedly returned, she had transferred this burdensome linkage of mortal sons to her husband, who towed them, hand in hand, into the chamber, commenting on how this must now seem a different towing than their previous exit with their mother. The play concludes with Theseus leading Herakles and his mortal father, hand in hand, to their burials at Athens. The stone monument where the Lady of the Chambers had sought asylum at the play's beginning awaits the father and his mortal son as the rock of their entombment.

# THE SON CONCEIVED IN DRUNKENNESS

# Chapter Eleven
# Arrow Toxins

### The Venom of the Hydra

Although both the hemlock of Nemea and the aconite of Taenarum could have served to anoint Herakles' arrows, this role was specifically reserved for the Hydra of Lerna.[447] Such was the unanimous opinion in antiquity. It is also this poison that will eventually end his mortal life when it finds its way back to him as a love potion through the misguided passion of his other wife Deianeira (Dejanira).[448]

Unlike the numbing coldness induced by the hemlock and aconite, the venom of the Hydra caused a burning sensation that could result in a terminal fiery immolation as spiritual transcendence. It was essentially a dermal agent inducing an extreme irritation. It could be administered in the form of an unguent smeared on a piece of clothing, and it was characterized by a noisome sulfurous stench probably associating it with chthonic subterranean volcanic activity.[449] The stench could kill all the birds

---

447  A version of this chapter was published as "The Myth of the Lernaean Hydra": 795-804, in Stefano Goffredo and Zuy Dubrinsky (eds.), *The Cnidaria: Past, Present, and Future: The World of the Medusa and her Sisters* (New York, NY: Springer Publishing, 2016).

448  Alcman, frag. 815; Sophocles, *Trachiniae*, 680 *et seq.* and 1140-1144; Pausanias, *Description of Greece*, 5.5.9; Diodorus Siculus, *Bibliotheke Historike*, 4.38.1; Hyginus, *Fabulae*, 30, 34; Ovid, *Metamorphoses*, 9. 129 and 158 *et seq.*, *Heroides*, 9.115 *et seq.*; Seneca, *Hercules Furens*, 44 and 1194 *et seq.*; Apollonius Rhodius, *Argonautica*, 4.1390 *et seq.*; Apollodorus, *Bibliotheke*, 2.80 and 2.157 *et seq.*

449  Walter Addison Jayne, *Healing Gods of Ancient Civilizations* (Whitefish, MT: Kessinger Publishing, 2003, reprint of 1900), 339.

within a twenty-mile radius and all the fish swimming in the surrounding waters.

After the ascension of Herakles' spirit to the celestial realm through the funeral pyre lit on Mount Oeta, above the thermal volcanic springs of Thermopylae at the northeastern base of the Delphic mountain of Apollo's Parnassus, the toxic bow passed into the possession of the tormented hero Philoctetes, whose noisome smell was characterized as the odor of rotting flesh from his gangrenous foot, whose toxins were further intensified by the venomous bite of a sacred serpent on the volcanic isle of Lemnos. His only food on the island has been the birds he has shot with the poisoned arrows, inevitably recycling the toxin as his sole source of nutriment. It is this toxic bow that is destined to end the long Trojan War by an arrow delivered to the heel of Paris,[450] the hero named for the *péra* of his exposure as an infant on the mountainside. This event signaled the transfer of the toxin to him as the final recipient and would occasion the cure of Philoctetes' toxicity.

The mountaintop of Herakles' immolation and the holy fire at the core of the volcano on Lemnos establish the axis for spiritual ascendance from the chthonic to the empyreal realms. As the fit of madness overtakes him in Sophocles' tragedy, Philoctetes begs, 'O burn me, please, take me and burn me in this Lemnian fire that I summon. Do for me what I did once for the son of Zeus in exchange for this poisoned bow'.[451] It is thematically significant that the isle of Lemnos was the site of a Mystery sanctuary of the chthonic little Kabeiroi creatures and that the caldera of the volcano there was the forge of the smithy god Hephaistos (Hephaestus), whose name itself means 'volcano'. In Latin, he is called Vulcanus (anglicized as Vulcan).

The Hydra venom could be likened to a kind of wine. When a tuft of wool imbued with it fell by chance into the sunlight on the ground, Deianeira was aghast to notice that 'it grew warm,

---

450 Sophocles, *Philoctetes*, 1409 *et seq.*
451 *Ibid.*, 799-803.

melted, and crumbled into pieces, like sawdust from a leveled tree, and from the ground where it lay, a clotted foam seethed up, like a libation of the rich potion from the Bacchic vine'.[452] Similarly, Philoctetes' fits of madness made him no fitting companion at the symposium and his fellow drinking partners abandoned him, unable to stand his wild shouting and terrible stench. It was all a matter of dosage since arrow toxins were commonly drunk recreationally as psychoactive additives to wine.[453]

## Lake Halcyon

Nothing remains today of the Lernaean Alcyonian Lake just south of the town of Argos along the eastern coast of the Peloponnesus, near the modern village of Mili (*Myloi*). Although in antiquity its depth was without limit and swimmers were dragged down, never to reappear,[454] it silted up into a malarial marsh and was finally drained away in the early nineteenth century, although the powerful karstic springs remain, which implies that there were once also accessible subterranean caverns. A karst spring is the termination of a cave system formed where a subterranean river reaches the surface, usually affording access to a vast system of underground chambers. These were often sacralized in antiquity and considered entrances to the netherworld. The limestone terrain is like the Mexican Yucatán with its sacred *cenotes* or sinkholes, and the tale of the disappeared swimmers probably indicates that the Lernaean Lake was once used for similar rites of human victims. The modern village of Mili (the 'Mills') is named for these springs. Herakles, had he failed, was intended to become one of these sacrificial victims.

The lake and its springs were associated with the myth of the Danaïds. The fifty Danaïds had supposedly arrived from Egypt with their father six generations before Herakles, which would be seven generations before the Trojan War and hence in the

---

452 Sophocles, *Trachiniae*, 695 et seq.
453 D.C.A. Hillman, *The Chemical Muse: Drug Use and the Roots of Western Civilization* (New York, NY: Thomas Dunne Books/ St. Martin's Press, 2008), 82-83.
454 Pausanias, *Description of Greece*, 2.37.4; Strabo, 8.3.18.

mid-second millennium BCE, and the controversy that had occasioned the murder of the husbands and the subsequent execution of the maidens involved the essential role of marriage in subjugating the female as subservient to her husband. Thus, in fetching the toxin of the female Hydra, Herakles was performing his paradigmatic role in suppressing the power of the goddess and reassigning the cosmos to his Olympian father. Perseus was descended from these Danaïds three generations later and his fetching of the toxic female Medusa head had a similar symbolism, indicated by his subduing into marriage a transmutation of that Medusa in the form of his bride Andromeda.

Perseus sought the advice of the water nymphs as he set out on his quest, which probably implies his great-great-aunts, the Danaïds, and that the pathway to the Gorgons was through the karst caverns of the Lerna Lake. Medusa means merely 'queen or female sovereign' of the sisterhood of Gorgons, and the same verbal formation underlies Andromeda as a 'man-sovereign', descriptive of the Medusa's male or hermaphroditic attribute as bearded, as well as her sovereignty over men. In the underworld, the waters of Lake Lerna welled upwards, either from the sieves that the Danaïds used to gather it or from the leaking urn into which they poured it. All one hundred of the corpses lay down there, fifty husbands and their wives (actually only twice fortynine), just beyond the Hydra that was the guardian of the gateway to the chthonic realm of the dead. The murderous wives had been found guilty of the murder of their intended husbands and put to death, tossed into the lake to join their dead mates. The maidens were supposedly gathering the water for their prenuptial bath as eternal penance for the matrimonial rite that they had refused, a rite that would have signified their acceptance of a husband's dominance over his wife.

One of the sisters, Hypermnestra, the only daughter of Danaüs to survive, as it turned out, did accept her husband out of love, the great-grandparents of Danaë, who was the mother of Perseus as the son of Zeus. Hypermnestra's love for her husband Lynceus is comparable to Hippodamia's selection of Pelops as her husband. The same motif of transition from matriarchy to marriage and patriarchy is indicated in the tradition that the river that fed the karst springs of the Lernaean Lake first flowed from the Danaïd Amymonë, who was abducted, without benefit of matrimony, by the god Poseidon. Although by Classical times, Poseidon was the lord of the oceans, his more ancient persona, as we have seen, associated him with sacred springs and freshwater fountains, since he was counted an Olympian deity who migrated with Zeus from the Indo-European homeland where there was no ocean, but only rivers and springs. It was in such a role that Poseidon figured as the maternal grandfather of Apollo's son Iamos, the eponymous founder of the prophetic priesthood at Olympia. The probable etymology of Poseidon's Latin equivalent as Neptune associates him with such springs.

The lake's name is a corruption of Halcyon, which despite its pleasant connotations of the 'halcyon days', which are the brief period of calm seas after the first storms of winter, masks the sinister reality that the halcyon bird supposedly lost her mate in such a storm at sea and the grieving little sparrow was granted respite of a few days, just long enough to lay her eggs safely on the lakeshore, while she lamented her dead husband. The halcyon bird is the kingfisher, which feeds almost entirely on aquatic prey, diving into the water to nab fish and crayfish with its powerful long straight beak. On one of its dives into the lake, it had followed the pathway of the victims into its bottomless depths. The grieving halcyon was the mother of the chicks, born with no living father, and hence they were counted as her offspring in matriarchal fashion. The halcyon builds its nest as a burrow on the shoreline, which would suggest the karstic caves of the sanctuary.

The Alcyonian Lake of Lerna was once one of the entrances to the underworld, where the Lernaean Mystery rites, sacred to Demeter, were performed. This was the route that Dionysus used when he descended to resurrect his dead mother Semele for her ascension to Olympus, a myth like the Christian Feast of the Ascension, or the Assumption, of the Virgin or the Orthodox Dormition. The mythic paradigm represents the elevation of the unwedded virginal mother to the celestial realm as the Queen of Heaven (*Regina Coeli*), the bride of her son, who was her former abducting inseminator, as the supreme self-begotten god.[455] This pattern is another instance of the reconciliation with female primacy as subservient to the ultimate dominance of the masculine principle presiding over the universe. The rescue of Semele is also the same celestial transcendence that was afforded by Herakles' mastery over the Hydra's venom as the toxin for his arrows.

The boatman who rowed Dionysus to the middle of the lake on the occasion of his descent to retrieve his dead mother had demanded that the god make love to him as recompense for facilitating his journey, but Dionysus cheated the boatman of his erotic payment by returning by a different route. When the god discovered that in the interim the boatman had died, he ritually fulfilled his promise by fashioning a phallus out of fig wood, which he applied to himself while sitting grieving upon the boatman's tomb. The death of the boatman, who was called Polymnos[456] (Poly-hymnus, the theme of 'Many Hymns'), masks the reality of his persona as one of these praiseworthy victims tossed into the waters, like the poor little halcyon's mate. The eroticism is an indication of the motif of shamanic rapture, similarly implied by the 'ecstatic' flight of the amorous water birds. The murdered husbands, whom the executed Danaïds joined in death, belong to the tradition of human victims of pubescent males offered to the waters of the Hydra's lake.

At the time of the boatman's death, probably dateable to the mid-second millennium BCE, Dionysus, however, had not yet

---

455 Carl A.P. Ruck and Mark A. Hoffman, *The Effluents of Deity* (Durham, NC: Carolina Academic Press, 2012). Van Eyck's *Ghent Altarpiece* (1432) makes this elevation explicit in using the same model for the Virgin of the Annunciation as well as the pregnant Eve for the enthroned Queen of Heaven presiding over the Marriage Feast of the Lamb, seated beside the Almighty, who is painted from the same model used for Adam.

456 Also, a dialectal version as Prosymnos, with the same meaning.

achieved his divine Classical persona as represented among the assemblage of the Olympian family, to which he originally did not belong, and even in later times he was considered somewhat marginal and an outsider, more at home in the chthonic realm of the netherworld. He is not counted among the twelve deities who comprise the Olympian family. Dionysus, in general, appears to be a latecomer to the Greek pantheon, and although wine drinking is a common theme in the Homeric poems (recorded in writing at the end of the eighth century BCE, but narrating events of the early twelfth century), the god plays no role in the action. His greater antiquity associates him with wild intoxicants, which in the course of his evolution will be transmuted into the inebriating potion manufactured by the subduing of fungal growths into the controlled and civilizing fermentation of yeasts grown on the juice of the grape. This primordial persona, balanced with his patronage of the wine, was essential to his dual symbolism and was repeatedly enacted in the rituals performed in all aspects of his worship. The plant-gathering revels, it is generally assumed, once involved the sacrificial death of a young male, like the rejected suitors of the Danaïds. This tradition underlies the role of Pentheus in Euripides' *Bacchae* tragedy, as well as the death of the Thracian Lycurgus, who similarly opposed the advent of the cult of the wine god. These figures represent the more ancient persona of Dionysus, associated with the wild psychoactive fungus.

The myth of the boatman was the etiology for the wooden phallus as a cultic item in the Mystery rite of the Alcyon Lake of Lerna and the god's employment of it as a dildo to fulfill his promise to the sacrificed boatman, as he sat on the tombstone mourning, suggests the anal application of the shamanic agent. Since tombstones are not suitable for use as seats, the tombstone probably was in the shape of a phallus, or was the dildo itself. Such phallic tombstones were often in the shape more correctly recognized as a mushroom.[457] In fact, 'mushroom', not only was a common

---

[457] Donna Kurtz and John Boardman, *Greek Burial Customs* (London: Thames and Hudson, 1971), 242-244.

term for the erect penis,[458] but it appears to have been a metaphor for the burial coffin or for the tomb itself.[459] In addition, rock-cut monuments as mushroom markers for organized necropolises or cemeteries occur throughout northeastern Greece (Thrace, Macedonia, Bulgaria, Anatolia), mostly in the Late Bronze Age and Early Iron Age (second millennium BCE), with some continuing to operate through the Classical, Hellenistic, and Roman eras. The mushroom marker is often a natural rock formation, sometimes showing signs of human intervention to improve the likeness to the fungus. Further carving in some instances depicts a doorway on the stipe, imparting the sexual metaphor of the vulva as the entrance to the world beyond and the bisexual or hermaphroditic symbolism of the mushroom.[460]

The myth of the long-beaked[461] halycon suggests the same phallic sacred dildo, since the erect penis was commonly a metaphoric bird, as amply elaborated in Aristophanes' *Birds* comedy. The dildo was still employed well into the late Roman period for the sacred application of ecstasy inducing toxins, both vaginally and rectally.[462]

Dionysus even up into the Roman period was summoned

---

458 Archilochus, frag. 34 (Diehl); cf. Hesychius, Herodian.

459     Suda, *s.v., muke.*

460 Carl A.P. Ruck (ed.), Mark A. Hoffman, Evie Marie Holmberg, Stavros Kiotsekoglou, and Vassil Markov, *Dionysus in Thrace: Ancient Entheogenic Themes in the Mythology and Archaeology of Northern Greece, Bulgaria, and Turkey* (Berkeley, CA: Regent Press, 2014).

461 Aristophanes, *Birds,* 299. The male halcyon was called *keirúlos*, affording a pun upon the long straight 'razor-beak' of a barber in the audience. In the comedy, the razor-beak is, of course, the choral member's phallus.

462 Juvenal, *Satires*, 6.314-319: *Nota Bonae secreta Deae, cum tibia lumbos incitat et cornu pariter vinoque feruntur attonitae crinemque rotant ululantque Priapi maenads. O quantus tunc illis mentibus ardor concubitus, quae vox saltante libidine, quantus ille meri veteris per crura madentia torrens!* ('The Mysteries of Bona Dea are famous: a time when devotees stimulate their groins with the stiff flute. Plying horns and wine with a singular purpose, these Priapic maenads roll their stunned heads and groan to the goddess. Such great desire for sex burns in their minds; their groaning is accompanied by explicit gyrations and produces a flood of undiluted sexual desire that flows down their medicated thighs'.) Compare the third-century CE Saint Cyprian, who performed similar rites as graveyard necromancy: Prudentius, *Peristephanon*, 13.21 *et seq.*

from the Lernaean Lake's depths as *Bougenes*, 'bull-begotten', with an archaic trumpet (testifying to the great antiquity of the rite), and a lamb was tossed into its waters as an offering to the Keeper of the Gate.[463] The Hydra was this guardian. The Gorgons where probably also lurking down there beneath the calm halcyonic watery surface, since they, too, were counted among the other traditional monsters as guardians of the gate to Hades.[464] The site was occupied as early as the fifth millennium BCE. Almost nothing is known about the Mystery, but as a secret mystical rite, it undoubtedly involved a psychoactive sacrament represented as the Hydra zoomorphism. No remains of the Mystery sanctuary survive, probably because the religion was practiced within the system of subterranean caverns. The offering of the lamb in Roman times is a pacified version of earlier victims of sacrifice, also suggested by the employment of the antique trumpet for summoning the god from the depths.

Dionysus, in fact, was not 'begotten of a bull'. He did, however, materialize in taurine form among the ecstatic revels of his female devotees in mountain rituals of herb gathering, in which the 'bull' was identified as a zoomorphism of the sacred mushroom.

> You seem to be a bull now leading me, and you've grown horns on your head. Were you always a beast, because you certainly have become a bull now?[465]

The epithet of bull-begotten could, however, be rightfully applied to Minos, born of Europa's abduction by Zeus as a bull, and to the Minotaur, born of Pasiphaë's passion for the bull of Minos. This would associate the very ancient rite of the Lernaean Mystery with the Cretan Minoan/Pelasgian stratum of Greek religion and the traditions of the labyrinth of Knossos.

---

463 Plutarch, *De Iside et Osiride*, 35 (364 F).
464 Vergil, *Aeneid*, 6.287 *et seq.*
465 Euripides, *Bacchae*, 918-921.

### Priapus

Since the grapevine, like the olive, requires annual pruning, Dionysus[466] and his son by Aphrodite, Priapus,[467] are the only other figures in Greek mythology who, like Perseus, are characterized with a *hárpe* pruning hook in their iconography. Priapus is actually an anthropomorphism of the god's phallus and lends his name to the medical abnormality known as priapism. From the Roman period there are depictions of devotees lowering themselves backwards onto the erect penis of his statues, suggesting that it was a cultic practice to employ him for an anal administration of some probably psychoactive preparation. It is not otherwise understandable to make love to a statue.

Priapus was commonly depicted as a misshapen gnome with a ridiculously enormous permanent erection, usually colored red, ridiculous because by several accounts he was impotent, like the well endowed but infertile ass, which was his sacrificial victim of choice. The ass implies the asshole.[468] Although more developed in the Roman period, the first extant reference to him is the *Priapus* comedy of the fourth-century BCE Attic Xenarchus. Ithyphallic statues of the god were commonly placed as trivialized ornaments in gardens and doorways as guardian figures, often hung with placards threatening obscene sexual assault to whoever transgressed the boundaries he protected. As such a guardian or apotropaic figure, he was commonly conflated with Hermes as a herm pillar, a quadrangular column with a sculptural portrait head and the male genitals at the appropriate height. A fresco from Pompeii humorously depicts Priapus with an enormous erection as a master thief, stealing from the thieving god himself, carrying the caduceus of Hermes/Mercury and his magical sandals.[469] Another shows him weighing his huge erection.

---

466 Philostratus, *Life of Apollonius of Tyana*, 2.8.
467 He is sometimes accounted the father of Hermes, or the son of Zeus or Pan.
468 A.E. Housman, "The Latin for Ass": 11-13, in *The Classical Quarterly*, vol. 24 (1930). The metaphor is enacted as the opening obscenity of Aristophanes' *Frogs* comedy.
469 *Ca.* 89-79 CE, Museo Archeologico Nazionale, Naples.

A particularly interesting Roman bronze figurine of the deity probably is a very sophisticated anthropomorphism of a mushroom intended for employment as a dildo. The statuette from northern Gaul is made in two parts. The upper portion of the cloaked figure, wearing a Phrygian cap and holding the pruning hook, can be lifted off to reveal an anthropomorphism of a phallus. The speculative identification of it as a Priapus depends solely upon the pruning hook. The little creature revealed lurking beneath the Phrygian-capped deity resembles a mushroom. It is not difficult to conclude that the item was intended for use as a sacred dildo, either vaginal or anal, or for oral application, these being the typical threats he aims toward women, boys, or men who transgress his boundary.[470] The sophisticated anthropomorphism of the device is not so much an obscenity, as a cultic implement meant to impart the correct theological implications of its employment.

### The Dermatological Affliction

Another mythical tradition about the famous lake of the Hydra at Lerna tends toward the conclusion and that the visionary sacrament or entheogen of the Mystery rite of the Halcyon Lake partook of the same symbolism of wild and cultivated fungal growths as was involved in the great Eleusinian Mystery. This involves the story about the Proïtids, who by one account were the half-sisters of Perseus. In this version, his father was not Zeus, but Proïtos (Latin Proëtus[471]), after whom the girls were named as his offspring by their mother Stheneboea (Greek Sthenéboia) of the citadel of Tiryns on the shore of the Mycenaean plain.

These maiden half-sisters of Perseus became afflicted with a bizarre mania, which would cause the death of the hero. In

---

470 *Haec cunnum, caput hic praebeat, ille nates. Per medios ibit pueros mediasque puellas mentula, barbatis non nisi summa petet.* 'The girl will give me her cunt, the man his head, the boy his buttocks. My dick will go through the middle of boys and girls, but for bearded men I aim only for the top'. Craig A. Williams, *Roman Homosexuality: Ideologies of Masculinity in Classical Antiquity*, New York, NY: Oxford University Press, 1999), 21.
471 To be distinguished from Proteús, the protean metamorphosing old man of the sea who tended seals (Homer, *Odyssey*, 4; Vergil, *Georgics*, 4).

matrilineal tradition they might be seen as the daughters, not of their father, but of their mother Stheneboea, who is named for the 'Strength of the Cow'. She was also known for her uncontrollable sexual lust, which would eventually cause the death of Bellerophon, who is a double for Perseus from a parallel version of the Medusa tale.[472] The maidens developed an extreme dermatological deformity, with their skin growing red and scabby characterized with white patches, which was accompanied by the delusion that they were metamorphosing into cows driven madly ecstatic with their sexual lusting for the bull, wandering the mountainside in uncontrollable estrus like maenads or bacchants, and when they came upon Perseus, they tore him to pieces.

Scholars have assumed that the affliction was scabies, psoriasis, leprosy, or elephantiasis, all of which are purely wild guesses and take no account of the delusion that they were becoming cows in estrus lowing like Gorgons for the erotic communion with the bull and the fact that they were maenads or bacchants, involved in the plant-gathering rites of the god's mountain revels. It is ludicrous to imagine the poor girls lugging their deformed leprous or elephantine limbs about the mountainside in a bacchanalian frenzy, or to divorce their bovine delusion from their sexual longing for the bull-begotten god. The nettlesome itching of their psoriasis required sexual gratification.

The girls were metamorphosing into a metaphor of the sacred mushroom, of the Amanita species, characterized by its red cap splotched with white scabs. They were becoming Gorgons. This is borne out exactly by a parallel version of the hero's death which claims that Perseus, thinking that the Gorgon-head had lost its power, turned and looked at it.[473] This would mean that the hero who had harvested and tamed the Medusa zoomorphism and its

---

472 Carl A.P. Ruck and Daniel (Blaise) Staples, *The World of Classical Myth: Gods and Goddesses, Heroines and Heroes* (Durham, NC: Carolina Academic Press, 1994), 154-161.

473 The fifth-century CE chronographer John Malalas, pp. 38-39, Dindorf; cf. eleventh-century Byzantine historian George Cedrenus. 1. 41; Daniel Ogden, *Perseus* (New York, NY: Routledge, 2008), 32-33.

fungal analogue finally succumbed to its deadly potential. Such is the common motif in the tales of the hero and his liminal or dichotomous potential or dual personae,[474] analogous to the fatal recycling of the Hydra toxins back to Herakles, as the hero who had formerly mastered them.

The seer Melampous is credited with curing the maidens by using the waters of the Lerna Lake polluted with the noisome sulfurous stench of the Hydra as a homeopathic agent.[475] In homeopathic medicine, minute dosages of the drug that caused an ailment are administered as a curative. The cure is variously narrated, and some claimed it involved the application of the toxic herb hellebore, which otherwise is known to induce madness, or the drinking of the milk from goats that had grazed on hellebore, or the application of a torch and brimstone, which would imply the noisome lethal fumes of the Lake's volcanic substructure.[476] Ingested hellebore causes a burning taste, and throat and oral ulceration, which can proceed to delusions and cardiac arrest. Various plants or species were identified as helleobre in antiquity. It was named as 'fawn-food' (Greek *hellós boreín*) and hence it is involved in the metaphor of the deer and the hunt for the sacred mushroom. This would identify the waters of the Alcyon Lake that effected the cure as the same mushroom that caused the girls' bacchanalian delusion of their bovine metamorphosis.

Melampous has the same name as Molière's Doctor Hellebore, the physician for madness, pursuant to a tradition well documented in antiquity. Melam-pous is named as 'Black-foot', which is descriptive of the symbolic homeopathic agent that also caused the delusions, since hellebore was also called *melampódion*.[477] Like Oidipous (Oedipus, 'Swollen-foot' or 'Know-foot'), his

---

474 Carl A.P. Ruck and Mark A. Hoffman, *Entheogens, Myth, and Human Consciousness* (Berkeley, CA: Ronin Publishing), 104 *et seq.*

475 Strabo, *Geographike*, 8.3.19.

476 James George Frazer, Sir, *Pausanias's Description of Greece: Commentary on Books VI-VIII: Elis, Achaia. Arcadia* (London/New York/Toronto: MacMillan, 1897, 1913), commentary on chapter 18.8.

477 Theophrastus, *Historia plantarum*, 9.0.4.

name suspiciously sounds as though he has but a single foot, like the 'black-foot' herb *melampódion*.

'Black Foot' is the common name for some mushrooms, such as the *Polyporus elegans*, and characteristically, the psychoactive *Amanita muscaria* is pulled from the earth with some black soil still adhering to its bulbous base, yielding a dirty foot. In the folklore of mushrooms, this becomes the black boots of the anthropomorphized little creature. Exemplars range from the popular Santa Claus, now commonly recognized as derived ultimately from the traditions of Siberian reindeer shamanism, to *nain rouge* ('red-dwarf'), a *lutin*, imported from Normandy, that has haunted the region around Detroit, Michigan ever since the early eighteenth century, and the redcap *powrie*, that inhabits the ruined castles along the border between Scotland and England. All gnomes are said to wear black boots. Fairies, who are now widely recognized as fungal anthropomorphisms, similarly have dirty feet.[478]

Some claimed that the cure of Melampous was accomplished at Sicyon,[479] near Corinth, where, as we have seen, the aboriginal people first sprouted from the earth as mushrooms that turned into men and where the hoopoe bird plays the same role as the raven. Since the delusion that visited the daughters of Proïtos was characterized as the lowing of cows for the bull, we should not inquire too closely into the method of administering the gnomish misshapen phallic black-footed antidote.

Dr. Black-foot, however, was no stranger to the sacred dildo. Herodotus credited him with introducing the phallic procession of Dionysus from the Egyptians. In these parades, women carried dolls or puppets about a foot and a half tall, fitted with a penis of about the same length and hinged to bob up and down by the mechanism of attached strings.[480] The Egyptians had an etiological myth for this oversized bobbing member, but the historian, to our

---

478 Herbert J. Thornn and John Trabert, *Gnome Chronicles* (Bloomington, IN: AuthorHouse, 2007).
479 Apollodorus, *Bibliotheke*, 2.2.2.
480 Herodotus, 2.48-49.

loss, declined to convey it.

## The Rusty Potion

We should recognize that Melampous never existed, except as a figure in myth, or as a title for a tradition of shamanic priests. There is still another tale about the famous Black-foot seer that suggests that the Mystery of the Hydra's Halcyon Lake partook of the same pattern that is discernable in the Great Eleusinian Mysteries, namely of a transition from the wild mushroom and the offering of human victims[481] to a communal experience of initiation into a shared vision of spiritual transcendence induced by the ergot potion, such as is indicated by the apotheosis of Herakles and by the resurrection of Semele, the mother of Dionysus, to the celestial empyrean. The participants in the ancient secret rites practiced in the cavern of the Lernaean Hydra well into Roman time obviously did not go there to be offered as victims, but to experience the Heraclean transcendence.

Melampous supposedly ruled as king in Argos, which neighbors the nearby Halcyon Lake of Lerna. There are two traditions that connect the famous supposed seer with ergot. In one, he cured a prince of impotence. Seeing his father about to geld a sacrificial offering, the boy ran away, suspecting that he was the intended victim, pursued by his father with the still bloody knife.[482] A gelding knife is usually curved, resembling a pruning hook. Hence, it is not difficult to imagine that this is not an historical event, but a sacred etiology with botanical implications. In fact, by one account, the father wasn't gelding rams, but using the knife to prune trees.[483] The father, to calm his son's suspicion, tossed the bloody knife aside, by chance lodging it in a tree, which according

---

481 Carl A.P. Ruck, *Sacred Mushrooms of the Goddess: Secrets of Eleusis* (Berkeley, CA: Ronin Publishing, 2006), 175 *et seq*. The tradition of human offerings at Eleusis underlies the plot of Euripides' *Suppliants* (423 BCE).
482 James George Frazer, Sir, *Apollodorus: The Library, Volume 2* (London/New York: William Heinemann/Putnam's, 1922, Loeb Library), appendix 3, 'Melampus and the Kine of Phylacus'. Apollodorus, *Bibliotheke*, 1.9.12.
483 Scholiast on Theocritus, 3.43.

to some accounts, was no ordinary tree, but a sacred tree, whose indwelling deity in consequence had cursed the boy. It might have been the same sacred oak that stood in front of the supposed house of Melampous and that harbored a brood of serpents, from whom the seer was said to have received his shamanic powers. The serpents imply something toxic and psychoactive associated with the tree, since it empowered the shaman, and the species as an oak obviously partakes of the sanctity of that tree in Druidic traditions as host for the mistletoe and the sacred mushroom. The episode of the gelding-pruning knife and the boy's anxiety probably masks the fact that the child was indeed the intended victim, not for castration, but as a human offering. Gelding, of course, would have harvested or pruned his mushroom.

As a shaman, Melampous could speak with birds. A vulture told him of the incident with the gelding-pruning knife, and when it approached the tree, it told the black-footed hellebore deer-food shaman the cure. The role of the vulture belongs to the tradition of the raven/hoopoe as associated with the theme of mushroom bread. The king was to remove the knife from the tree's trunk, boil it, and give the boy the rusty water in wine to drink, wine being the customary mode of administering drugs. The sacrificial knife that rusted in the oak represents the transition from the Druidic sacred tree that is host to the parasitic mistletoe and the *Amanita muscaria*, linked in symbolism and sanctity, to the cultivated psychoactive agent derived from rust.

One of the common names for ergot in Greek, as in English, was 'rust' (*erysíbe,* Latin *robigo,* 'red'). It served also as an epithet of the goddess of the Eleusinian Mystery. It is descriptive of the color, but implies as well the metaphor of the rusting of iron, which signifies the reversion of the manufactured metal back to the primitive ore from which it was extracted. Hence it is a symbolic mediation of the dichotomy between the wild and the cultivated antitheses. The ergot-infested kernels of barley, in fact, appear to provide a seed for the otherwise seedless growth of mushrooms, since as with all fungi, the mycelium under suitable conditions of moisture sprouts into the fruiting bodies, recognizable as mushrooms to the unaided eye.

A similar tale of rust as a cure was told about Telephus, a son of Herakles. The story of his infancy displays all the mythical motifs that would identify him with the attributes of fungal consubstantiality. He had received a wound from the spear of Achilles that would not heal, and the oracle at the Delphic sanctuary advised that what had caused the wound would be its cure. The cure for the incurable wound of Telephus was the rust scraped from the blade of the magical spear of Achilles.[484] This weapon, like the club of Theseus, was no ordinary blade, but had been forged in the volcanic caldera of the god Hephaestus. The tale was the subject of tragedies by both Sophocles and Euripides. Pliny interpreted the cure not as sympathetic magic, but assumed that there was some kind of homeopathic remedy involved. Scholars have commented on his naïveté, but in reality we might have assumed that Achilles would not let his blade rust, or that the workmanship of the volcanic smithy might have produced a weapon not susceptible to corruption.

### Ass's Ears

Still another tradition about the famous balck-footed hellebore seer leads to the same conclusion about the fungal toxins of the Hydra zoomorphism. It involves Melampous with King Midas. The ergot kernels suggest another metaphoric description as 'ass's ears'.[485] As king of Phrygia, Midas wore a Phrygian cap, which is perhaps the most ubiquitous representation of the *pileus* or 'cap' of the *Amanita muscaria* and its involvement in the myth of Perseus and in the symbolism of Mithraism and the secret initiatory societies derived from it. Midas judged the famous musical contest between Apollo and the satyr Marsyas. The presence of

---

484 Apollodoros, *Epitome*, 3.20; Hyginus *Fabulae*, 101; Propertius, 2.1.63 *et seq*; Ovid, *Ex Ponto*, 2.2.6; Pliny, *Natural History*, 25.42 and 34.152.

485 Carl A.P. Ruck, Mark Hoffman, and José Alfredo González Celdrán, *Mushrooms, Myth, and Mithras: The Drug Cult that Civilized Europe* (San Francisco, CA: City Lights Books, 2011), 77-86.

the satyr obviously implies the theme of a bacchanalian revel, and the fact that Marsyas ended up flayed alive indicates that this is another instance of a human offering, joining the ranks of Pentheus and Lycurgus as personae of the harvested mushroom that embodied the Apollonian-Dionysian deity that predated the evolution of viticulture. The Gorgon Medusa is also involved, since the instrument that Marsyas played for the contest was the flute that Athena invented to imitate the hissing of the serpents of the decapitated head. When the king judged the satyr victor, Apollo called him an ass and gave him ass's ears, which the ashamed king kept hidden beneath his Phrygian cap, which is to say, his Amanita hat. He was inseparable from his defining mushroom cap. Only the barber knew, since the king would have to remove his cap for his haircut, but he was sworn to secrecy.

The secret proved more than the barber could bear. He dug a hole by the banks of the Pactolus River and shouted his secret into the ground and then buried it. Unfortunately reeds grew from the secret burial site and as the wind blew through them rustling, they whispered that the king had ass's ears.[486] The rustling reeds, of course, are like the sheaves of grain bearing their infestation of ergot. This was the same river, moreover, where the king washed away his notorious affliction that turned all that he touched to gold.[487] It is another case of homeopathic therapy, and the golden touch is probably metaphoric for alchemical transmutation and the primordial mushroom analogue of the ergot fungus.

## The Sting of the Medusa

The Hydra is named simply as a water monster, imagined as an erect serpent rising to a multiplicity of heads in the likeness of a branching tree, suggesting an ultimate botanical original. As depicted in vase paintings and art, it bears a remarkable similarity to the hydrazoon, which the Dutch natural scientist Leeuwenhoek

---

486 Ovid, *Metamorphoses*, 11.172-193.
487 *Ibid.*, 11.140-144.

was the first to name after the mythical prototype in 1702.[488] The hydrozoa are only a few centimeters in length (roughly 0.6 inches) and barely visible to the naked eye, but with the aid of the microscope, Leeuwenhoek noted and drew several of its fundamental characteristics. It is unlikely that the actual hydra animal was ever seen in antiquity and served as the model for the mythical monster, nor do any ancient sources notice its existence. The Swiss naturalist Abraham Trembley, unaware of Leeuwenhoek's precedent, nearly half a century later published his own observations on the freshwater polyp, which he discovered with his two young pupils while acting as tutor for the Earl of Portland's children.[489] In the interim, the Swedish devisor of the system of binomial nomenclature Carl Linnaeus, who made little use of the microscope,[490] in 1735 had debunked the famous taxidermied remains of the quite sizeable seven-headed monster preserved in Hamburg as a pious fraud, assembled from weasel jaws and feet and the skins of serpents, probably the work of monks attempting to create the beast of John of Patmos' *Revelation*.[491]

The multi-cellular freshwater stinging invertebrate polyp is assigned in the Linnaean scientific nomenclature to the phylum of the *Cnidaria*, named from the Greek *knízein*, 'to nettle or sting', which includes the jellyfish or 'medusa', so called in English as early as 1758, and the stinging corals, which according to myth first came into existence from the spilled blood from the severed head of the Medusa. Before submerging into the sea, coral was

---

488 Anthony van Leeuwenhoek, "Part of a Letter from Mr. Antony van Leeuwenhoek, F. R. S., concerning Green Weeds Growing in Water, and Some Animalcula Found about Them": 1304-1311, in *Philosophical Transactions of the Royal Society*, vol. 23, no. 283 (1702-1703).

489 Abraham Trembley, *Mémoires pour servir à l'histoire d'un genre de polypes d'eau douce*, 1744, translated into German in 1791 as *Abhandlungen zur Geschichte einer Polypenart des süssen Wassers*.

490 Brian J. Ford, "The Microscope of Linnaeus and his Blind Spot": 65-72, in *The Microscope*, vol. 57, no. 2 (2009).

491 Carl Linnaeus, *Systema Naturae per regna tria naturae, secundum classes, ordines, genera, species, cum characteribus, differentiis, synonymis, locis* (1735).

soft and spongy like a fungus.[492] The Greek verb equally means 'to provoke, tickle, eroticize'.

The mythical Hydra had the ability to regenerate its branching array of tentacles, which represented its multiple serpent heads. Only one of them was mortal, indistinguishable and protected by the others. The number varied, sometimes as many as one hundred, one for each of the fountain wells. The hydrazoon is now recognized as potentially immortal, avoiding senescence by continual regeneration. Its toxins are being investigated for their potential medical benefit in geriatrics.[493] Herakles could defeat the Hydra only by cauterizing the wounds with a torch before each head could regenerate or multiply.

The hydrazoon, moreover, and other *Cnidaria* actually shoot barbs infected with a paralyzing toxin at their prey. Since the animal is so tiny, it can cause no harm to humans, although its jellyfish medusa relatives can deliver a lethal sting. With modern technology, the hydralysin toxins can be concentrated by ultra-filtration and demonstrate paralytic and other effects similar to certain mushroom and toad toxins.[494] Herakles used the mythical Hydra's venom to poison his arrows,[495] and then finally killed the beast homeopathically by shooting the deadly arrows back at the animal.[496] This is clear analogue to the deer-food hellebore as the only cure for the madness that it induces and to the ultimate demise of Perseus by viewing the harvested Gorgon head.

Although the hydra protozoon's venomous barb offers a perfect analogue for an arrow, it is obviously not lethal enough to serve as the hero's arrow toxin. Nor does the Mediterranean area

---

492 Ovid, *Metamorphoses*, 4.735-762. Ruck and Hoffman, *The Effluents of Deity*, 70 et seq.
493 Martin K. Ettington, *Immortality: A History and How to Guide* (MKEttingtonbooks.com, 2008), 60.
494 Daniel Sher, Yelena Fishman, Mingliang Zhang, Mario Lebendiker, Ariel Gaathon, José-Miguel Mancheño, and Eliahu Zlotkin, "Hydralysins, a New Category of Beta-Pore-forming Toxins in Cnidaria": 22847-22855, in *The Journal of Biological Chemistry*, no. 280 (2005).
495 Apollodorus, *Bibliotheke*, 2.77-80; Pausanias, *Description of Greece*, 2.37.4.
496 Diodorus Siculus, 4.11.5; Hyginus, *Fabulae*, 30.

even provide a suitably deadly water snake Hydra monster. Even the bite of the moray eel *Murena helena* is not a good candidate. Cooking destroys its toxins and it was considered edible in antiquity. Its deadliness resides in its potential feeding upon human flesh. Vedius Pollio, a friend of the Emperor Augustus, was said to have fed a slave to his pool of culinary eels as punishment for breaking a crystal cup, and then eaten the eel to taste his revenge. The anecdote was often cited in antiquity as an exemplar of exorbitant luxury and cruelty. The eel's fresh blood, however, does remain toxic, and as little as one-tenth of a milliliter per kilogram of prey is sufficient to kill small mammals. The eel, nevertheless, provides a poor parallel to the mythical Hydra, inasmuch as it has but a single head and is generally not a freshwater animal.

The *knída* after which the *Cnidaria* are named is the common stinging nettle, *Urtica dioica*. The fifth-century CE lexicographer Hesychius of Alexandria speculated that the verb *knízein* meant that the herb's effect was like a 'bite'. Its many hollow stinging hairs on its leaves and stems offer another intriguing analogue of the toxic arrow and act like hypodermic needles, injecting chemicals that produce a stinging burning sensation, hence its common names as burn nettle, burn weed, and burn hazel. The genus *Urtica* is so named from the Latin verb *urere*, 'to burn'. This, too, provides an intriguing comparison to the burning robe that Deianeira presented to Herakles anointed with the Hydra toxin, which was the forerunner to his approaching immolation in the funeral pyre lit atop Mount Oeta. The chemicals include serotonin and methyl-tryptamine hallucinogens, found also in certain mushrooms and toad venoms, and nettles are brewed into alcoholic cordials and country beers to access their psychoactive potential. The nettle, however, loses its stingers when cooked and is considered a quite edible and healthful vegetable food, and its fibers are used, like cannabis, for weaving cloth. It was employed since antiquity as a beneficial pharmaceutical for a wide array of afflictions.

The *knída* was also identified as the sea nettle (*Actinia equina*) or anemone, which has the same stinging barbs as the hydrazoon, but is large enough to present a likeness with the unaided eye to the multiple heads of the mythical Hydra. Its polypeptide toxins are a possible source for a psychedelic agent similar to LSD.

The sea nettle is lethal to crabs. As Herakles struggled with the mythical Hydra, Hera sent a crab to aid the monster. This is a bizarre element in the tale since in no other heroic exploit does the monster have an ally. It is this crab that became the constellation of Cancer. Vase paintings sometimes include the crab in the depictions of the hero's encounter with the Hydra, or even other crustaceans, hence linking the freshwater Hydra with marine creatures like the anemone and corals, and probably also with the metaphor of the Medusa's blood transformed into sponges and coral.

The crab, moreover, has a botanical analogue. It was thought in antiquity that crabs from the seashore turned into scorpions if their claws were removed and then planted in the ground, from which it would sprout like an herb, with only a single venomous tail in place of its claws.[497] The crab, however, probably figures in the myth as an element of the mythical paradigm of the single-footed autochthonous creatures. It bit Herakles on his foot, which is a motif in a series of maimed, often toxic feet that includes Philoctetes, bitten by the serpent, and Achilles, who will be shot in his heel with an arrow delivered by Paris, who in turn would be shoot in the same way by Herakles' toxic arrow delivered by Philoctetes as the final settlement of the Trojan War.

Scorpion venom also offers hallucinatory and lethal potential. Ultimately, of course, the mythical Hydra has serpent heads, which provide a wider range of possibilities for the identity of the venom for the hero's arrows. As a weapon of combat, the arrow's toxin would have to be fast acting,[498] which few of these candiates for the Hydra toxin supplies, although arrows were also commonly dipped in excrement to assure scepsis of the wound. Certain serpents, however, like the cobra, as well as toads spit their venom

---

497 Ovid, *Metamorphoses*, 15. 369-371.
498 Adrienne Mayor, *Greek Fire, Poison Arrows, and Scorpion Bombs, Biological and Chemical Warfare in the Ancient World* (New York/London: Penguin, 2009).

at their prey and offer a more suitable paradigm for a poisoned arrow.

In all probability, however, the similarity of the hydra and its Cnidarian relatives to its Classical namesake is completely fortuitous and the vaunted toxin of Herakles' bow is a purely mythical construct derived from the deadly offerings of human victims to the Hydra lurking in the depths of the Lernaean Lake and the mystery rites enacted there as a rite of fiery spiritual transcendence.

Neither the mushrooms nor the ergot are suitable as actual toxins for arrows and are only metaphoric in the entire mythical complex of human victims and shamanic transcendence. The mushroom figures also in the botanical pharmaceutical symbolism of several other Labors of Herakles, such as his encounter with the giant Antaios and his dwarfish fairytale brothers, and in the episode of the Cattle of Geryon.[499]

The mares of Diomedes, however, implicate a different botanical original for the zoomorphic object of Herakles' heroism. The four horses were mad, enraged by their diet of human flesh. Their horse-madness supplies the common name for *hippomanés* ('horse-mad'), the psychoactive datura species (*Datura stramonium*, jimsonweed). Horses frequently are poisoned by grazing upon datura and other toxic plants (locoweed, crazyweed), causing them to to exhibit erratic behavior as if possessed or intoxicated. The equine metaphor, however, belongs to the Medusa zoomorphism as well, and to her magical horse son Pegasus and the centaur hybrids, and like the legendary horses of the Thracian Rhesus, it is an element of the symbolism of the sacred mushroom. In Sophocles' *Ajax* tragedy, the hero harvested his madness in a meadow of *hippomanés*, experiencing a severe delusional state in which he butchers cattle mistaking them for his intended victims, his fellow Greek soldier.[500] Hercules supposedly founded the city of Abdera in Thrace, in memory of his boyfriend lover, who had been consumed by the mares. Thus, the figure of the

---

499 Ruck *et al.*, *The Hidden World*, 165, 256 *et seq.*
500 Sophocles, *Ajax*, 143.

flesh-eating mares again implicates rituals of human offerings supplanted by the hero's successful conquest. He accomplished this by digging a trench around the horses, isolating them on an island at the site of the city that he founded, and then he used his shovel to kill their master Diomedes. The shovel is, of course, an implausible weapon of heroism. The mares became tame after they were sated homeopathically upon the corpse of their former master, and athletic contests, as is the recurrent motif, were inaugurated in honor of the dead lover. The tamed horses where eventually dedicated at Olympia, where wolves unfortunately devoured them, although the famous horse of Alexander the Great was supposedly descended from their bloodline. The horse was named Boucephalas ('Cow-head') for the defining white spot on its forehead.

The essential mythical attributes of Herakles' arrow toxin is its superiority to all other venoms, its involvement in the bizarre rites of Lake Halcyon, the bacchanalian delusions of the Proïtid sisters, and most significantly the role of the volcanic forge as the caldera for alchemical spiritual transcendence.

# Chapter Twelve
# The Club from the Volcanic Calera

**The Club-man with a Single Foot**

Although Theseus, too, wielded a club as his unlikely weapon of choice, it was an implement of a different sort. It was made of bronze and fashioned by Hephaistos for his son, Periphetes, the 'Wielder', also known as Korynetes (Corynetes), the 'Club-man'. He had only a single serviceable foot, being lame in one leg, and, even more suspect as an attribute of the anthropomorphized fungus, he had but a single eye.[501] Surely, this is beyond credibility as ordinary history. As the product of the volcanic forge of Hephaistos, the club would have been fashioned by his three workmen, the single 'Orb-eyed' Cyclopes, who were also the manufacturers of the thunderbolts of Zeus, the fiery bolt from the heavens that incased empyreal fire in the wetness of matter, causing mushrooms to sprout and mistletoe to hang from the golden boughs of sacred trees. The Cyclops of Homer's *Odyssey* was a Thracian associated with the especially potent wine of Maron, which was fortified with Amanita toxin, still even into the Roman period.[502]

---

501 Apollodoros, *Bibliotheke*, 3.15.8; Pausanias, *Description of Greece*, 2.1.4; Ovid, *Metamorphoses*, 7.436; Hyginus, *Fabulae*, 38; Diodorus Siculus, 4.59.2; Plutarch, *Theseus*, 8.
502 Carl A.P. Ruck (ed.), Mark A. Hoffman, Evie Marie Holmberg, Stavros Kiotsekoglou, and Vassil Markov, *Dionysus in Thrace: Ancient Entheogenic Themes in the Mythology and Archaeology of Northern Greece, Bulgaria, and Turkey* (Berkeley, CA: Regent Press, 2014).

Certain fungi are commonly called 'club mushrooms' (*Clavariadelphaceae*) because of the inescapable likeness they present to a club, including ergot, called *Claviceps* or 'club-head', although most mushrooms resemble a club at some stage of their growth. Coral, also, the spongy fungal petrifaction derived from the Medusa's blood, displays the likeness of a club, and one is actually named the 'hard bolt-club of Theseus' (*Sclerobelemnon theseus*). Although made of bronze, the club of Periphetes as depicted in ancient art was a metal imitation of the olive club. Ovid called it a 'knobby sprout' (*nodoso stipite*)[503] or 'sucker', such as what is pruned off trees, and it was a club with three such knobs (*trinodi clava*, 'triple knobbed club').[504] There could be no workmen more skilled than the fungal anthropomorphized Cyclopes of Hephaistos in the art of transmuting the mushroom into the alchemical brazen olive club.

The Club-man was the first of the Labors of Theseus, and the hero thereafter used the club as his weapon of choice, elsewhere, but specifically in his major feat of heroism, namely his encounter with the bull-man Minotaur of Crete.[505] The hero was said to have tricked his opponent Periphetes into letting him hold the club to check that it really was made of bronze, since it looked so much like the olive club of Herakles. He then administered the homoeopathic blow by clubbing the Club-man. Scholars have trivialized the club of Theseus, as merely a chauvinistic Athenian imitation of the Dorian hero Herakles, but that is not case, as we shall see. Ancient mythographic pedantry could not anticipate or invent motifs of such archetypal perfection.

The site for the encounter with the Club-man was just a short distance along the shore northwest of the place where Theseus was born, at the sanctuary that would later be known as the healing spa of Asklepios (Asclepius, Latin Aesculapius) at Epidauros (modern Epidavros) and reputed as his birthplace as a son of Apollo. This

---

503 Ovid, *Heroides*, 10.101.
504 *Ibid.*, 10.101.
505 Ovid, *Heroides*, 4.115; 10.101; Nonnus, *Dionysiaca*, 47.434 *et seq.*

would mark the site as the place where Apollo transitioned from his role as 'wolf' (*lykos*) to 'light' (*lux*) and from the cause of disease and plague to the alleviation of the same afflictions through the ministrations of his physician son. The cult is attested as early as the sixth century BCE, but the mythical time of Theseus would have been nearly a millennium earlier.

**The Healing Spa**

The site was the most celebrated healing center in the Classical world, ambitiously enlarged and reconstructed in the fourth and third centuries, and although looted and plundered several times, it continued as a healing center into Christianity as late as the mid-fifth century, until it was irreparably damaged in the earthquakes of 522 and 551 CE. There was a theater, still in use today, and a stadium, where athletic contests were celebrated, as was common for these sanctuaries that benefited from the reorganization commemorated in the etiological mythical traditions of the hero's encounter with the previous monstrous occupant or guardian of the site. Diagnosis was accessed by incubation in a mass open-air sleeping portico, and the dormitory where the patients lodged during the consultation, which could occupy several days, had accommodations for one hundred sixty patients.

The sleeping, which was meant to imitate the motif of death and rebirth, would no doubt have been accessed through the administration of a soporific. The god appeared to them in dreams, which the priests would interpret for each person as an individual prescription for a cure, a precursor of what in the modern period would be called psychoanalysis. Obviously, the only feasible procedure was the use of some drug, as in the Delphic Trophonion Cave, since insomnia or a dreamless slumber would be an unacceptable outcome. Since sacred serpents, either in reality or as aspects of their delusional dreams, are known to have slithered among them as they slept, some kind of medication would certainly have been necessary to calm the patients' anxiety, if they were ever to fall into the required slumber.

## An Eyewitness Account

In Aristophanes' *Ploutos* comedy (408 BCE), the slave only feigns sleep, but manages to stay awake to spy on the scene through the holes in the miserably thread-worn blanket covering his face. He watches the old god of 'Wealth' be rejuvenated and cured of blindness by the administering of serpents that licked his eyes while he slept.[506] The scene, as described, has Asklepios himself and his obviously allegorical daughters Panacea ('Cure-all') and Iaso ('Druggist', from the root complex as Iamos, Ion, Iason, and Iole, and *iatrós* for 'doctor') compounding ointments and tending to the patients. In reality, of course, they would have to have been hallucinations or materliazations from another dimension. Since this is a comedy, the feigning slave also sees the attendant priest steal the food offerings from the sacred table; and following his example, he steals a pot of porridge that lay just beyond the head of an old woman lying next to him.

When she heard him, she put out her hand, which he bit, hissing like a serpent. She was so frightened that she quickly pulled back under her coverlet, letting out a burst of flatulence that fouled the air. The slave did the same after downing the stolen porridge. It was hardly frankincense, he says; he really had a foul-smelling wind.

The daughters of Asklepios squeamishly turned their heads aside, but the smell didn't bother their father since as a physician he was used to tasting stools. (*Scatophagy:* one of the oldest medical diagnostic tests was the examination of the effluents of the body to assess its physical condition.) Then the god prepared a caustic stinging salve that he maliciously applied to the eyes of a patient known to be a perjurer in the Athenian democratic Assembly, before finally ministering to old Ploutos. The bad guy ended up blind, and the good Wealth Ploutos was restored to sight. The restoration of his sight signified the renewal of the world since henceforth Wealth could distribute his bounty to the correct recipients.

---

506 Aristophanes, *Plutus*, 653 *et seq.*

## The Birth of Apollo's Son

As the place where Asklepios, the healing god, was born, it is also the site of his mother's death. She was the daughter of Phlegyas ('Flaming red-brown'), king of the Lapiths, who were neighbors of the centaurs that roamed Mount Pelion, and who were, probably, also centaurs, the good ones, as opposed to the bad, lascivious, and drunken ones, the ones who tried to rape the marriage bride, the horsewoman Hippodameia. It is the event depicted, as we have seen, in the sculptural group of the western pediment of Zeus' Temple at Olympia. Theseus and his centaur friend Peirithoös (Pirithoüs) fought to rescue the horsewoman from the drunken revel of the centaurs at her marriage feast. Asklepios, himself, learnt the medical art from the good centaur Cheiron, who was the tutor of most of the heroes in the lore of drugs and arrow toxins.[507] The centaurs, who first sprouted from the rainfall of the 'mistletoe' Ixion's 'cloud-maiden' Nephele, in all proability were equine zoomorphisms of the sacred mushroom.

The mother of Asklepios is named as a 'Crow-woman' (Koronis, Korone, Coronis, Latin *coxnix, covus*, Greek *kórax*, 'crow'), and while already pregnant with Asklepios, supposedly by Apollo, she had sex either with the 'Halcyon-man', Alcyoneus,[508] or a 'Wolfman', Lykos.[509] Both of these figures are probably fungal personae of Apollo in his pre-Olympian evolution and the female's name as the 'crow' suggests the whole metaphoric complex of the raven/hoopoe/vulture and mushroom bread. The hoopoe and the halcyon kingfisher are classified as *Coraciiformes* or 'raven-like'. The white crow that Apollo had stationed as her keeper tattled to him of the infidelity of the maiden Koronis, and the god burned the feathers of the tattling crow, so that crows now are forevermore black like the raven. He then called upon his sister Artemis to kill

---

[507] Carl A.P. Ruck, Blaise Daniel Staples, and Clark Heinrich, *The Apples of Apollo: Pagan and Christian Mysteries of the Eucharist* (Durham, NC: Carolina Academic Press, 2000), 98-92.

[508] Antoninus Liberalis, *Metamorphoses*, 20.

[509] Lactantius Placidus, on Statius, *Thebaid*, 3.506; Second Vatican Mythographer, 128.

Koronis with her arrows, but as the girl was burning on her pyre, obviously suffering the same chromatic metamorphosis as her namesake, the crow, Apollo relented and removed his fetal son from her incinerating womb.

The infant was exposed on Mount Titthion ('Nipple') above the later sanctuary, where he was nursed by a goat and guarded by a dog. The name of the mountain makes Asklepios a child of the mountainside, like the fantasized mother of Oedipus on Mount Kitharion. The milk of the goat was no doubt psychoactive or magical from the herbs of the satyrs that she grazed upon and the dog is a pacified version of a wolf. In fact, when the goatherd found him, he was afraid at first to pick him up, since lightning was flashing from his body.[510] All these details are suggestive of the motif of the botanical infant exposed upon the mountainside.

### A Good Place for Dying

The myth of the god's miraculous birth masks a transition from earlier times, when Epidauros was the site, not for physical healing, but the ultimate healing of mortality by the offering of human victims. This would have been the nature of the figure that Theseus confronted as the 'Wielder' of the alchemical club. Thus, Koronis is also counted as one of the sacrificial victims to the Minotaur, and another so named maiden was a bacchanalian maenad in Thrace, and still another Koronis was daughter of a 'Club-man' (Coronaeus) and changed into an actual crow by Athena. In the ethnobotanical context, the crow maidens evoke the metaphor of the *Amanita muscaria* as 'Raven's bread'. All these crow maidens are probably versions of the same motif. Thus, the tradition of the bacchant Thracian daughter of the Club-man strongly suggests that Asklepios was another son conceived in drunkenness; and that, furthermore, she is another version of Athena's former persona as a Gorgon.

The motif of death as the cure for the affliction called life was

---

510 Pausanias, *Description of Greece*, 2.26.1-7.

a commonplace. As the last words recorded for Socrates as he drinks the lethal hemlock potion, Plato in the *Phaedo* dialogue has the great philosopher acknowledge his debt to the god of healing: 'Crito, we owe a cock to Asklepios. Don't neglect to pay it'.[511] As on the isle of Delos, at Epidauros no one was allowed to die, or even worse, be buried within the grounds of the sanctuary, for fear, symbolically, that it would evoke the site's former rituals of the ultimate healing as the transition to paradise.

Asklepios himself was destroyed by a thunderbolt of Zeus, forged by the volcanic Cyclopes, for going too far in calling back to life a man already dead. This was the son of Theseus, Hippolytus, the beloved of Artemis, who inveigled her nephew to restore him to life. Although revived, he eventually fell as human victim to the goddess when he wandered into her grove in Italy, the grove of mistletoe, known in antiquity as the Golden Bough.

## Dog Mount

The original Epidaurian sanctuary stood on the Kynortion Hill ('Dog-mount'), northwest of the theater complex, near the modern town of Palaiá Epídavros ('Old Epidauros'). It was a Mycenaean site dedicated to a goddess, founded in the sixteenth century BCE, about the supposed time of Theseus, built over an earlier Pelasgian/Minoan settlement of the Early and Middle Bronze Age (2800-1800 BCE).[512] There is no reason to suppose that in its earliest manifestation it was used for healing. The activity of Periphetes as a murderous highwayman would suggest that, like many Mycenaean and Minoan sanctuaries, it was a place where human victims were offered,[513] in the context of dog/wolf lycanthropy, as attested on Mount Lykaion in nearby Arcadia. At the sanctuary of Lykaion, whoever feasted upon the heart of the

---

511 Plato, *Phaedo*, 118a.5.
512 Eric H. Cline, *The Oxford Handbook of the Bronze Age Aegean* (Oxford/New York: Oxford University Press, 2012), 269.
513 Rodney Castleden, Mycenaeans (Abingdon, Oxon/New York: Routledge, 2005), 155 *et seq.* Dennis D. Hughes, *Human Sacrifice in Greece* (Abington, Oxon/New York: Routledge, 1991).

human victim turned into a wolf, and whoever cast a shadow inside the sacred grounds died within the year.[514] At some sanctuaries of Asklepios, in addition to the slithering serpents, sacred dogs licked the patients.

Epidauros passed into the control of Apollo in the seventh century BCE, supposedly through the god's indigenous son Malos, who became replaced in the persona of Asklepios. Apollo at Epidauros had the epithet of Apollo Maleoticus,[515] a name that designates the homophonous word in Greek for 'apple' and 'sheep, goat, ram' (*mélon/málon*), and hence implicates the tradition of both the Apples of the Tree of the Hesperides and the Golden Fleece of Medea as metaphors for the sacred mushroom. This explains the strange bursts of lightning from the exposed infant's head when the goatherd picked him up off the mountainside.

The final application of the club as the unlikely weapon to defeat the Minotaur of the Cretan labyrinth had a similar thematic motive, most explicitly as the termination of the offering of human victims in the bull dance and the transition of Apollo and Artemis from their former identities as recipients of such sacrifices into their newer Hellenic personae as the twin children of Zeus, as commemorated at their birth site on the sacred isle of Delos.[516]

## The Rod of Asklepios

The healing god had a serpent twined about a staff of olive wood as his emblem, which became the cult symbol of the physicians who constituted the professional brotherhood of the Asklepiads. It represents the ultimate transmutation of the olive and the club-bearing murderer who haunted the site until Theseus tricked him into relinquishing his brazen weapon. The rod of Asklepios was the weapon of choice of the healing god and the physicians

---

514 Pausanias, *Description of Greece*, 8.38.7.
515 Second Vatican Mythographer. 215. (Vatican Regina Christina of Sweden, lat. 1401).
516 Carl A.P. Ruck and Daniel (Blaise) Staples, *The World of Classical Myth: Gods and Goddesses, Heroines and Heroes* (Durham, NC: Carolina Academic Press, 1994), 95-122.

who followed him as their etiological ancestor. The rod-staff implies that Asklepios, like the other creatures born from Earth, had trouble at first in walking, or that like his Apollonian brothers, Ion at Athens and Iamos at Olympia, he had a botanical persona.

In the fourth-century BCE cult statue at Epidauros, Asklepios was molded from ivory and gold, seated, with the serpent and the rod separate on either side of him, his hand resting on the serpent's head. A dog lay at his feet, and bas-reliefs on the throne depicted Perseus decapitating the Gorgon Medusa and the parallel motif as Bellerophon (a doublet for Perseus) defeating the Chimera.[517] Both of these conquered monsters are a zoomorphism of the sacred drug-plant, and their depiction upon the throne of Asklepios would be a bizarre choice if meaningless.

It is assumed that the serpent was harmless, identified as the rat snake *Zamenis longissimus* (formerly called *Elaphe longissimus*), which is as much as two meters in length. There is, however, no basis for this identification, other than the mistaken assumption that a long ('very long' *longissimus*) non-venomous serpent is required. The rod of Asklepios has been adopted as the insignia of modern physicians. Similarly, the serpent twined about the potion cup has been invented as the insignia of pharmacists[518] and called the 'Bowl of Hygieia', the god's daughter Hygiene. In the early twentieth century, the rod of Asklepios was confused with the caduceus of the god Hermes, when it was mistakenly adopted as the insignia of the U.S. Army Medical Corps. The caduceus has two serpents entwined about the staff, which is often depicted with wings.

## Never Do Harm

Hippocrates of Cos (*ca.* 460-*ca.* 370 BCE) is claimed as the founder of modern medicine and of the professional association of physicians who termed themselves the 'sons of Asklepios'.

---

517 Pausanias, *Description of Greece*, 2.27.2.
518 First used of the pharmacy profession as early as 1796, and depicted upon a coin minted for the Parisian Society of Pharmacy.

Physicians today repeat the Hippocratic oath at their inauguration, swearing by Apollo, Asklepios, and Hygieia. This is an element in the entire idealization of Classical culture. It is likely that the mythical Asklepios was more in the tradition that survives today as shamanic healing, where the doctor and often the patient as well enter a trance state accessed with drugs. Just as chemistry and astronomy as modern disciplines have distanced themselves from the theological implications of their predecessors, alchemy and astrology, ancient doctors are cast in the mold of the modern professsionals, although a large element in the ancient practice was merely the determination of prognosis, which is to say, the prophetic art.[519]

To identify the Asclepian/Aesculapian snake as the harmless rat snake deprives the physicians and the pharmacists of their medicine cabinet. The Greek doctors were called *iatroí*, 'druggists', and they swore from their expertise in toxins never to give a lethal potion. Pausanias claimed that the Epidaurian serpent had a peculiar yellowish color,[520] but the Greek language did not distinguish yellow from green. The European cat snake (*Telescopus fallax*) is a better candidate. The rat snake at two meters in length is too long probably to twine about a rod of closer to a meter, which is the length of the cat snake. It is *opisthoglypous*, with backward pointing fangs, which make it inept in biting humans. If a longer snake is really required, the Montpellier snake (*Malpolon monspessulanus*) grows to two meters, and although quite venomous, it, too, is 'back-fanged'. The toxins of the back-fanged serpents are complex and are intended to paralyze the snakes' prey, which rarely is human, and the actual bite upon a human almost requires self-infliction. All three candidates would fall into the yellowish-green spectrum of color.

The Medusa is already sufficiently toxic from the venomous

---

519 Mark Holowchak, "Interpreting Dreams for Corrective Regime: Diagnostic Dreams in Greco-Roman Medicine": 382-399, in *Journal of the History of Medicine and Allied Sciences*, vol. 56, no. 4 (October, 2001).
520 Pausanias, *Description of Greece*, 2.28.1.

serpents that constitute her *chevelure*. Minoan females were commonly depicted handling serpents, a ritual that persisted into the rites of the female devotees of the god Dionysus in their mountain revels. It is probable that the women are milking the reptiles of their venom for the preparation of psychoactive sacraments.[521] Ancient medical writers describe the use of snake venoms in potions and ointments, and the serpent on the rod of Asklepios, the patron of doctors, is a clear declaration of such expertise. The use of cobra venom as a vision-inducing toxin by holy men is reported from India,[522] and the Greek lands have numerous venomous vipers as a source of medicinal and psychoactive coumpounds.

## Viper's Venom

The god's hand resting above the serpent's head in the cult image suggests that the serpent was indeed one of those milked to provide a toxin, at least symbolically, for the healing ceremony. Serpent toxins, moreover, were often not lethal when drunk. Galen claimed that Asklepios himself appeared in a dream and prescribed a cure for a patient that involved a daily regime of drunk and anointed viper's venom. In fact, Apollo was said to grow his own snakes as sources of medicine.[523]

The identity of the serpent, however, doesn't really matter. The Aristophanic parody indicates that the god's serpent was commonly suspected of biting, and hence fearful, and it symbolically

---

[521] D.C.A. Hillman, *Original Sin: Ritual Child Rape and the Church* (Berkeley, CA: Ronin Publishing, 2012). 41-43. Cynthia Palmer and Michael Horowitz, "Introduction": 21-22, in Cynthia Palmer and Michael Horowitz (eds.), *Shaman Woman, Mainline Lady: Women's Writings on the Drug Experience* (New York, NY: William Morrow and Co., 1982). Philip Gardiner, *Secret Societies: Gardiner's Forbidden Knowledge: Revelations about the Freemasons, Templars, Illuminati, Nazis, and the Serpent Cults* (Pompton Plains, NJ: ReadHowYouWant, 2008), 107-108.
Explict mention of extracting serpent venoms as intoxicants: Seneca, *Medea*, 731-732: *serpentium saniem exprimit*, '([Medea as she concocts her poison] squeezes out the venom of snakes'); Demoshenes, *De corona*, 18.260: *toús ópheis toús pareías thlíbon* ('pinching the cheeks of snakes').
[522] John C. Murphy, *Secrets of the Snake Charmer: Snakes in the 21$^{st}$ Century* (Bloomington, IN: iUniverse, 2010).
[523] Nicander, *Theriaca*, 440.

represents the wide-ranging contents of the medicine cabinet. The parody also assumes that two levels of reality or perception were involved in a consultation, the actual thieving priests and the visionary ministration of the god and his allegorical daughters, who can only be seen as materialized from another dimension or as a dreaming hallucination. Votive plaques piously depict the same two levels of reality. The patient lies asleep, wrapped by the serpent licking his wound and attended by the priest, while simultaneously the dream world is depicted as the god himself ministering to the wound.

The rod of Asklepios, moreover, is a symbolic cult item, and as such, it represents the transmutation and pacification of all the venomous monsters into the olive tree that provides the wood for the staff. Hence, it is the mythological replacement for the bronze club of Periphetes of Epidauros, and the substitution of physical healing for the metaphysical cure of mortality though a sacred offering in death.

## The Alchemical Serpent of Renewal

The serpent, itself, was recognized in antiquity as emblematic of transcendence, rebirth and renewal, sloughing off its old skin like a disease and emerging rejuvenated.[524] Ovid specifically linked the motif of the serpent's rejuvenation to the agency of the mere fragrance of the magical herbs that Medea gathered as she flew in her chariot searching for the ingredients of her fiery potion.[525] The representation of the olive club as the bronze exemplar wielded by Periphetes carries the symbolism of transmutation one step further, indicating that it has undergone transcendence through the forge of his father Hephaistos.

The serpent staff of Asklepios bears comparison to the Hebrew *nehushtan*, which as a name dates from the seventh century BCE, but was mythologized back to the time of Moses, roughly

---

[524] James H. Charlesworth, *The Good and Evil Serpent: How a Universal Symbol Became Christianized* (New Haven, CT: Yale University Press, 2010), 258 *et seq.*
[525] Ovid, *Metamorphoses*, 2.117 *et seq.*

contemporaneous with the heroism of Theseus. The name is a pun on words meaning 'serpent' and 'bronze', and it was supposedly the fiery serpent wrapped on a pole, with which Moses cured the Israelites from a plague of venomous snakes.[526] A sacred exemplar was preserved as a pious forgery in the Temple in Jerusalem, and it represented the Canaanite snake cults documented in archaeological sites going back to the Bronze Age. In a contest of magic, Aaron and the sorcerers of the pharaoh cast down their staffs, which all turned into serpents and Aaron's serpent devoured the others.[527]

The rod of Aaron had a long history. It became a fragment of the Tree of Eden, a symbol of the Incarnation, the sign that chose the Virgin as the wife for Joseph, and ultimately the Cross of the Crucifixion.

## The Asklepia Festival

As response to the Great Plague in fifth-century Greece, the cult of Asklepios was introduced into Athens in the year 429 BCE, perhaps through the influence of Sophocles, who was a priest of the god and his Athenian counterpart Alkon (Alcon), the son of Erechtheus, and hence the brother of Ion's mother Kreousa. Alkon was so gifted an archer that he rescued his son from a serpent wrapped about his body with an arrow that struck only the serpent.[528] Virgil mentions this Alcon as merely a possible poetic theme for a contest between pastoral goatherds (*si... Alconis habes laudes*),[529] but the poet's fourth- to fifth-century commentator Servius identifies Alcon as a Cretan instead of an Athenian. Unfortunately, we never got a chance to hear the poem that Virgil might have sung. Alcon was probably a version of the Halcyon of the Lernaean Lake, and hence, like Asklepios, a pacified persona of Apollo. His supposed Cretan lineage suggests the Minotaur,

---

526 *Numbers*, 21.6-9.
527 *Exodus*, 7.12.
528 Valerius Flaccus, *Argonautica*, 1.399 et seq.
529 Vergil, *Eclogues*, 5.11: 'if you have any praise for Alcon'.

whom Theseus vanquished with the Epidaurian brazen club or serpent rod.[530]

The great tragedian maintained the god's sacred serpent in his house until it was lodged in the new sanctuary prepared for the god on the slope of the Acropolis beside the Theater of Dionysus. The festival of the Asklepia was introduced at the same time, for which Sophocles wrote an anthem called a paean.[531] It addresses Apollo with the epithet of *Paíon*, supposedly as the 'Healer', although the word actually identifies him homeopathically as just the opposite, 'the one who smote them' with the plague.[532] Paion was the physician of the Olympian gods, and mythologically he almost fell as a sacrificial victim to his jealous teacher Asklepios/Apollo, but Zeus turned him into a medicinal plant that materialized on the slopes of Mount Olympus at the very last moment to save him.

As the cause of plagues, Apollo is a less efficacious intercessor than his son Asklepios for its removal. Both Ion and his brother Asklepios were called upon to bear the burden of their father's problematic involvement in the rituals of pre-Olympian times. This is the common motif for the god's favorites. Thus, Ion was not openly acknowledged as the god's son, and Asklepios lost his life for resurrecting the dead Hippolytus for his aunt Artemis as her beloved boyfriend. Oedipus paid a similar debt for his alliance with Apollo. Similarly, the god's brothers Hermes and Dionysus take over at Delphi when the rituals revert to the sanctity of the primordial Korykian Cave.

The new Asklepia festival was celebrated to coincide with the dramatic festival of the Greater Dionysia in March. Six months later they added a day to the sequence of events in the Great Eleusinian Mystery. This was the Epidauria, to accommodate Asklepios and Hygeia, who had arrived too late to participate in the ceremonies. On this fourth day of the initiation observances, the

---

530  Ovid, *Heroides*, 4.113 *et seq.*; 10.99 *et seq.* Nonnus, *Dionysiaca*, 47.434 *et seq.*
531  Philostratus, *Life of Apollonius of Tyana*, 3.17.
532  Ruck *et al.*, *Dionysus in Thrace*.

candidates rested indoors, while an accelerated ritual was enacted to allow the latecomers to catch up with the preliminaries for the initiation, following the precedent set by the late arrival of Asklepios and his daughter.[533]

In this way, the heroism of Theseus with the brazen club was incorporated into the cycle of death and renewal celebrated by the drinking of the mixed potion, the Eucharist of the Eleusinian Mystery.

## The Sword of Aegeus

Although Theseus is depicted employing the brazen club to clobber the Minotaur,[534] as well as its thematic analogue as the Bull of Marathon,[535] sometimes identified as the same bull from which Pasiphaë conceived the Minotaur, the hero also frequently is seen with a sword, often using it to decapitate the head of the bull-man Minotaur.[536] It was generally agreed that Theseus overcame the Minotaur by decapitation, for which the sword would be a necessary implement. This would be a thematic requirement if he were to master the monster to display it as his weapon,[537] like the Gorgon-head of Perseus, although it is a very implausible manner in

---

533 H.W. Parke, *Festivals of the Athenians* (London: Thames and Hudson, 1977), 63-65.

534 Theseus and Minotaur mosaic, fourth-century CE Roman villa, Loigersfelder, near Salzburg, Kunsthistorisches Museum, Antikensammlung, Vienna, Austria. Theseus and Minotaur, Villa of Theseus, floor mosaic third-fourth century CE, Paphos, Cyprus. Etc.

535 Theseus and the bull of Marathon, Attic red-figure *calyx-krater*, attributed to the Polygnotos Group, *ca.* 440-430 BCE, Metropolitan Museum, New York, #56.171.48. Theseus and the Marathon bull, Attic red-figure *kylix*, attributed to the Codrus Painter, fifth century BCE, British Museum, London E84, #217213. Etc.

536 Theseus and the Minotaur, Attic red-figure *stamnos, ca.* 500-450 BCE, British Museum, London E441, #202709. Theseus and the Minotaur, Attic red-figure amphora, ca. 550-530 BCE, Rhode Island School of Design, Providence, RI, RISD 25.083. Theseus Killing the Minotaur, *ca.* 530-520, black-figure amphora, in the manner of the Lysippides painter, Chrysler Museum, Norfolk, VI, #2003.18. Etc.

537 No works from antiquity survive with Theseus holding the decapitated head. A bronze figurine in the ancient style by an unknown artist of the seventeenth century depicts the hero with Minotaur head held aloft, and his club held downward in his other hand.

reality to slaughter a bull.

The bull-man represents the antithetical potential of the hero's dichotomous persona. The two are opposite versions of a single entity, and thus belong together in an agonistic embrace. Thus, Theseus can also be seen locked in a wrestling hold with the monster, hardly a likely way to overcome a bull.

The sword is identified as the same sword that Aegeus (Aigeus, named for the 'goat'), the father of Theseus, deposited beneath the rock at Troizen as a token of his son's identity. The motif of the magical sword derives from Persian-Iranian traditions, and appears later as the swords of Beowulf and King Arthur and others.[538] The Persian Indo-European origin would suggest that the motif participates in the thematic complex of the same psychoactive fungal sacrament as the Gorgon Medusa and Zoroastrian Mithraism. The Theseus version, however, adds the significant detail that Aegeus placed sandals as well as the sword beneath the rock, or in a cache within the rock, thereby making the child's identity consubstantial with the rock, and that Aegeus then departed for Athens, leaving his unborn son with the mother upon whom he had begotten the child in the episode of the drunken revel.[539]

Theseus lifted the rock at the start of his heroic career as he set off for Epidauros and its Club-man. The fixity of the sandals beneath the rock or in the rock represents the motif of the initial difficulty in walking encountered by the indigenous creatures sprung from earth. Thus, the Minotaur typically is shown attempting to counter Theseus with a rock as his weapon, sometimes a stone of substantial magnitude, but at other times no more than a symbolic pebble in his hand or in both hands, enacting the decadent/descendant version of Theseus, not as the one who as settler places a rock upon the tomb of a friend, but as settled instead, as he was when Herakles found stuck to the rock in Hades. The stone of

---

[538] C. Scott Littleton, "Theseus as an Indo-European Sword Hero, with an Excursus on Some Parallels between the Athenian Monster-Slayer and Beowulf": online electronic essay un-paginated, in *The Heroic Age: A Journal of Early Medieval Northwestern Europe*, no. 11 (May, 2008).

[539] Apollodorus, *Bibliotheke*, 3.15.7.

Theseus is a recurrent theme, and the other opponents of Theseus also typically counter the hero with a stone that they attempt to place upon him. When Theseus sets out with the tokens to find his father, his journey has the same significance as Ion's 'moving' from matrilineal fixity toward the transition to paternal acceptance.

The sword motif also occurs in the Perseus myth in the context of sexual maturation, its mushroom pommel, the plucking of the mushroom, and the encounter with its zoomorphism as the Gorgon. The Metropolitan Museum Polygnotos vase makes the same metaphoric associations quite explicit.[540] As Theseus prepares to clobber the bull of Marathon with his brazen club, he grasps the head of the bull with his other hand. The hero is nude, with genitals clearly displayed. At his side, slung on a strap around his neck, is the sheath for his sword. Extending from its top, aligned to his penis as if to identify it as a metaphor, is the pommel for the sword's blade, an explicit depiction of its fungal shape. He is crowned as victor with a wreath of olive as emblematic of the transmutation of the bull's toxin into the traditional cultivar. The bull, moreover, has no details of its hide, except for the spotted markings on its head. The Minotaur itself frequently is depicted with multiple spoty scabs all over its hide, resembling the multiple 'eyes' that characterize the herdsman Argos of the cow maiden Io; and Theseus, like Perseus, usually impersonates Hermes in the god's conquest of the monster Argos. Thus, Theseus, here in the Polygnotos vase, as elsewhere, has but a single item of clothing, the petasos cap of Hermes. The scabby skin of the Minotaur participates in the same fungal metaphor as the bovine delusions and dermatological affliction of the maenadic daughters of Proïtos and of the cowherd Argos, guardian of the cow maiden Io, tied in mycorrhizal symbiosis to the sacred olive tree.

Two other figures are shown in the Polygnotos vase. Behind the bull is an elderly man, probably identifiable as Aegeus. To the right in front of the bull is a young woman with a jug and a

---

540 Metropolitan Museum, New York, #56.171.48.

libation salver in her hands. She has been identified as Medea. The scene, which may derive from Sophocles' lost *Aegeus* tragedy, depicts the moment that Theseus has managed to bring the bull back to Athens, and the jug contains the poison that Medea will now use to try to kill the hero whom she had sent to fetch the bull, intending him to fall as its victim.[541]

The pair of sandals, moreover, that empowered the hero to move with the scabbard of the sword with its mushroom pommel toward the recognition of his father and the displacement of Medea recalls the motif of Jason's fungal identity as the one-sandaled protégé of the centaur Cheiron, who came down from the mountainside with his muddy foot and missing sandal.

In the year 476/5 BCE, the Greek aristocratic general Kimon (Cimon), pursuant to the command of the Delphic oracle, found the bones of Theseus. He uncovered them at a mound on the island of Skyros, where the mythical Theseus was reputed to have met his death at the hands of a 'Wolf-lord' named Lykomedes. An eagle (raven/vulture/hoopoe) tearing up the ground with its talons indicated the site to him. Although the tale is probably another pious forgery,[542] Kimon supposedly found the coffin of a man of extraordinary size, as befitted the stature of a legendary hero. He didn't find the club, but a 'spear' (*aichmé*) of bronze had replaced it, and beside it was the sword of Aegeus. Kimon brought the bones and the relics back to Athens, where they were received with a splendid torch-lit procession and buried in the center of the city, near the gymnasium.[543] Thus Theseus was accorded the same burial stone that he had offered to so many other heroes.

---

541 Susan B. Matheson, *Polygnotos and Vase Painting in Classical Athens* (Madison, WI: University of Wisconsin Press, 1995), 221.
542 Adrienne Mayor, *The First Fossil Hunters: Paleontology in Greek and Roman Times* (Princeton, NJ: Princeton University Press, 2000), 110 et seq. Brian M. Lavelle, *The Sorrow and the Pity: A Prolegomenon to the History of Athens Under the Peisistratids, c. 560-510* (Stuttgart: Franz Steiner Verlag, 1993), 48 et seq.
543 Plutarch, *Life of Theseus*, 36.1-4; *Life of Kimon*, 8.3-6.

# Bibliography

Allegro, John M. (1970). *The Sacred Mushroom and the Cross: A Study of the Nature and Origins of Christianity within the Fertility Cults of the Ancient Near East*. London: Hodder and Stoughton.

Arakawa, Osamu, Hwang, Deng-Fwu, Taniyama, Shigeto, & Takatani, Tomohiro. (2010). "Toxins of Pufferfish that Cause Human Intoxication" In A. Ishimatsu and H-J Lie (eds.), *Coastal Environmental and Ecosystem Issues of the East China Sea.*, 227-244 Tokyo:TERRAPUB and Nagasaki University Press.

Astour, Michael C. (1967). *Hellenosemitica: An Ethnic and Cultural Study in West Semitic Impact on Mycenaean Greece*. Leiden: Brill.

Bates, William N. (1911). "Two Labors of Heracles on a Geometric Fibula". *American Journal of Archaeology: The Journal of the Archaeological Institute of America.* 15. 1-17.

Bennett, Chris. Osburn, Lynn. & Osburn, Judy. (1995). *Green Gold and the Tree of Life: Marijuana in Magic and Religion*. Frazier Park, CA: Access Unlimited.

Bernal, Martin. (2006). *Black Athena: The Linguistic Evidence*. Piscataway, NJ: Rutgers University Press.

Bragg, Lois. (2004). *Oedipus Borealis: The Aberrant Body in Old Icelandic Myth*. Cranbury, NJ: Fairleigh Dickinson University Press.

Bremmer, Jan N. (2012). "Demeter in Megara" In Attilio Mastrocinque & Concetta Giuffré Scibona (eds). *Demeter, Isis, and Cybele: Studies in Greek and Roman Religion in Honor of Giulia Sfameni Gasparro*. 23-38. Stuttgart: Franz Steiner Verlag.

Calimach, Andrew. (2002). *Lover's Legends: The Gay Greek Myths*. New Rochelle, NY: Haiduk Press.

Campbell, A.Y. (1931). "The Boy, the Grapes, and the Foxes" *The Classical Quarterly*. 25, 2. 10-102.

Campbell, Joseph. (1949). *The Hero with a Thousand Faces*. Princeton, NJ: Princeton University Press.

Cantarella, Eva. (1989) *Pandora's Daughters: The Role and Status of Women in Greek and Roman Antiquity*. Baltimore, MD: Johns Hopkins University Press.

Castleden, Rodney. (2005). *Mycenaeans*. New York: Routledge.

Charlesworth, James H. (2010). *The Good and Evil Serpent: How a Universal Symbol Became Christianized*. New Haven, CT: Yale University Press.

Cline, Eric H. (2012). *The Oxford Handbook of the Bronze Age Aegean*. Oxford: Oxford University Press.

Cook, Arthur Bernard. (1925). *Zeus: A Study in Ancient Religion*. London: Cambridge University Press.

Cooper, Frederick A. (1996). *The Temple of Apollo Bassias*. Princeton, NJ: American School of Classical Studies at Athens.

Daley, John W., H. Garraffo, Martin & Spande, Thomas F. (1993) "Amphibian Alkaloids": in Arnold Brosse (ed.), *The Alkaloids: Chemistry and Pharmacology V43: Chemistry and Pharmacology*. 186-274. San Diego, CA: Academic Press.

Davidson, J.F. (1987). "Anacreon, Homer, and the Young Woman from Lesbos." *Mnemosyne*. 40, 1-2, 132-137.

Davidson, John. (1995). "Zeus and the Stone Substitute" *Hermes*. 123,3, 363-369.

Dawson, David. (1992). *Allegorical Readers and Cultural Revision in Ancient Alexandria*. Berkeley: University of California Press.

Dempsey, T. (2003). *Delphic Oracle: Its Early History, Influence and Fall*. Whitefish, MT: Kessinger Publishing.

Detienne, Marcel. (1994). *The Gardens of Adonis: Spices in Greek Mythology*. Princeton, NJ: Princeton University Press, 1994.

Devereux, George. (1992). "Why Oedipus Killed Laïus: A Note on the Complementary Oedipus Complex in Greek Drama." 132-141. In Wayne R. Dynes and Stephen Donaldson (eds.). *Homosexuality in the Ancient World*. London: Taylor and Francis.

Dikov, Nikolail Nikolaevich. (1999). *Mysteries in the Rocks of Ancient Chukotka: Petroglyphs of Pegtymel.* U.S. Department of the Interior, National Park Service, Shared Beringian Heritage Program.

Dover, KJ. (1992). "Greek Homosexuality and Initiation" In Wayne R. Dynes and Stephen Donaldson (eds.), *Homosexuality in the Ancient World.* 127-146. London: Garland Publishing.

Eliade, Mircea. (1986). *Zalmoxis, the Vanishing God: Comparative Studies in the Religions and Folklore of Dacia and Eastern Europe.* Chicago: University of Chicago Press.

Ellens, J. Harold. (ed.) (2014). *Seeking the Sacred with Psychoactive Substances; Chemical Paths to Spirituality and God.* Santa Barbara, CA: ABC-CLIO.

Ettington, Martin K. (2008). *Immortality: A History and How to Guide.* Available: http://www.MKEttingtonbooks.com.

Farnell, Lewis Richard. (1909). *The Cults of the Greek States.* Oxford: Clarendon Press.

Fedigan, Linda Marie. (1982). *Primate Paradigms: Sex Roles and Social Bonds.* Chicago: University of Chicago Press.

Fernández, Ramón Gómez. (1999). *Las Plantas en la Brujería Medieval.* Madrid: Celeste Ediciones.

Ford, Brian J. (2009). "The Microscope of Linnaeus and his Blind Spot. *The Microscope.* 57,2. 65-72.

Frame, Douglas. (1978). *Myth of the Return in Early Greek Epic.* New Haven: Yale University Press.

Frazer, James George Sir. (1922). *Apollodorus: The Library, Volume 2.* London: Putnam's.

Frazer, James George Sir. (1897). *Pausanias's Description of Greece: Commentary on Books VI-VIII: Elis, Achaia. Arcadia.* London: MacMillan.

Gardiner, Philip. (2008). *Secret Societies: Gardiner's Forbidden Knowledge: Revelations about the Freemasons, Templars, Illuminati, Nazis, and the Serpent Cults.* Pompton Plains, NJ:ReadHowYouWant.

Geniusz, Wendy, M. (2009). *Our Knowledge is Not Primitive: Decolonizing Botanical Anishinaabe Teachings (Iroquois and their Neighbors).* Syracuse, NY: Syracuse University Press.

van Gennep, Arnold. (1960). *The Rites of Passage*. Chicago, IL: University of Chicago Press.

Gershenson, Daniel E. (1991). *Apollo the Wolf God*. Ann Arbor: University of Michigan, Institute for the Study of Man.

Gourley, Kath. (2001, September 2). 5,000-year-old pub found on Orkney served real dung ale. *The Independent*.

Graves, Robert. (1955). *The Greek Myths,*. Harmondsworth, UK: Penguin Books.

Guia, M. Valdés. (2005). "The Cult of Aglauros (and Aphrodite) in Athens and in Salamis of Cyprus: Reflections on the Origin of the *Genos* of the *Salaminioi*". In Gocha R. Tsetskhladze (ed.), *Ancient West and East*. Leiden: Brill. 4, 1. 57-76

Harrison, Jane Ellen. 1906. *Primitive Athens as Described by Thucydides*. Cambridge, UK: Cambridge University Press.

Hartlieb, Johannes. 1465. *Das Puch aller verboten Kunst, Ungelaubens und der Zaubrey*. Augsberg.

Hastings, James. (2003). *Encyclopedia of Religion and Ethics*. Whitefish, MT: Kessinger Publishing.

Hatsis, Thomas. (2014). "Medieval Witches and Flying Ointments." *Psychedelic Press UK*. 2.

Harvati, Katerina. Panagopoulou, Eleni. & Runnels, Curtis. (2009). "The Paleoanthropology of Greece" *Evolutionary Anthropology*. 18,131-143.

Hillman, D.C.A (2008). *The Chemical Muse: Drug Use and the Roots of Western Civilization*. New York: St. Martin's Press.

Hillman, D.C.A. (2012). *Original Sin: Ritual Child Rape and the Church*. Berkeley: Ronin Publishing.

Hillman, D.C.A. (2001) "The Salamander as a Drug in Nicander's Writings, *Pharmacy in History*, 43, 93-96.

Holowchak, Mark. (2001). "Interpreting Dreams for Corrective Regime: Diagnostic Dreams in Greco-Roman Medicine" *Journal of the History of Medicine and Allied Sciences*. 56, 4, 382-399.

Hooper, Richard Walter. (1999). *The Priapus Epigrams from Ancient Rome*. Urbana, IL: University of Illinois Press.

Housman, A.E. (1930). "The Latin for Ass." *The Classical Quarterly*. 24, 11-13.

Hughes, Dennis D. (1991). *Human Sacrifice in Greece*. New York: Routledge.

Illes, Judika. (2009). *The Encyclopedia of Spirits: The Ultimate Guide to the Magic of Fairies, Genies, Demons, Ghosts, Gods, and Goddesses*. New York: Harper Collins.

Isager, Signe, & Skydsgaard, Jens Erik. (1992). *Ancient Greek Agriculture: An Introduction*. London: Routledge.

Jayne, Walter Addison. (2003). *Healing Gods of Ancient Civilizations*. Whitefish, MT: Kessinger Publishing.

Keewaydinoquay. (1984). *The Miswedo in Anishinaabeg Life* with an introduction by R. Gordon Wasson. Verona: Stamperia Valdonega. From the hand-corrected master proof of the unpublished printing, sequestered from access in the Wasson Archives, Harvard Library.

Kenens, Ulrike. (2012). "Greek Mythography at Work: The Story of Perseus from Pherecydes to Tzetes." *Greek, Roman, and Byzantine Studies*. 52,147-166.

Kiriyak, M.A. (2007). *Early Art of the Northern Far East: The Stone Age*. U.S. Government Printing Office.

Kozorog, Miha. (2003). "Salamander Brandy: A 'Psychedelic Drink' between Media Myth and Practice of Home Alcoholic Distillation in Slovenia" *Anthropology of East Europe Review*. 21,1,63-71.

Kurtz, Donna. & Boardman, John. (1971). *Greek Burial Customs*. London: Thames and Hudson.

Larcher, Pierre Henri. (1829) *Notes on Herodotus: Historical and Critical Remarks on the Nine Books of the History of Herodotus*. London: John R. Priestly.

Lavelle, Brian M. 1993. *The Sorrow and the Pity: A Prolegomenon to the History of Athens Under the Peisistratids, c. 560-510*. Stuttgart: Franz Steiner Verlag.

Lawler, Lillian (1964). *The Dance in Ancient Greece*. Iowa City, IA: University of Iowa Press.

Lawler, Lillian. (1946). "The Geranos Dance—A New Interpretation" *Transactions and Proceedings of the American Philological Association.* 77, 112-130.

van Leeuwenhoek, Anthony. (1703). "Part of a Letter from Mr. Antony van Leeuwenhoek, F. R. S., concerning Green Weeds Growing in Water, and Some Animalcula Found about Them" *Philosophical Transactions of the Royal Society.* 23, 283, 1304-1311.

Lévi-Strauss, Claude. (1967). *Structural Anthropology.* New York: Doubleday Anchor Books.

Littleton, C. Scott. (2008). "Theseus as an Indo-European Sword Hero, with an Excursus on Some Parallels between the Athenian Monster-Slayer and Beowulf". *The Heroic Age: A Journal of Early Medieval Northwestern Europe,* 11.

Lobeck, Christian August. (1829). *Aglaophamus, sive, De theologiae mysticae Graecorum causis libri tres.* Berlin: Gebrüder Borntraeger Verlag.

Markantonatos, Andreas. (2002). *Tragic Narrative: A Narratological Study of Sophocles' Oedipus at Colonus.* Berlin: Walter de Gruyter.

Matheson, Susan B. (1995). *Polygnotos and Vase Painting in Classical Athens.* Madison, WI: University of Wisconsin Press.

Mayor, Adrienne. (2000). *The First Fossil Hunters: Paleontology in Greek and Roman Times.* Princeton, NJ: Princeton University Press.

Mueller, Melissa. (2010). "Athens in a Basket: Naming, Objects, and Identity in Euripides' Ion." *Arethusa.* 43, 3, 365-402.

Murphy, John C. (2010). *Secrets of the Snake Charmer: Snakes in the 21st Century.* Bloomington, IN: iUniverse.

Nulton, Peter Edward. (2003). *The Sanctuary of Apollo Hypoakraios and Imperial Athens.* Providence, RI: Brown University, Center for Old World Archaeology and Art.

Ogden, Daniel. (2013). *Drakon: Dragon Cult and Serpent Cult in the Greek and Roman Worlds.* Oxford: Oxford University Press.

Ogden, Daniel. (2008). *Perseus.* New York: Routledge.

Ott, Jonathan. (1996). *Pharmacotheon: Entheogenic Drugs, their Plant Sources and History.* Kennewick, WA: Natural Products Co.

Pache, Corinne Ondine. (2004). *Baby and Child Heroes in Ancient Greece*. Urbana, IL: University of Illinois Press.

Pahlow, Mannfried. (1993). *The Healing Plants*. Hauppauge, NY: Barron's Educational Series.

Palmer, Cynthia. & Horowitz, Michael (eds.) (1982). *Shaman Woman, Mainline Lady: Women's Writings on the Drug Experience* . New York: William Morrow and Co.

Parke, H.W. (1977). *Festivals of the Athenians*. London: Thames and Hudson.

Plommer, Hugh. (1979). "Vitruvius and the Origin of Caryatids" *The Journal of Hellenic Studies*. 99, 97-102.

Rank, Otto. (1993). *The Trauma of Birth*. In Marcia Ian (ed), *Remembering the Phallic Mother: Psychoanalysis, Modernism, and the Fetish*. Ithaca, NY: Cornell University Press.

Rigoglioso, Marguerite. (2011). *The Cult of Divine Birth in Ancient Greece*. New York: Palgrave Macmillan.

Rigoglioso, Marguerite. (2010). *Virgin Mother Goddesses of Antiquity*. New York: Palgrave Macmillan.

Robertson, Noel. (1996). "The Ancient Mother of the Gods: A Missing Chapter in the History of Greek Religion" In Eugene M. Lane (ed.), *Cybele, Attis and Related Cults: Essays in Memory of M.J. Vermaseren*. 239-304. Leiden: Brill.

Robertson, Noel. (1999). "Callimachus' Tale of Sicyon ('SH' 238)" *Phoenix*. 53, ½, 57-79.

Robson, James. (2013). "The Language(s) of Love in Aristophanes" In Chiara Thumiger, Chris Carey, and Nick J. Lowe (eds.) *Erôs in Ancient Greece*. 251-266. Oxford: Oxford University Press.

Rose, H.J. (1959). *A Handbook of Greek Mythology*. New York: Dutton and Co.

Rosenzweig, Rachel. (2004). *Worshipping Aphrodite: Art and Cult in Classical Athens*. Ann Arbor, MI: University of Michigan Press.

Ruck, Carl A.P. Staples, Blaise Daniel, & Heinrich, Clark. (2000). *The Apples of Apollo: Pagan and Christian Mysteries of the Eucharist*. Durham, NC: Carolina Academic Press.

Ruck, Carl A.P. (2014) "Aristophanes' Parody of Socrates as a

Pothead and the Spartan Cult of the Wolf": chap. 4 in J. Harold Ellens (ed.), *Seeking the Sacred with Psychoactive Substances; Chemical Paths to Spirituality and God*, vol. 1, History and Practices. Santa Barbara, CA: ABC-CLIO.

Ruck, Carl A.P (2013). "Democracy and the Dionysian Agenda": 343-385. In John A. Rush (ed.), *Entheogens and the Development of Culture: The Anthropology and Neurobiology of Ecstatic Experience*. Berkeley, CA: Atlantic Books.

Ruck, Carl A.P. (ed.), Hoffman, Mark A., Holmberg, Evie Marie, Kiotsekoglou, Stavros, & Markov,Vassil. (2014). *Dionysus in Thrace: Ancient Entheogenic Themes in the Mythology and Archaeology of Northern Greece, Bulgaria, and Turkey*. Berkeley, CA: Regent Press.

Ruck, Carl A.P. (1976) "Duality and the Madness of Herakles." *Arethusa*. 9,53-76

Ruck, Carl A.P, & Hoffman, Mark A. (2012). *The Effluents of Deity*. Durham, NC: Carolina Academic Press.

Ruck, Carl A.P, Bigwood, Jeremy, Staples, Danny, Ott, Jonathan & Wasson, R. Gordon. (1979). "Entheogens": 145-146, in *Journal of Psychedelic Drugs*. 1, 145-6.

Ruck, Carl A.P, & Hoffman, Mark A. (2010). *Entheogens, Myth, and Human Consciousness*. Berkeley: Ronin Publishing.

Ruck, Carl A.P. (2010). "Fungus Redivivus: New Light on the Mushroom Controversy": 351-381. In John Allegro, *Sacred Mushroom and the Cross: a study of the nature and origins of Christianity within the fertility cults of the ancient Near East*. Los Angeles, CA: Gnostic Media Research and Publishing.

Ruck, Carl A.P. (1997). "Gods and Plants in the Classical World": 131-143, in R.E. Schultes and Siri von Reis (eds.), *Ethnobotany: Evolution of a Discipline*. Portland, OR: Timber Press.

Ruck, Carl AP. Blaise, Staples, Daniel. Hoffman, Mark A. & Celdrán, José Alfredo González. (2007). *The Hidden World: Survival of Pagan Shamanic Themes in European Fairytales*. Durham, N.C.: Carolina Academic Press.

Ruck, Carl A.P. & Hoffman, Mark A. (2013). *Mushrooms, Myth, and Human Consciousness.* Berkley: Ronin Press.

Ruck, Carl A.P., Hoffman, Mark A., & Celdrán, José Alfredo González. (2011). *Mushrooms, Myth, and Mithras.* San Francisco, CA: City Lights Books.

Ruck, Carl A.P. (1976). "On the Sacred Names of Iamos and Ion: Ethnobotanical Referents in the Hero's Parentage" *Classical Journal.* 71,3, : 235-252.

Ruck, Carl A.P. (2006). *Sacred Mushrooms of the Goddess: Secrets of Eleusis.* Berkeley, CA: Ronin Publishing.

Ruck, Carl A.P. & Larner, Robert. (2013). "Virgil's Edible Tables": in John Rush (ed.), *Entheogens and the Development of Culture: The Anthropology and Neurobiology of Ecstatic Experience.* 387-449. San Francisco: North Atlantic Books.

Ruck, Carl A.P. & Staples, (Blaise) Daniel. (1994). *The World of Classical Myth: Gods and Goddesses, Heroines and Heroes.* Durham, NC: Carolina Academic Press.

Rue, Leonard Lee III. (2000). *The Deer Hunter's Encyclopedia.* Guilford, CT: Lyons Press.

Rykwert, Joseph. (1999). *The Dancing Columns: On Order in Architecture.* Cambridge, MA: MIT Press.

Shelley, Cameron and Thagard, Paul. (1996). "Mythology and Analogy": 152-186, in David R. Olson and Nancy Torrance (eds.), *Modes of Thought: Explorations in Culture and Cognition.* Cambridge, UK: Cambridge University Press.

Sher, Daniel. Fishman, Yelena. Zhang, Mingliang. Lebendiker, Mario, Gaathon, Ariel, Mancheño, José-Miguel, & Zlotkin, Eliahu. (2005). "Hydralysins, a New Category of $\beta$-Pore-forming Toxins in Cnidaria" *The Journal of Biological Chemistry.* 280, 22847-22855.

Shlain, Leonard. (1998). *The Alphabet Versus the Goddess: The Conflict Between Word and Image.* New York: Viking Penguin.

Teeter, Donald E. (2007). *Amanita Muscaria: Herb of Immortality.* Manor, TX: Ambrosia Society.

Thompson, E.A. (1944). "Neophron and Euripides' *Medea*". *The Classical Quarterly.* 38, ½,10-14.

Thornn, Herbert J. &Trabert, John. (2007). *Gnome Chronicles*. Bloomington, IN: AuthorHouse.

Toporov, Vladimir Nikolaevic. (1985). "On the Semiotics of Mythological Conceptions about Mushrooms." *Semiotica*. 53, 4, 295-357.

Topper, Kathryn. (2010). "Maidens, Fillies, and the Death of Medusa on a Seventh-Century Pithos," *Journal of Hellenic Studies*.130, 109-119.

Trembley, Abraham. (1744). *Mémoires pour servir à l'histoire d'un genre de polypes d'eau douce.*

Trendall, Arthur Dale. & Lonsdale Webster, Thomas Bertram. (1971). *Illustrations of Greek Drama*. London: Phaidon.

Turner, Victor. (1969). *The Ritual Process: Structure and Anti-Structure*. New York, NY: Aldine de Gruyter.

Ulansey, David. (1989). *The Origins of the Mithraic Mysteries: Cosmology and Salvation in the Ancient World* . New York, NY: Oxford University Press.

Vinci, Felice. (2006). *The Baltic Origins of Homer's Epic Tales: The Iliad, the Odyssey, and the Migration of Myth*.Rochester, VT: Inner Traditions.

Walsh, David. (2009). *Distorted Ideals in Greek Vase-Painting: The World of Mythological Burlesque*. Cambridge: Cambridge University Press.

Wasson, Valentina Pavlovna, & R. Gordon Wasson. (1957). *Mushrooms Russia and History*. New York, NY: Pantheon Books.

Wasson, R. Gordon, Kramrisch, Stella, Ott, Jonathan & Ruck, Carl A.P. (1986). *Persephone's Quest: Entheogens and the Origins of Religion*. New Haven, CT: Yale University Press.

Wasson, R. Gordon. (1972). *Soma: Divine Mushroom of Immortality*. New York, NY: Harcourt Brace Jovanovich.

Wasson, R. Gordon, Hoffmann, Albert. & Ruck, Carl A.P. (1978). *The Road to Eleusis: Unveiling the Secret of the Mysteries*. New York: Harcourt Brace Jovanovich, Inc.

West, M.L. (1997). *The East Face of Helicon: West Asiatic Elements in Greek Poetry and Myth*. Oxford: Clarendon Press.

Williams, Craig A. (1999). *Roman Homosexuality: Ideologies of*

*Masculinity in Classical Antiquity*, New York: Oxford University Press.

CARL A.P. RUCK is a professor in the Classical Studies department at Boston University. He is an authority on the ecstatic rituals of the god Dionysus. With the ethno-mycologist R. Gordon Wasson and Albert Hofmann, he identified the secret psychoactive ingredient in the visionary potion that was drunk by the initiates at the Eleusinian Mystery. In *Persephone's Quest: Entheogens and the Origins of Religion,* he proclaimed the centrality of psychoactive sacraments at the very beginnings of religion, employing the neologism "entheogen" to free the topic from the pejorative connotations for words like drug or hallucinogen.

Printed in the USA
CPSIA information can be obtained
at www.ICGtesting.com
BVHW041215300723
667919BV00002B/9